AMERICAN FIELDNOTES:
Collected Essays of an Existentialist Anthropologist

Paul Durrenberger

To Suzan and Ayshe

Published by Draco Hill Press
1398 Franklin Ave., West Branch, Iowa 52358

Cover Photo:
Suzan Erem and Paul Durrenberger at Emma Goldman's grave, Waldheim Cemetery,
Chicago, 1999

Introduction

An occupational hazard of being an anthropologist is an un-conventional outlook that comes from trying to shed my own cultural conventions to better understand those of other people. When I place things I see and hear in the wide scope of the five million years of human evolution it puts a different spin on something as transient as a single lifetime, political movement or historical period. When I see the same things as part of the kaleidoscopic pattern of the range of human cultures around the planet it gives a whole 'nother definition to "normal." Where is our homeland? How do *we* practice human sacrifice?

The only thing that can make any sense of the constant flow of strange stories I listen to and read in the news is a vast sea of assumptions we are never supposed to question. Anthropologists call these "culture." It's a revelation to learn that we have one, just as different, reasonable, sensible and reality-based as those assumptions that helped Aztec, Inka, Maya, Nazis, and every other people that has trod our planet make sense of their worlds. Which one is right? Empirically? Ethically? If you believe in magic does it work? What about money? Democracy?

What if you do question those assumptions that define your realities? Flip a coin and call, "edge"? Your world begins to waver. This askew view of the world that lifts up a corner of our culture to look underneath makes me an existentialist in a philosophical sense if you want a label for it. What does that mean? Accepting the absurdity of living in a world we can never fully understand and continuing to try even though we know we can't. To fully understand the world, you can take the leap of faith of a political ideology or a religion, a kind of intellectual suicide. Or you can despair of the whole enterprise and kill yourself. Or you can accept the absurdity of it all and appreciate the sense of passion, humor, goodwill, generosity and intensity in life; a sense of heroism and humanism. In some of these essays I've tried to explain how existentialism bears on Anthropology.

But I am an American. No matter how much we try, we can never really shed our cultures. Americans believe all people were created equal. That should make us all anarchists who reject hierarchy and authority. We also believe that a corollary to equality is democracy. That should settle the matter once and for all. So to me, anarchism is as American as apple pie, which, I've heard, is actually French. That's the thing about culture.

Anthropology aids and abets these two tendencies—anarchism and existentialism. If you question rather than just accept your and everyone else's culture, if you reject authority that justifies itself, that's where you land.

So, to my mind anarchism, existentialism and anthropology go together or mutually imply one another as a philosophy, a political outlook, and as a way of understanding the world and the people in it. It's one thing to take seriously the idea of describing cultures or economic systems and developing the methods and habits of observation that make that possible. Trying to explain those things leads to a kind of formal academic writing. But something else happens when those habits of mind ricochet and bounce back on the stuff of your own culture, the stories of daily life we hear and read about in the news or themes that you see repeated so often they become commonplace. Have you ever heard of a university that strove for adequacy? No, every one of them struggles for nothing less than excellence. What kind of culture calls a retail worker that makes too many mistakes stupid and fires her while giving massive bonuses to bankers who do the same thing and calls them smart? Why is everyone so busy? Why are there so many conspiracies about so many things? How does our country manage as well as it does when we're all whacked out on our national drug of choice? Can corporations own people? Why are there still witches among us? What is the American Dream? What gods do we hold to be so holy that we sacrifice human beings to them?

These are some of the subjects I've written about and collected in these American fieldnotes.

Acknowledgements

In the essays I also make reference to the people closest to me, my wife Suzan Erem and her daughter Ayshe Yeager. Some of the essays reach back to the time when I was married to Dorothy Durrenberger and mention her. These are events that I discuss more fully in a memoir entitled, *At the Foot of the Mountain: Existentialism, Anthropology and Life.* I include the prologue to that book in this collection. But in these essays when I mention my friend in Chicago, I mean Suzan and when I mention my young friend, I mean Ayshe.

Some of the essays were broadcast on National Public Radio's evening news program, *All Things Considered.* I thank Ellen Weiss who edited and directed the ATC commentaries. Another group were broadcast on the morning news program of Penn State's affiliate station, WPSU. Cindy Deutschmann was an able editor and producer of these; her skillful editing of both tape and print made me sound much better on the radio than I could in reality. For every essay I recorded there were several that I sent in at the same time, in those days on paper, that were not broadcast. I include some of those as well. Another body of material I published in the *Society for Applied Anthropology News.* Michael Whiteford was the editor at that time and I thank him for allowing me the freedom to express my various opinions in the pages of the newsletter. To round out the collection are some pieces I published in *Anthropology and Humanism,* a review essay from the *American Anthropologist,* and a piece from *Culture and Agriculture,* all publications of the American Anthropological Association.

I thank both Dorothy Durrenberger and Suzan Erem for reading and discussing many of these pieces with me, especially the radio broadcasts.

War and Peace

Homelands

All Things Considered 10/2/1995

The news is full of stories of the various Balkan factions fighting for their homelands, of folks in the Middle East negotiating boundaries of ethnically defined states, of ethnic nationalist movements in the British Isles and on the Continent of Europe, in Africa, Asia, and in the Americas. These speak of primordial attachments and beginnings. They proclaim that we are all first and foremost Serbs, Palestinians, Hutus, Mon, Texans, or whatever because from the beginning we have always been thus.

When I think of the beginning, I think of Olduvai Gorge, that place in East Africa where we know our Australopithecine ancestors lived. They and their ancestors no doubt lived in other places, but my imagination places them in Olduvai where the Leakeys found their remains. When I think of what is important about ethnicity, my thoughts go to the beginning and I see us walking out of East Africa, out of our homeland, and going to other places, moving north and east and west from that navel of our species to stop off anywhere we could make a living a while before moving on to the next place. I wound up in Iowa.

So, when I hear people preach, dream, and talk of beginnings, of holy lands, of homelands, of lands of the ancestors, I imagine that process backwards—I imagine all of the Americans of European descent walking toward the Atlantic Ocean; those of Asian descent, heading west across the Pacific; those of African descent going toward the Atlantic; Native Americans going north returning to Asia across the Bering Straits, Polynesians, Melanesians and Australians paddling back toward Malaysia. I imagine a vast milling majority who can't decide which way to go because they know their inheritance comes from all directions—those whose four grandparents, eight great-grandparents, sixteen great-great-grandparents—all the way back to Olduvai—represent all points of the compass.

But, to continue the vision, I imagine the Americas and the Pacific islands empty of people; and I imagine all of the Europeans and Asians walking south toward Africa until we all converge on Olduvai. That is our homeland. Everything in between has just been a stepping stone to where we are now, spread as we are all over the planet. We could all return to the native homeland to stand on each other's shoulders and hunt frogs and mice with pebble tools as our Australopithecine ancestors did. Homelands have always been the temporary stopping-off points of a species on the move. I can't help but think that this talk of national and ethnic identity is a weapon local elites use against the people who are closest to them. If we cannot take our sense of identity from our species in the aggregate, if we cannot take our passion for place from our planet as a whole, our species does not deserve to be called "sapiens," wise.

San Francisco Speaks

WPSU 6/7/2000

When I was San Francisco recently I felt like the city was speaking to me. It was like reading the divination from a fortune cookie. I was getting messages of ideals in the concrete and of failures in the flesh.

The bronze letters at my feet declared, "To promote the social progress and better standards of life in larger freedom." As I copied them out, I was vaguely aware of the hum of an engine, but I didn't look up until a voice said, "Shopping for prices?"

"No," I answered the policeman in his cruiser, "Copying the words."

"No problem," he answered. The next inscription proclaimed, "To promote tolerance and live together in peace with one another as good neighbors and to unite our strength to maintain internal peace and security."

And the next, "To insure . . . that armed force shall not be used save in the common interest." The symbol of weapons-carrying authority that had accosted me drove over the words of peace and solidarity to keep an eye out for other suspicious characters loitering in the farmer's market at the United Nations Plaza.

Two days before, the guard at the Veterans' Building had directed me to the new location of the Art Museum and advised me not to walk as there was a pretty rough area between the civic buildings and downtown. As I walked I found out that he meant the Tenderloin district and the U.N. plaza.

On the wall of a dry fountain, "The structure of world peace cannot be the work of one man, or one party, or one nation. . . . It must be a peace which rests on the cooperative effort of the whole world."

So said FDR to the Congress in 1945. A sign warned against sitting or lying near the fountain. The wall reeked of stale urine. The shopping cart village of homeless people of all races and genders had disappeared to make way for the Sunday farmer's market, an alternative to California's famous industrial agriculture. The musty organic stench provided lingering evidence a global economy whose only sustainable product seems to be homelessness and joblessness.

There were more messages. A man carried a signboard proclaiming, "Fallen, Fallen is Babylon. . . " and a dire Biblical warning to us all. On the window of a Brooks Brothers store: "It's a personal thing. A Suit should be worn how you want to wear it. You want something different. . . . . Three button ventless jacket and pleated trousers. . . ." Across the street a sign on a sporting goods store stated, "Never Stop Exploring." Another on the corner of a building commanded, "Change." A second look showed it was synonym for money, not an instruction. The other corner said "Cambio." But a billboard for Apple Computers ordered, "Think Different."

Words of world peace underfoot in a cleared out camp of homeless that cops patrol to make room for a farmers' market; Biblical words of damnation; words of individuality on the window of the store where you go to look like everyone else; an instruction to change our thinking.

On the way to the airport the next day I saw a billboard advertising Forbes dot com. It said, "Capitalism served fresh daily." Whatever words the fortune cookie city offered, that was the reality of the people who lived in the plaza of the brave declarations of freedom and justice for all, that rough area between the government buildings and downtown where the guard had advised me not to walk.

Good and Evil

WPSU 10/2/2001

I had another commentary I wanted to record, about our identity as Americans. Maybe later. It doesn't seem important right now.

Now I hear of good and evil and wonder how we Americans can live our principles of freedom, democracy, equality, liberty and justice for all. A priest explains there is evil in the world but Christ taught forgiveness. An American Imam explains that when evil interferes with our lives there must be some intervention. A person of the Taliban explains that they, like Osama bin Laden, bear the duty of the righteous to stop evil. Our president tells us it is our duty to bring these evil people to justice.

An old labor union song says, "Without our brain and muscle not a single wheel can turn." Lots of people have to do their parts to make any system work. The Nazi system worked for genocide. Every policeman, fireman, engineer, builder, lawyer, factory worker, cook, cleaner, every person who carried a gun for the Nazis participated in that evil. To bring it to an end we fire-bombed Dresden and Berlin and invaded Europe. Every person who followed the Emperor contributed to the evil of Japanese fascism. To bring that to an end we nuked Hiroshima and Nagasaki. In these acts of terror we killed untold numbers of civilians—women and children. It was their brain and muscle that turned the wheels of fascism. Are they not culpable?

It didn't matter. To exchange understanding and forgiveness for revenge and retribution we created a myth of evil leaders who duped their people.

Because we understood the causes of fascism in the political and economic systems that gave rise to it, we changed those systems with massive transfers of wealth.

Today, we Americans, a minority of the world's population, use the majority of the planet's resources to fuel our consumption habits. Our defense of freedom does not extend to lands where our power supports corporate and government oppression to maintain the flow. People in these lands do not enjoy our freedoms, rights, or prosperity. If we lived in lands of poverty and oppression would we not resent the evil land that caused our misery?

Do we not all contribute to this evil when we turn the wheels of America?

No, we know we are just people doing the best we know how to do, living good lives from one day to the next. If we are not evil, then we must absolve the Germans, the Japanese, the Taliban, and the terrorists.

Defining others as evil makes us comfortably righteous with good reason to use violence. We can gas them, nuke them, fire-bomb them.

We become the evil we combat.

The problem is the assumption that there is evil.

Maybe we should not dichotomize the world. Maybe we should substitute understanding and forgiveness as we did after the Second World War, but make it planet-wide. This is the task of governments. What can we do?

Let us all step out of the process to a place with no evil and bend our efforts to create lives and lands and governments that work for the benefit of all rather than against any part of humanity.

Then we give meaning and truth to our American principles of freedom, democracy, equality, liberty and justice for all.

Memorial Day/Labor Day

2001 *SfAA News* 12 (3)

Summer has Memorial Day on one end and Labor Day on the other. Where there is consciousness of classes, Labor Day is May 1 to commemorate the Haymarket—the attack of the Chicago police on strikers during the struggle for an 8-hour workday, the retaliatory bomb, the trumped up charges and the five hangings. With no reference to historical events or class, our American September Labor Day is part of our great magic trick to make classes disappear in a cloud of debate and rhetorical smoke and bolster our illusion of a classless middle-class society. When I was growing up in Texas we did not much notice Memorial Day. One of the towns that claims to have initiated the day as a time to remember their Civil War dead is Boalsburg, Pennsylvania. Since I came to central Pennsylvania, I have gone there to celebrate the day and mark the beginning of summer.

This year, on the way through the cemetery to the town square, I saw men dressed in Union regalia tending cannons close to the statue of the women who first decorated the graves of the Union dead there.

Near the grave of a two-month baby I saw a marker inscribed with the birth dates of 1909 and 1910 waiting for its ninety-something owners to claim it. The streets were teeming with all of the generations, people with white hair and their kids with their own kids. Toddlers and teenagers and new parents with new babies. I sat on the grass in the center of the village and listened to the fiddlers and the report of cannons in the background.

I remembered my father's father's father had come to Texas to claim a land grant as a reward for serving in the Union Army. I remembered the book that showed pictures of my mother's mother's people in their Confederate uniforms. I remembered my father's letter, postmarked "1944 Navy," that started, "Why was it necessary for my father to write 'Happy Birthday' on my first birthday will no doubt ramble through your mind many times in the future. This is no simple matter for any living human being to explain."

I remembered my uncle who was aboard the first minesweeper into Japan. I remembered my uncle who was injured by a Japanese bomb in the Pacific and how he lost his civilian job when he was called back to serve in the Korean War shortly after he returned. I remembered the anxiety of the phone ringing and waiting tensely for my dad to be called back too. I remembered practicing for the inevitable atomic holocaust and our own deaths in elementary school duck and cover drills. I remembered starting awake at night when a plane would fly over and thinking that if we were bombing Koreans, surely they would bomb us.

I recalled a grizzled old retired sergeant telling stories of killing Italian soldiers with his helmet when he ran out of ammunition and how he'd been machine-gunned in Korea, his chest one mass of scars. I recalled my colleague who had been one of the experimental subjects of the atomic bomb tests and how his bones and flesh were rotting inside him. I remembered the mobilization for Vietnam. My brother joined the Army; my sister, the Air Force. I knew that if no one went there could be no war. I remembered an Iowa friend, a big Swede, one of the first Marines into Vietnam, who saw Hispanic Marines on all sides when he landed in Santo Domingo and wondered, "If the shooting starts, which way are these guys going to shoot?"

On the stage, the fiddler introduced a medley of Civil War tunes. He said on this side of the Mason-Dixon Line people might not know the words to some of them but I found myself singing "for Southern rights hurrah, hurrah for the bonnie blue flag that bears the single star." Southern rights? The rights of aristocrats to own slaves? I stopped singing. Then the crowd sang, "Look away Dixieland." Indeed. Look away.

During the Battle Hymn of the Republic I sang the only words that came to my mind—*Solidarity Forever*— "Is there aught we hold in common with the greedy parasite who would lash us into serfdom and crush us with his might?. . . It is we who plowed the prairies; built the cities where they trade; dug the mines and built the workshops; endless miles of railroad laid. Now we stand outcast and starving midst the wonders we have made . . . we have laid the wide foundations; built it skyward stone by stone. It is ours not to slave in, but to master and to own. . . .They have taken untold millions that they never toiled to earn, but without our brain and muscle not a single wheel can turn. . ." The fiddlers ended with the plaintive strains of Jay Unger's *Ashokan Farewell*, the tune that runs through Ken Burns' Civil War films and makes your face swell for losses remembered.

I remembered that these wars all had one thing in common— working people were fighting and killing other working people. Japanese workers built the bomb that injured my uncle. My mother's people fought my father's people. The scarified storyteller had killed Italian working people and Korean working people tried their best to kill him. It wasn't working people who did my colleague harm. It was other Americans. After a while in the Marine Corps it was all too obvious to my Iowa pal who was harming whom. I thought maybe we should remember and celebrate the difference between the people who wage wars and the people they send to fight them. It doesn't matter what country or when. An atomic bomb as much as a bayonet is a weapon with working people at both ends.

Labor Day would make sense if it were a time for working people all over the world to remember that they share the fact of being working people. To make war is to kill our own kind whatever country they are from, whatever language they speak. Making war is killing one of us, not one of them. If we remember that hard enough and long enough, maybe next time they call us or our sons or our grandsons, our brothers and our sisters, no one will answer the call. Without our brain and muscle not a single wheel can turn. In time—in enough time—there will be people who have no war dead to remember. Then we can stop commemorating Memorial Day and have a big picnic on May 1 to rejoice in what we have in common with the rest of the world. Then we could celebrate our hopes for the future rather than the sorrows of the past.

Ethnography at Home Teamsters Speak on War in Iraq

2003 *SfAA News* 14 (1)

The news is full of troop movements to the Middle East, call ups of reserves, and the administration's denial that war with Iraq is inevitable. It's not so full of stories about the resistance to the war. At a demonstration in Washington D.C. late last year, I saw the usual suspects. There were lots of people; so many that we couldn't see the speakers. Thanks to the sophisticated sound system, though, we could hear their words. The usual cast Al Sharpton, Susan Sarandon, the Ben and Jerry ice cream guy who had just written a book. And so on. But that's what you expect at a peace rally. That's the kind of place where you'd expect tree-huggers and peaceniks and university people to hang out and agree with each other. There were even the curvaceous sirens gently swaying as though stoned holding the obligatory "make love not war" sign. The signs were clever.

That night, after the bus ride back to central Pennsylvania, I watched the speakers on CNN and could see them better than I did from the middle of the crowd.

What I didn't expect was for a bunch of truck drivers to agree.

Get off Chicago's Green Line train at the Ashland Avenue stop. Go down the long metal stairway to the street and past Union Park on your left, past the residential hotel with decaying cars in its parking lot. As you walk you see a couple of churches on the other side of the street along with K-Fried/Taco Bell fast food station. On the left side of the street you see the regional headquarters of the United Electrical Workers (the union that represents the graduate assistants at the University of Iowa), a dumpy red-brick building famous for its colorful murals inside and out. Then comes the fortress-like building for UNITE!, the clothing workers' union. You can see why this stretch of street is still called "Union Row." Finally, you come to a broad lawn with two tall 1960's glass and aluminum buildings—not tall by Chicago standards, maybe, but 7 or so stories. In front of them is the low-slung auditorium that other unions and families can rent for celebrations. This is "Teamster City."

Across the back of the auditorium that faces the buildings is a mural of the Janus-like two horse Teamster symbol and the slogan, "705 Fighting for the Future."

On the seventh floor are the offices of the 22,000-member strong local 705, Jerry Zero Secretary-Treasurer, their principal officer.

There's also a spacious parking garage with wide turns. "For the Cadillacs they used to drive," explained my collaborator, Suzan Erem as she parked there. The reference is to the more traditionally centralized business oriented union that had been trusteed a few years before.

There's a parking lot where the reps park. Members park there when they come in for the monthly meetings. One bargainer commented, as we pulled in after a day of negotiating with an oil company, "Some things never change," and pointed to the Cadillac SUV parked facing his more modest vehicle. On the way to one meeting, we saw one member maneuvering his shiny black Mercedes.

I was accustomed to union presidents who wore fancy suits, elegant footwear, silk neckties and the other trappings of power to let the politicians and bosses know that they were all moving in the same circles.

The 705 reps and negotiators don't. They don't need to, they explained. They have a powerful union.

Teamsters stood in front of the auditorium smoking, joking, and talking. As we went in, people handed us printed copies of resolutions that they would bring before the meeting.

I had a survey instrument ready for the October meeting. The president, a long time Army sergeant and Vietnam vet, opened the meeting and introduced Suzan who took the podium to explain the survey as her nine-year daughter and I passed them out to the 300 or so members sitting in the folding chairs. People actually paid attention to the minutes, financial statement, and announcements. They heard who had been suspended for what and who had charged whom of what. Then came time for the open microphone.

There was resolution in support of the West Coast Longshoremen who were locked out. A speaker said that Bush used Taft-Hartley against the Longshoremen, used war scare tactics. Bush used that against unions. "If your people speak out, it's against us. Using that as a front is disgraceful!"

There was applause.

Another guy took the mike. "Since PATCO [Air Traffic Controllers Union that Reagan busted in 1981] there's been a war on labor. Now Bush is damaging unions. Transportation on a global scale has changed. Docks-rail-UPS are all linked. They go after the docks, then they will go after teamsters. That's their game plan. We need to support them [Longshoremen]."

There was applause again and the resolution passed.

Jerry Zero spoke from the podium. "There are new federal regulations about Commercial Driver's Licenses (CDL). Three strikes and you're out including operating a non-commercial vehicle. Including improper changing of lanes. They have written exams, physicals, drug exams, drug tests. That's to drive a truck. If you care to fly a plane into the country and crash it into a building, you don't have any problem." Applause. "This comes to us right from the Bush-whacker. It's getting out of hand." The negotiating team for the freight contract would meet in room 300 right after the meeting, he announced.

Then the resolution against war in Iraq. "I have no quarrel with the working class people of Iraq. It takes billions from schools and acts as a cover for his corporate corruption. 705 stands for justice. Therefore against war. 705 seeks others who are against the war."

Another guy comes to the mike and says, "My dad was a Marine. He did two tours in Vietnam. He was a translator and knew the Vietnamese. 60,000 Americans died. But a lot of others' heads were fucked up. No friends of Bush are gonna die. Hussein is evil. But I have no beef with ordinary people and they want us to go kill those people and we got to think about this and take a stand against it."

Another Teamster. "Congress gave Bush the ticket. In Vietnam nobody knew what they were fighting for. As union members we are still fighting for our freedom against our own government. I need an excuse to fight against the people of Iraq. As for sending our guys in to protect oil interests, I'm totally against it."

Another. "I served three years in the Marines. My brother is screwed up. I'm not in favor of war. History makes war seem full of glory. There is no glory. The government pulls the wool over our eyes on oil. It belongs to oil barons that built the oil refineries. The people over there didn't build it. Bush was there—Desert Storm—three days and it's over. How come you're burning our oil? Get out. . . ."

Another. "My dad served in Vietnam. He has all kinds of personal problems. Drugs. Alcohol. I say no more blood for oil."

Another "There hasn't been a debate on this in our country. Our union is strong enough to have a debate. Our congress won't do anything but give Bush a resolution for war. Current policy is the Bush administration can do anything it wants to anyone. It makes the lives of people like us worse. My uncle died of Agent Orange. In the eyes of the Pentagon, we're collateral damage. We need to fight for justice here and not for oil profits abroad."

And so it went. The next guy was wounded in Vietnam. His brother was killed. Another said this was for corporations. One guy said his mother was a Marine and supported it.

Jerry Zero said it was a good resolution. "I see no connection between Sadam and Bin Ladin. I have seen a lot of proof that people who blew up our buildings came from Kuwait or Saudi Arabia. Our friends. They didn't come from Iraq. Let's talk to Saudi Arabia and police their people. Or Kuwait. We might want to look into some of these countries and see why these things happen. The Vietnam War supported drugs. Reagan's war supported drugs. Why not find hot why people use drugs? It's a waste of money and lives."

When they voted the auditorium resounded with "Ayes." There was one dissenting vote.

The motion:

"Whereas, we value the lives of our sons and daughters, of our brothers and sisters more than Bush's control of Middle East oil profits;

"Whereas, we have no quarrel with the ordinary working-class men, women, and children of Iraq who will suffer the most in any war;

"Whereas, the billions of dollars being spent to stage and execute this invasion means billions taken away from our schools, hospitals, housing, and social security;

Whereas, Teamsters Local 705 is known far and wide as fighters for justice;

"Be it resolved that Teamsters Local 705 stands firmly against Bush's drive for war;

"Further Resolved that the Teamsters Local 705 Executive Board publicize this statement, and seek out other unions, labor and community activists interested in promoting anti-war activity in the labor movement and community."

Once again, moving with the people of this country gave me reason to feel proud.

I Ain't Gonna Study War No More

2003 *SfAA News* 14 (2)

I went to Chicago to put in a week with Teamster's Local 705 during Penn State's spring break on my way to the SfAA meeting in Portland.

I'd been sitting in contract negotiations, grievance hearings, riding with reps to their barns, and hanging around the hall to learn what was going on. Sunday was a membership meeting billed as the most contentious of the year because people would vote on changes to the bylaws. Members, reps, steward and officers spoke and voted for and against each of the seven proposals. It was contentious. But nobody could say it was not democratic.

After the meeting the principal officer of the local, Jerry Zero invited me and Suzan to ride with Teamsters in the local's van to the peace rally downtown at Daley Plaza. At the Picasso sculpture. In front of the Federal Building.

Someone told me it would be the biggest rally Chicago had seen. I said that there had been that Haymarket thing about a hundred years ago and then there was that thing in 1968, but there were a lot of people at the plaza—vegans and Baptists; guys in friar robes and clerical collars; Marine moms, Vietnam vets against the war and atheists against the war. There were labor union presidents and staff folk milling around with the peaceniks and International Socialists and even the Industrial Workers of the World, the Wobblies, had a big sign. Waving in the breeze were earth flags, peace flags, Palestinian flags, and American flags. I even saw a brief flutter of the Red and

Black of the Spanish Civil War Anarcho-Syndicalists. Theologians said this war was heresy. Labor leaders said it was a waste of resources that should better be used at home. Baptists sang, "I ain't gonna study war no more."

That flashed me back to 1964 when I'd learned that song from my professors as they led students in marches against the war in Vietnam. One of the MCs said "Those of us who were active against the Vietnam War have been waiting a long time for this, but now labor has joined us." There were students as well. In Portland, I learned that one of my former students was on the other side of the Picasso.

Each student announced her high school or university. They were from Northwestern and the University of Chicago, from DePaul, and lots of high schools. One of the guys from the University of Chicago mentioned that the students had walked out of their classes at noon the Wednesday of the previous week.

Penn State students joined that action. I teach a class entitled, "Global Processes and Local Systems" from 11:15 to 12:05. The students had asked whether we would meet. I said, yes, we'll meet—till 11:45. True to the example of those who taught me the most, I led the students from my class to the steps of Old Main to join the crowd while I went up the steps to make the brief talk I had promised the organizers.

The war started while we were in Portland. A colleague with kin connections there had let us know of the anti-war gathering across from the Federal Building. Suzan and I joined the crowd and met colleagues there. Some of them had been around for the anti-Vietnam War activities; some had not.

The Portland people were superbly organized. The Black Cross medics were there with a truck; the legal defense team had people write their phone number on their arms; Critical Mass was there with their bikes. Again, theologians—and Pagans for Peace—and labor were there, including Longshore Workers Local 5. We anthropologists returned to our meetings while some of the several thousand who had gathered dispersed for various actions through the night.

The next evening at our SfAA business meeting, I offered a resolution against the war and we passed it unanimously. Then, with tears in our eyes and voices, we sang the old anthem, "How many roads must a man walk down….How many times must the cannon balls fly….How many deaths will it take till … too many people have died?…How many times can a man turn his head pretending he just doesn't see….The answer, my friend, is blowing in the wind."

The war in Iraq may be finished by the time this newsletter comes out. If it is, we will be a long time picking up the pieces. And we will know that too many people have died. It seems to me that we who have voices should add them to those of our students, labor, clergy, atheists and pagans.

Let us all raise our voices until those who represent us in Washington know that we want our national wealth spent on health-care, on schools, on alleviating poverty, and not to build death machines and destroy the working people of other lands. It seems to me that it is the obligation of we who can speak to do so.

Memorial Day, 2005

2005 SfAA News 16(2)

Americans remember our war dead on the last Monday of May. It was early April, walking from our hotel to the SfAA meetings in Santa Fe when Suzan and I stopped into the Monroe Gallery to look at the display of Carl Mydans's black and white photographs. He worked for the Farm Security Administration during the Depression and then for *Life* magazine.

A woman demanding the right of workers to organize, 1936. Italian fascist ministers' fancy cars parked for a 1940 meeting. A French resistance fighter, 1944. Marines hoisting the flag at Iwo Jima, Mac Arthur at Luzon, the Japanese surrender, 1945. An old woman collecting water from a broken water pipe amidst ruins of Hiroshima, 1947; General Tojo's war crimes trial, 1948.

An American corpsman holding a wounded comrade in Korea, 1950; a Korean woman fleeing Seoul with a baby at her breast and her possessions on her head; a Turkish sentry in Korea, 1951. The joyous family greeting of an American POW returning from Vietnam, 1973.

I remembered the letter I found among the wartime correspondence of my mom and dad. It was from my dad, addressed to me, dated 1944.

"Why was it necessary for my father to write 'Happy Birthday' on my first will no doubt ramble through your mind many times in the future," he wrote. He said it wasn't simple, that many had tried to explain it to their sons through history. When he was falling asleep in history classes, he never thought he would have to do it, but now, awaiting assignment after Navy boot camp, it was his task. He wrote that when he was born, our land was fighting the Germans and now it was happening again with the addition of the Japanese.

Obviously to develop the richest nation in the world took individual ingenuity as well as hard work. We, the people, possessed these qualities as we did this very thing.... We made mistakes but we knew no harm came of telling the truth and facing facts.

Other powers had only a few men ruling them.... They did not rule themselves and did not think for themselves....When they had their people in the right state of mind they began to build up armies, air forces, navies...a powerful machine of war....

In doing this the government thought for its people. Told its people lies and stimulated hate....When this machine was finished, they began to take the smaller nations one by one.

In the meantime we Americans would not hate these people....We are peace loving people....

We were attacked one Sunday morning, December 7, 1941.

We, the citizens of the United States, united every bit of our strength to a common cause...first in the manufacturing of the weapons of war....We supplied the allied forces and manufactured arms so they might continue to fight.

He explained that the time came for every able bodied citizen to use this equipment and how draft boards of neighbors and "the President of these United States (Franklin D. Roosevelt)" had called him to serve. He ended with, "May each and every other birthday be just a little happier and more enjoyable."

That letter ran through my head as I looked at the photos in the gallery. I thought of my uncle who was on the first mine sweeper into Japanese waters, of another uncle wounded by Japanese bombs in the Pacific, and of my Dad who was assigned to the fleet post office to do handle mail as he did in civilian life until shortly before he died.

Most of the people in the gallery photos were nameless French, American, Korean, Japanese, Turkish workers and soldiers of all countries like my Dad and uncles fighting the wars on behalf of the named—Churchill, MacArthur, Tojo.

I looked at the photos and recalled recent photos of the war in Iraq and thought that we are doing now what my dad said the bad guys were doing back then. A few men ruling the country, telling lies, telling us not to think for ourselves, and building a war machine to take wealth from the rest of the world.

In a couple of back rooms were other photos—some of celebrities of yester-year in scanty clothing to take our minds off the relationships and struggles depicted in the main gallery. One of the scantily dressed celebs was the one who taught us that if we use the violence of the rulers, we become the people who use violence against us, the person who taught us that "no" is the most powerful word in any language, Gandhi.

Corporations

The Placebo Effect

Not broadcast.

New medical research testifies to the efficacy of the placebo effect. At least some times, if people think a procedure is effective, it really helps them, whether physicians can think of any reason it should or not. This would not have been any news to my doctor, a confirmed practitioner of placebo medicine.

I learned about carpal tunnel syndrome when I had done several long sessions of removing paint from the woodwork in our house. My neck began to ache, then my right shoulder, then my arm, and my wrist. Soon my right arm was hanging useless at my side and I went to the emergency room where they called my doctor. He had some X-rays made and asked me some questions. He showed me the X-rays and some pictures in a book, called it repetitive motion syndrome, explained about tendons swelling in the small space of the wrist bone, and said, "Don't worry, it'll get better in a little while."

I complained. "But it hurts when I do like this," and without smiling he said the punch line to the old doctor joke, "Don't do that." That was that. Some pictures and the assurance that everything would be alright. He was right. It got better in a little while.

When a wart on my foot had been bothering me for some time, I made an appointment to see what he could do. He dutifully looked at it, and then told me that the best treatment I could get would be from some witches in London. He went on to describe research on warts that showed that whatever witches in London do is more effective than other treatments. He said there wasn't much he could do about warts, that the only reason to cut it off or burn it off would be if his son needed a new pair of shoes, and since his son, also a physician, was doing quite well for himself, he didn't see any reason to do anything but wait. He gave me some citations so I could look up the research at the medical library, and sent me off. The wart went away in short order. I hadn't even been to London.

"Wait a while and it'll get better," is probably good advice for most problems. Then again, maybe he just didn't have any investments in drug companies. The new medical research showing how effective placebos can be may be vindicating my doctor's minimalist approach. If they are on the ball, the drug companies should be able to patent his approach and find a way to profit from the placebo effect.

Intellectual Property

2001 *SfAA News* 12 (4)

Take a step into the near future. A guy from a Zapotec village in Oaxaca comes up to the Rio Grande where he's going to cross into the United States to get a minimum wage job doing agricultural, janitorial, or construction work. He can cross legally since the U.S. has dropped all the barriers to workers coming north. The border patrol person takes a drop of blood and asks him to wait a while. In a few minutes, the official comes out with forms for him to fill out. One form tells him that 2 cents of every dollar he earns will be deducted before he is paid to go directly to the DuPont Corporation.

At first he can't understand. He thinks maybe his English isn't that good. He thinks he's being informed that two percent of his wages are automatically going to the DuPont Corporation. When he asks, the guard shows him to the line waiting to see a social worker. Half a day later, the social worker explains that it's intellectual property. The blood test shows the tell-tale trace of DuPont corn. The DuPont Corporation patented the corn that made the tortillas that were the mainstay of his diet, and since he is a product of proprietary corn, he owes two percent of his value to the DuPont Corporation. "It's just like beef," the social worker explains, bored with having to go through this for the hundredth time today. "You feed your cattle DuPont corn; you gotta pay the DuPont Corporation when you sell the beef. Two Percent. Same deal."

The worker protests that he's not a side of beef. Maybe not, thinks the social worker, but you are Mexico's chief export. Labor on the hoof.

"Look, I don't make the law," the social worker reasons. "It's just the law. The farmer had a choice. He didn't have to feed DuPont corn to his cattle. If his cattle got fatter faster and he made money, then he owes part of that to DuPont. Farmer uses the seed, gets a better crop, he can pay DuPont some of the difference. He has a choice. Nobody's making him do it."

The worker is thinking about his neighbor's corn field that was pollinated by DuPont corn. The court said he had to pay royalties, even though he never planted DuPont corn. That farmer had no choice. Not sure his English is up to that, he drops it.

"Your mom had a choice," the social worker says, "She didn't have to feed you tortillas made from DuPont corn. If you grew up to be healthy and strong and able to work, well . . . you owe it to Du Pont. Part of everything that comes from that corn belongs to DuPont. It's the law. Like I say, I didn't make the law. You want to go on or go back?"

If you're hearing the theme song from *The Twilight Zone* and expecting a voice-over from the ghost of Rod Serling, you're in the same boat with a lot of Mexican farmers, ranchers, and consumers of corn these days. DuPont has a patent all but approved in the European Community for a variety of corn that's nearly identical, some say identical, to one that many Mexican farmers grow. Feed it to cattle, DuPont claims a percentage. DuPont's patent on a common variety of beans that many Mexican farmers plant gives the corporation the right to a percentage of each sale.

You grow it, you sell it, you pay DuPont. Why? Because they've patented the genetics of your beans. They own the intellectual property rights.

Adam Smith and Karl Marx agreed that the market price of commodities would converge on how much it costs to produce the next one. That cost includes the price for labor, rent, machines, raw materials and any other costs of production. They couldn't imagine a commodity that people could produce with no labor or raw materials. If the machines and rent are paid for, that makes the marginal cost of production zero. That is an oxymoron—a commodity that you would—what? Give away? But commodities are things you sell. You don't give them away. But what about this 0 marginal cost commodity? If you have such a thing, how can you sell it and make a buck? A government has to make it possible through policy.

Can you own an idea? Maybe not. But you can own a specific statement of it. Romeo and Juliet was an old story when Shakespeare stole it. Then there was Westside Story—same story, different statement. If the government says so, you can own it. That's what intellectual property is all about. That's what DuPont is claiming—ownership of the genetic code of varieties of corn and beans even if they were in common use before the patent—and they want a fee for every use.

A recent law case brought by the National Writers Union decided that if you write something, you get the copyright to it, and any time anyone reproduces and sells it in print or electronically they have to pay the writer. What's the marginal cost of producing the next one? The price of photocopying, or, if it's electronically done, nothing at all. Individual writers could never have enforced that. It took collective action to make it work for writers like it does for corporations.

You write a song and anyone who sings it has to pay you for the use of it. It's easier for corporations to enforce than song writers. So if they've bought the song from the writer they can put the kaibosh on outfits like Napster that would give away their 0 marginal cost product.

Toward the end of August of 2001, the *Wall Street Journal* quoted Bill Gates on what happens when you put major money into developing a 0 marginal cost product and then someone else comes out with a different but equivalent product. A different version of Romeo and Juliet, a different drug that does the same thing, a different song with the same message, a different genetic code for the same corn. The only way to recover costs and make an honest buck is through monopoly practices—controlling the market.

Toward the end of August, 2001 the *Wall Street Journal* reported that geneticists are on to a gene for longevity. How's that going to work if that ever gets made into the kind of life prolonging drug they were talking about? You pay Merck two percent of your pension for every year of life after you start taking their drug? Seems reasonable don't you think? And if someone brings out an equivalent one? Then figure out a way, by hook or by crook, to make everyone buy your product.

So our future worker starts to sign the paper, but the social workers says, "Jeez, look, the blood test shows DuPont beans too, and they didn't give you the form for deduction of 2 percent of your wages for that. You'll have to go back to the first line and get that form too."

The worker knows the sense of futility that generations have known as they gave their rulers flowers and candles and wished them well and well gone, but he says, "What the hell is this, the United States of DuPont?"

A puzzled look crosses the social worker's face as he answers, "No, not at all, I mean Sony, AOL-Time-Warner, Disney, Pioneer Seed, Monsanto, ADM, Dow Chemical, IBM, Microsoft, Merck, Johnson and Johnson—they got rights too, you know."

American Dreaming

2006 SfAA News 17 (1)

The other night I put on a Blondie disk while I was cooking supper and over the rock beat heard about how she meets a guy at a restaurant who knows she is no debutante and, "Dream dream: even for a little while. Dream dream: filling up an idle hour… imagine something of your very own; something you can have and hold. I'd build a road in gold just to have some dreaming. Dreaming is free." Of course, that made me think of Marvin Harris. In the prologue to *Cows, Pigs, Wars and Witches* he says that from ignorance, fear and conflict politics fashions a collective dreamwork that prevents people from understanding what their social life is all about.

Never has this been more true than now. We live in an age of what Harris elsewhere called mind control that is more Orwellian than Orwell ever imagined. Even NPR has caved to the power of the right and stopped identifying their sources from the Heritage Foundation and other right-wing ideology mills as conservative much less "corporate sponsored fascists." Several films show how Fox News is the ideological arm of the Bush administration.

Even more insidious is David Horowitz's innocuous-sounding Center for the Study of Popular Culture. The anti-labor, anti-corporate regulation, pro welfare-reform Bradley Foundation funds them. So does the Scaife Foundation, which also funds the Heritage Foundation that incubates and sponsors ideologies of the religious and corporate right. With such backing Horowitz has founded a national organization called Students for Academic Freedom with 150 chapters across the country that sponsor "academic freedom" bills in state legislatures, such as House Resolution 177 that the Pennsylvania General Assembly is discussing.

This bill would create a state committee to supervise the hiring, firing, curriculum content and political affiliations of faculty members and judge student complaints of faculty bias at any university in the commonwealth that receives state funding. Accused professors would have to defend themselves to a committee in Harrisburg (the capital) within two days. The Republican House majority voted down an amendment to require that the Select Committee to hold hearings across the Commonwealth be composed equally of Democrats and Republicans. This majority Republican Select Committee of the House has held hearings at Harrisburg, Temple University in Philadelphia and University of Pittsburgh, and central Pennsylvania, where Penn State is, is on the schedule for early summer.

Horowitz is using a rhetoric of diversity to disguise the use of ignorance, fear, and conflict to constrain education and inquiry. Being a conservative is not the same kind of thing as being Black, Hispanic, Native American, gay, lesbian or transgendered. Most conservatives may be born to it, but it isn't necessarily a life-long condition. Education helps.

This well-funded corporate-sponsored Astro-turf (fake grassroots) movement is inculcating ignorance, fear, and conflict to feed our collective dreamwork to prevent people from understanding their social lives. Similar bills have passed or are before legislatures in Georgia, Indiana, North Carolina, Colorado, Washington, Tennessee, Massachusetts, Indiana, Maine, Ohio, Minnesota, and Florida. The inquisition is coming to a campus near you soon.

We anthropologists are continually challenging cultural assumptions when we teach about kinship terms for cousins, different terms for colors, different marriage rules, different political and economic and religious systems. Almost anything we teach about from cultural relativity to evolution is likely to challenge someone's cultural assumptions about something. Not accepting our own cultural definitions of reality is what defines anthropology and frees us for the scientific study of other societies and cultures and our own. Who is more vulnerable to accusations of bias than those who don't teach the dream?

We anthropologists already have to cleave through massive collective dreamwork to gain any insight into the workings of any social, political and economic order. These fantasies are just as calculated as this latest attack on academic freedom. In her book, *Worked Over: The Corporate Sabotage of an American Community* (Cornell University Press, 2003) Dimitra Doukas outlines the great cultural revolution that shaped our current dream world. From the end of the 19th century, trusts, precursors to today's corporations, orchestrated and purchased legislation to grant them access to space, cheap utilities, and exemption from taxes. They sponsored a cultural revolution to make corporate rapacity acceptable, to make it seem natural and normal.

Andrew Carnegie sponsored Herbert Spencer's lecture tours across the United States to spread the gospel of wealth—that people get what they deserve and deserve what they get; that wealth is the product of wealth, not of labor. Affluence comes from the concentration of wealth to produce technical progress. Penn State has a Carnegie Hall. That's just one of many buildings named for a capitalist. These same capitalists endowed university chairs for economists who would create the religion to justify corporate rapacity under the guise of science.

Doukas discusses these developments from the worm's eye view of the ethnography and history of working people in Central New York's Mohawk River Valley. The cultural revolution of a hundred years ago made "the market" seem as natural as weather. The current cultural revolution is expanding that market and its religion of the acquisitive individual to all corners of the planet and all niches of our lives, including our dreams. Its corporate sponsors are buying legislators wholesale as they did a hundred years ago.

So, welcome to the American Dream, the corporate dream world enforced by legislative action and policed by corporate foundations that mold the news, concepts of what proper science is, culture and consciousness. These dreams are far from free. They come at the cost of honest and open scientific inquiry, at the cost of freedom of thought and expression. Most of all, they come at the cost of democracy.

AAA POLICY BRIEF #1

September 2007
http://www.aaanet.org/issues/policyadvocacy/
ctions/upload/AAAPolicyBrief_092707.pdf

POLICY AREA Labor

POLICY ISSUE Right of Employees to Organize Unions

POLICY INITIATIVE Employee Free Choice Act (H.R 800, S.1041).

ABSTRACT Ethnographic research supports the underlying assumption of the Employee Freedom of Choice Act—that there is significant management interference in employees' right to freedom of choice and association. Such interference constitutes a human rights violation that the Act is intended to remedy.

BACKGROUND The International Covenant on Civil and Political Rights—ratified by the United States in 1992—affirms the right of free association, including the right to form and join trade unions. US law (1935 National Labor Relations Act, or, the Wagner Act) grants employees the right to form, join, or assist labor organizations, to bargain collectively, and to engage in other activities for mutual aid or protection.

Income inequality is currently at historically high levels in the U.S. and around the world while workers' self-organization has reached historic lows (Human Rights Watch 2000). Human Rights Watch concludes, "Both historical experience and a review of current conditions around the world indicate that strong, independent, democratic trade unions are vital for societies where human rights are respected. Human rights cannot flourish where workers' rights are not enforced and these rights are not being enforced in the U.S."

Currently, 7.4 percent of private sector workers are represented by unions. However, a recent survey shows that 53 percent of workers would elect to be represented by a union if they had a choice. While polling reveals that management opposition is one cause of the disconnect (Freeman 2007), detailed ethnographic fieldwork, such as that cited herein, leaves no doubt.

Since the 1990s, antiunion consulting firms have become a multi-million-dollar industry aggressively creating demand for their services by inculcating in management fear that unions are an avoidable catastrophe. Research shows that two-thirds of employers faced with organizing campaigns hired such consultants (Logan 2002, 2006). The chances that an employee who favors a union will be unlawfully fired are one in five (Schmidt and Zipperer 2007). In 2005, more than 31,000 employees received back pay because of illegal employer discrimination for activities protected under the National Labor Relations Act (NLRB 2005)—a 500 percent increase since the late 1960s (HRW 2000). Such sanctions against corporations are minor and come too late to be effective. Even after employees vote for a union, 45 percent of employers deny the elected union a contract (Federal Mediation and Conciliation Service 2004).

Among the topics that anthropologists have addressed related to labor unions in the U.S. is the process of organizing a union. Whereas sociologists typically base their studies on national level data, anthropologists focus on specific ethnographic details. This was the strategy of Brodkin (1988) in North Carolina, Brodkin and Strathmann (2004) in Los Angeles and of Durrenberger and Erem (2005) in Chicago.

THE EMPLOYEE FREE CHOICE ACT The legislation this research addresses is the Employee Free Choice Act (H.R. 800, S. 1041, or EFCA). During the second stage of the current two-stage voting process, corporations routinely intimidate, harass, coerce and even fire workers who try to form unions. The EFCA would eliminate the second stage and allow employees to form unions at the first vote, when they sign cards authorizing a union to represent them. It would also institute stronger penalties for violation of employee rights (to increase the costs of corporate law-breaking) and provide mediation and arbitration for first-contract disputes (to end long term stalling of negotiations after a union is authorized). The EFCA is supported by a bipartisan coalition in Congress. Senator Edward Kennedy (D-MA) introduced S.1041 on March 29, 2007 and it is now being considered by the Health, Education, Labor and Pensions Committee. The Act has passed in the House of Representatives.

KEY RESEARCH FINDINGS Fine-grained ethnographic fieldwork (Brodkin 1987, 2007, Brodkin and Strathmann 2004, Durrenberger and Erem 2005) documents that:

• Management consultants organize supervisors to incorporate them into a "management team" with the objective of defeating unions. Those supervisors who favor the union, want to remain neutral, or are unwilling to commit unlawful acts are ostracized or fired.

• Management consultants coach supervisors on both legal and illegal methods of persuading workers to oppose the union.

• Management bombards workers with anti-union letters saying that that workers can adequately represent themselves individually to a benevolent management, and that unions
    1) remove any choice from workers,
    2) make them strike, and
    3) could cause them to lose their jobs.

• Management consultants work to reinforce hierarchical relations of workers with management, and define management as workers' only source of information, affirmation, and confirmation.

• Management consultants disrupt social relationships among workers who might establish alternative horizontal channels of communication, confirmation, and affirmation.

• Management depicts itself as powerful and willing to yield nothing to a union, and issues pamphlets designed to intimidate workers and disparage the union.

These and other studies (Zlolniski 2007) show that these practices disproportionately affect women, immigrants, minorities, and people of color. The studies also document other practices designed to inhibit union organization, such as contracting of service work.

ANTHROPOLOGICAL SIGNATURE Ethnography seeks to understand the ways in which people live, relate to one another, and understand the world, their communities, and themselves through on-site observation and analysis of human behavior. Although the discipline of anthropology was initially developed to research distanced "others," ethnographic sensibilities and practices have changed over time. North American workplaces, systems of production, power structures, and legislation are now viewed as potential sites and subjects of ethnographic research.

In their ethnographic study of organizing in Los Angeles, Karen Brodkin and Cynthia Strathmann learned about consultants' use of "… coercion and psychological warfare" (Brodkin and Strathmann 2004:4) to create interpersonal dissension among workers. Such tactics also aim to isolate people who favor the union, sow ethnic conflict, target pro-union employees for conspicuous surveillance and harassment, and humiliate workers in front of others. In this instance, ethnography yielded the following account:

"A management consultant takes a gun from his briefcase and speaks into a tape recorder addressing the union organizer by name. 'I have a license to carry this revolver. I will protect myself. I will protect all the workers who don't want to vote for the union.' Afraid of violence, the organizing committee tells the organizer that people want the union to go away. When the consultant starts his act after the next shift, the workers squirt him with water pistols the organizer purchased. This kind of fear tactic is routine for management consultants. Humorous responses may defuse the tense situations they engineer."

This ethnographic research exposed a previously concealed dimension of management-worker communication: actions of consultants that are often extreme and highly coercive. Because ethnographic research makes visible such factors, it is necessary for making fully-informed policy decisions regarding labor organizing practices.

POSSIBLE POLICY RAMIFICATIONS Anthropology provides sound evidence for the premises of The Employee Free Choice Act, namely that current organizing processes do not allow employees to express their desire to join unions because: 1) there are insufficient disincentives to managerial law-breaking in its resistance to unions; and 2) management uses tactics of intimidation and fear to coerce workers to vote against unions.

References Cited

Brodkin, Karen.1987. Caring by the Hour: Women, Work, and Organizing at Duke Medical Center. Urbana. University of Illinois Press.
2007. Making Democracy Matter: Identity and Activism in Los Angeles. New Brunswick. Rutgers University Press.

Brodkin, Karen and Cynthia Strathmann. 2004. The Struggle for Hearts and Minds: Organization, Ideology, and Emotion. Labor Studies Journal 29(3):1–24.

Durrenberger, E. Paul and Suzan Erem. 2005. Class Acts: An Anthropology of Service Workers and their Union. Boulder. Paradigm Publishers. Federal Mediation and Conciliation Service annual report, 2004.

Freeman, Richard. 2007. Do Workers Still Want Unions? More Than Ever. Economic Policy Institute Briefing Paper # 182.

Human Rights Watch. 2000. Unfair Advantage: Workers' Freedom of Association in the United States under International Human Rights Standards http://www. hrw.org/reports/2000/uslabor/

Logan, John. 2002. Consultants, Lawyers, and the 'Union Free Movement' in the US Since the 1970s. Industrial Relations Journal 22(3):197–214.
2006. The Union Avoidance Industry in the United States. British Journal of Industrial Relations. 44(4):651–675. National Labor Relations Board annual report, fiscal year 2005, Table 4.

Schmitt, John and Ben Zipperer. 2007. Dropping the Ax: Illegal Firings During Union Election Campaigns. Center for Economic and Policy Research. http://www. cepr.net/ documents/publications/ unions_2007_01.pdf

Zlolniski, Christian. 2006. Janitors, Street Vendors, and Activists: The Lives of Mexican Immigrants in Silicon Valley. Berkeley. University of California Press.

Policy, politics and politicians

On Walking

All Things Considered 11/13/1995

We live in an abstract world.

A lot of our food is abstract. We never touch it or feel it, much less raise it or kill it, even if we do open the packages and microwave it. Most of us know the abstraction of fast food from chain shops.

We travel abstractly. From higher and higher in an airplane, the generations of labor that fashioned the Middle West's farms recede into kaleidoscopic patterns. The endless labor and ingenuity that built the railroads and highways and dams on the Mississippi River and the industry to process the raw materials of the nation's commerce become fast moving exercises in an abstract art form way up there. Interstate highways are unvarying tunnels through varied geographic and cultural landscapes.

All of this abstraction frees us to travel great distances and to eat quickly.

But we also deal with people as abstractions.

People without any way of supporting themselves get summed as the unemployment rate. Or the homeless problem. Politicians and public and private administrators criticize others or pride themselves in moving up or down the scales. Like food processors and transportation providers, they increase speed and distance and quantity, but every abstraction decreases comprehension of the people below that build the abstract patterns.

We can only understand what we experience in human terms and we can never experience abstractions.

I can't offer any big solutions to the big problems but I think a small solution to the ills of abstraction is to walk. Walking makes me feel connected. I know the cold of Iowan's winters against the skin of my face and feel it in my ears and cheeks. I feel the crispness or sogginess of the snow or the slipperiness of the ice and know that day's precipitation for what it is. I feel the dampness of the fog in spring and the mugginess of the heat in the summer. I smell the coming thunder storms, sense the darkness, hear the thunder, and feel the rain. I see the houses and I can see other pedestrians as people doing what I am doing. Cars seem like angry growling beasts pointlessly racing against one another.

Maybe if administrators and politicians all walked a couple of miles each day they could feel themselves as people in human terms and be more capable of seeing others as people like themselves. Walking binds us to the planet for a while, puts us in a human scale of experience. Bound to the details of the concrete, we can't perceive big abstract patterns and do big things, but maybe our weakness is trying to do things in a big way instead of a human way.

Presidential Polling

All Things Considered 11/20/1995

It's started again. It's more than a year before the presidential election of 1996. This happens every four years in Iowa as regularly as leap year. It's just supper time and the telephone rings. A woman's voice asks in the nasal tones of the Middle West if Mr. Doringer is in. This is a hint. My surname has more syllables than most Americans are willing to scan—so many pick up the first and last and sort of fake the middle ones. "Who is calling?" I ask, defenses up. The voice tells me that it wants to ask me some questions about the issues in the presidential campaign. I ask, "Who is sponsoring the poll?" The voice sounds shocked at my question and responds that it can't really say. I say that if the polling organization cannot reveal the sponsor of the poll, I can't answer the questions, thank her, and hang up.

This will continue right up until Iowans meet with neighbors in public places to support the candidates they favor in our caucuses, the first official say in the presidential selection process. This process forces me to think deeply about what the press and pollsters call "the issues" so I can answer the questions when the callers dare to identify themselves. I am often presented with a menu of issues and asked to rank them—the environment, the economy, foreign affairs, the deficit, energy, crime, drugs, healthcare, whatever, the list changes from time to time, but only a little.

I think this approach to political discourse skims the surface of worry, looking for the keywords to unlock the emotional responses that advertising people can amplify to trigger voting behaviors. It misses almost all of the interesting and important issues and informed electorate should be thinking about and acting on. That shows in the results of the process, the selection of two guys that might as well be peas in a pod.

Have you ever tried to talk to a pollster? The poor person on the other end of the phone is just trying to make a living and has to fill in one of the blanks on the response sheet. If you go off into never-never land with some line of thought, the pollster will bring you firmly back to the task of constructing reality with a, "Will that be economy, foreign affairs, the deficit, or crime?" I've learned that the only relatively polite way to get through the exercise is to second guess the process with my own categories. I say that I think the most important issue of the election is the metric system. "I beg your pardon?" "The metric system. We've been talking about converting ever since the 19th century and it's never come to more than talk. I think it's time we did it." This, by the way, is sheer hypocrisy because I like the English system fine just as it is, but, hell; it seems to me just as significant a political issue as any of the artificially delineated categories on the pollster's menus that nobody is serious about really understanding or addressing. And I imagine that it gets firmly in the "other" category or "none of the above" or just thrown out of the whole process.

Speed Limits Revisited

All Things Considered 11/29/1995

When I get into my car I feel in control. I know I am an independent and rational individual making good decisions second by second as I adjust to the conditions of the road, weather, and traffic. Especially on interstate highways I am always on the lookout for developing danger so I can give it wide berth. When I get where I'm going, I delight in discussing the details of the trip—the weather, the craziness of other drivers, and the inevitable debate about the best route.

That illusion of control dissipates only when I am stuck in go nowhere traffic jams on the freeways of Chicago or Dallas or in the middle of Iowa. From the driver's seat I only rarely think of myself as playing a game of chance with death. When I do, it's enough to make me want to pull over and walk.

The rate of murder in the United States is well under half the rate of traffic fatalities. If the murder rate approached that of traffic fatalities, there would be terror through the land, we'd call out the National Guard, and the jails would overflow. But traffic deaths don't raise an eyebrow. People who gasp in horror at the thought of ancient Aztec priests ripping the throbbing hearts from their fellow human beings in sacrifice to their gods don't bat an eyelid at our Congress when it abolishes the national speed limit and increases our death rate from a similarly bloody brutality. And there's not even a religious justification to celebrate the deaths. I'm not saying it's the fault of Congress, because in this we vote with our feet.

Only six percent of the drivers on a freeway around Des Moines obey the 55 MPH speed limit. And that's in law-abiding Iowa. In Texas, my father-in-law once explained to me, it's unsafe to drive anywhere near the speed limit because other drivers will ram you from behind. I was once told that a particular hundred-mile trip in Arizona was about an hour's drive. I'd asked because while my kinetic sense—and speedometer—warned me that I was going fast, my visual sense advised that I was standing still as a steady stream of traffic passed on my left.

We have been willing to pay for speed with blood. The speed of traffic regulates the rate of traffic deaths just as surely as the feet of drivers regulate the speed of traffic. Traffic engineers predicted precisely the cost of the 65 MPH speed limit in human lives. Why do we pay this price? Where else in our daily lives do we get the illusion of control that driving brings? Whatever we say or think, our practice tells us that faster speeds are worth dying for. It looks like we've done the Aztecs one better in inventing a secular means of human sacrifice to gain a sense of control in an uncertain universe.

Conspiracies

All Things Considered 5/21/1996

Sometimes there is a current of warm water called El Nino in the Pacific off California. Meteorologists said that Iowans owed the mildness of the last couple of winters to it, but because it was breaking up we could expect harsher weather. We surely got the harsh weather and now I want to who know who is responsible.

There seems to be a conspiracy theory for everything. Assassinations and terrorist attacks go without saying. People in California blame immigrants for their brush fires. Militias blame "the government" for everything. Some folks mutter about the Trilateral Commission and the Federal Reserve Board. Batman, Superman, and Wonder Woman are constantly working to foil such conspiracies.

If we don't live in a land of constant conspiracy, why are conspiracy theories so widespread and credible? Nobody conspired to make a hole in the ozone layer and create the conditions for global warming, and if they had tried, they probably couldn't have pulled it off. But it happened anyway as a by-product of business as usual.

Do corporation executives conspire to give each other outrageous compensation packages? No, they just recognize quality when they see it. Because they sit on each other's boards of directors and know what folks just like themselves are worth they don't have to meet in dark corridors and plan it any more than filling station owners conspire to set the prices for gas at the pump. But it's always the same price in the same area.

Given the pattern of real conspiracies like Watergate and Iran-Contra, whenever something inexplicable happens, people don't have to be very imaginative to suppose that there is a conspiracy at work. Conspiracy theories offer us the comfort of letting us think that someone is in control, even if they are malign, so we don't have to suppose that things just happen because of the way our system is organized.

If there are conspiracies we can blame the bad guys, bring them to justice as the super heroes do, get the bad people out, and save the day so there is hope for the future. If our system is at fault, we have no one to blame but ourselves and we have to fix it. If there's no conspiracy disrupting El Nino, I can't hope to prevent its dissipation on the disagreeable weather that will follow. I'll just to have to get used to the cold.

Doctors and Lawyers in Fantasy Land

WPSU 6/23/2003

Everyone who invested in Enron or World Com lost their shirts. But not everyone can hope to recoup their losses by soaking someone else.

But that's what insurance companies are doing. The companies that are supposed to make an uncertain world safe by evening out the inevitable bumps are making the world more dangerous for us all by their greed and mismanagement. They are claiming that they are going broke by paying off claims, not by gambling on the stock market. That shifts the blame to the folks who buy insurance and justifies hiking everyone's rates.

Doctors swallowed that hook, line, and sinker. When the insurance companies raised their malpractice rates in Pennsylvania, some doctors closed up shop, left their patients to their own devices, and headed to Harrisburg. They asked the legislature to limit the insurance companies' liability for malpractice suits. That's supposed to stop the insurance companies from raising their rates to doctors and threatening to put them out of business.

But if the legislature limits the amount that victims of medical malpractice can get by suing the doctors, it would threaten to put some attorneys out of their fancy suits and cars if not out of business. So the trial lawyers turned against the doctors.

This created the spectacle of two of our land's most despised professional groups—lawyers and doctors—duking it out with each other on the steps of the legislature.

We can hope their current level of awareness prevails and that they *don't* figure out that the insurance companies are pulling the wool over their eyes. If they did that, they might get together. No telling what would come of that kind of unholy alliance.

But, on second thought, if they ever figured out what is going on in the real world, they might demand that insurance companies be responsible and get out of the business of playing the stock market. If they used their power in a responsible way like that, we might all benefit.

But I wouldn't hold my breath waiting for *that* to happen. People as self-interested as these doctors and lawyers are not likely to have anyone else in mind.

Reinventing Government

Not Broadcast

Not too long ago a friend of mine from Minnesota and I were in Washington, D.C. Both of us were struck by the fussing and fretting, the rush of important people doing monumental tasks, each more significant than the other, all vying for attention, money, votes, influence, power, all trying to get their own way.

Neither of us is from the Middle West, but after living there for some years, both of us had come to appreciate some of the virtues of that region. One of those is a down to earth human scaled sanity that kind of wears off on people of the coasts if they stay long enough.

It may have something to do with believing in people and respecting people. I think that in turn rests on some ideas of how people ought to be. You should do your share, take your turn, and be on time. You shouldn't take more than your share, interrupt, put yourself forward too much, brag, or be pushy. You should listen more than you talk and not be too sure of anything. You can sum it up in terms of a widely available negative role model: don't act like a hog.

We weren't in Washington pushing any big or important agendas or trying to get the attention of Congress or the President or the media, but we didn't notice much of that human scaled sanity we had become accustomed to. My friend concluded that there is no sense of reality inside the beltway. He was musing on the idea that it all gets lost in the rush and hurry and the press of politics—everybody acting like a hog.

And all of this important activity of important people is dissociated from the everyday lives of ordinary people. But my friend had a solution. He suggested the seat of government should be moved to Oshkosh, Wisconsin. That, he thought, would bring a sense of reality to the deliberations and the decisions. And maybe some sanity.

And it might slow things down a bit so people could act with more thought and craft and skill and attention to the needs of the land rather than just putting themselves forward all the time and being pushy.

I said I thought it might be a good idea, and I tried to imagine a government that was calm and quiet and deliberative and sane and that believed in its own people, a government that respected its people. It was such a stretch that while I allowed that his idea was pretty good, I wasn't sure it would work. Not just now, anyway. And it would probably ruin Oshkosh.

Encounter with a Goddess

Not Broadcast

I experienced an Epiphany waiting in the check-out line at the drugstore the other day. A display of refrigerator magnets featured Marilyn Monroe's celebrated breasts. The goddess of femininity was frozen in various poses of her fleshy voluptuousness as an icon to reproductivity.

All of a sudden I understood why the Equal Rights Amendment had not passed.

Not that it was Marilyn Monroe's fault. It was just because guys in legislatures voted on it and they understand their own focus on the reproductive dimensions of women—breasts, vaginas, sexual intecourse—the stuff of the propagation of the species, and the control of it all.

These guys know about herd management and that's what makes them sufficiently anxious that they can't bring themselves to grant women equality.

Any animal food production system centers on lots of females to supply the products of reproduction, the milk and honey of biblical images of plenty. You need one male to provide some sperm and you artificially inseminate the females so they produce offspring to eat and milk to drink. The males have no reproductive role, so you castrate them and fatten them up to eat. It's about the same for sheep, goats, pigs, chickens, or turkeys. If it's bees, you keep a couple of drones till they breed with the queen in their death flight and throw the rest out of the hive so the females can get on with producing the honey necessary for reproduction.

So as long as male legislators focus on the reproductive role of the females of their own species, they are going to see themselves in the same position as the males of other species they manage and feel nervous about it.

What are the excess males for? Decoration? Distraction? Dinner? What? That's worrisome. Especially to legislators who can't find much in the way of a convincing answer.

It all fell into place in a flash in that moment of contemplation of Marilyn Monroe's prominently displayed mammary glands by the check-out counter of the drug store. Moments later I reached the cash register, paid up, and left, satisfied with my encounter with the goddess and the enlightenment she had brought to me that morning.

The Paralysis of Choice

Not Broadcast

Not long ago I read an article about a packing plant that was recalling a batch of luncheon meat because they feared it might have been contaminated with salmonella.

What caught my eye was that the same stuff had been sent out under more than a dozen different brand names. This reminded me of a guy I used to know who worked in a shortening factory. He told me about changing the labels on the cans during the same production run and the many names for the same product.

This is what paralyzes me when I'm looking for instantaneous and miraculous relief from a cold in the drug store or cornflakes in the grocery store. I see fifteen different packages, each proclaiming its superiority. I read the microscopic text on the labels and discover they are all the same stuff. They are the same formulas if not from the same batch of the same factory.

It's even more insidious. Here in Iowa, farmers have to buy seed for hybrid corn every year. Many of the brands that compete with each other are precisely the same genetic make-up which originated with publicly funded research in agricultural colleges. The only way to know that, though, is to do genetic testing on the seed itself or somehow figure out its origins, usually a closely guarded secret just to protect the companies from the competition such revelations would bring. So there's a whole industry based on the well-protected secret that many products are precisely the same.

What kind of a society calls the same stuff by fifteen different names and pretends they are different. Why?

In Columbia, when the drug cartels were accused of contributing heavily to political campaigns, they protested that they gave to all sides. They didn't care who was elected, they just wanted to have the inside track to whoever it was. Maybe it's the same in the United States.

The problem facing any right thinking representative of an organized group with a political agenda and some money to buy influence is the same one that faces me in the super market. Pity the poor lobbyist, like a farmer buying seed corn, looking at the same thing in different wrappers, equally for sale to the highest bidder, with lots of effort on brand differentiation. There's not even a hint about contents in any hard-to-read-and-understand fine print.

It's not what brand of cornflakes you buy but that you buy some cornflakes to preserve your status as a consumer and get some breakfast. Is that corrupt? Or just business?

Keeping Bees

Not Broadcast

I learned a lot about people from keeping bees. I worked with an old beekeeper to learn a little of the art. He showed me how to calm excited bees by blowing smoke at them. Later, I started my own hives. I marveled at the concerted teamwork and enterprise of my bees and opened their hives more than necessary just to watch them working and admire their sense of methodically hexagonal geometry. The first year they made just enough honey to get through the winter and start a new hive, but the next summer I had to keep adding new boxes to hold the surplus honey.

Then, as winter approached I asked the old beekeeper how to get the bumper crop of honey away from the bees. He told me to take all of the boxes down and let all of the bees from the three hives mix up together. "They'll be confused," he said. "If you keep bees confused enough, you can do anything you want with them." He was right. Before the bees sorted out who was who, I made off with their honey, put the hives back together, and made my escape leaving them to regroup for winter.

I had to quit keeping bees when I came down with an anaphylactic reaction to their stings just as the Cold War was grinding down. The way I managed those bees was a lot like the governments of the world manage their people.

When I was in school learning the survival skills for a complex society, I had to practice my own death with duck-and-cover drills for the inevitable nuclear Armageddon.

I was well rehearsed when Jack Kennedy played chicken with the nukes over Cuba. The American, Soviet, European, and Asian governments so scared their people with such dramas and tales of diabolical foes and mutually assured destruction fabricated by our respective Drs. Strangelove that people, afraid and unorganized, let their governments do what they would.

To manage people, just keep them disorganized and blow plenty of smoke. Keep people worried about murder rather than traffic or industrial accidents. Keep attention focused on teenage pregnancy rather than the powerlessness of women in poverty. Keep people apprehensive about a drug problem rather than a tobacco or gasoline or alcohol problem. Keep people frightened about a criminal underclass and gangs rather than unemployment and hopelessness structured into our economy. Focus on welfare to deflect attention from the concentration of wealth in fewer hands and blame the problems on those who suffer the consequences.

My bees made honey for me alright--dark and complex heady stuff that made commercial honey seem like stripped down carbohydrates worthy of a name like "honey lite." And all I had to do was blow smoke and keep them confused.

Information

Not Broadcast

I heard a story of an East German woman who married a man because of his dissident beliefs and practices, had kids with him and only during the disclosures after the re-unification learned that he was an agent of the secret police who had been reporting all of the details of her daily life to the authorities ever since they had met. Though her friends envied her attentive husband, she divorced him when she found it was just his job.

I wondered at a system that bothered to collect, file, and archive such information on its people. Who would care? At times our FBI would have liked to have had such a system, and they tried, but even with J. Edgar Hoover's blackmail, they never had the budget to collect and maintain that kind of detail on that many people. They could never afford to hire half the people to watch the other half.

Then I thought about all of the information about me that is collected, archived and stored and how paltry the FBI's efforts have been in comparison. In this age of electronic billing and credit and debit cards, our economic lives are open books to anyone who cares to check up on how and where we spend our money. It's cheap because we inform on ourselves. Computers keep track when we pay our debts and the information merchants map our consumer preferences by zip-code.

Some people worry that all of this information, available at the stroke of a computer's mouse, opens our inner-most secrets to strangers. Money is at least as private to us as sex and no one wants strangers looking at such intimate matters. The idea that someone knows more than we do about our money feels like an invasion of privacy.

Others suggest that such detailed economic information simply opens the way to true democracy via the workings of the magic of the invisible hand of the market. If you want to be able to benefit from niche marketing, manufacturers and merchandisers have to know what niche you are in. If you want to take advantage of all of the technological advances in any realm of everyday life from diapers to dishwashers, it behooves you to let people know who you are and what you are about so they can supply your every desire.

The better the information, the less hit and miss the market can be, the better it can serve our needs, the more accurate our dollar votes, and the more democratic the provision of life's necessities.

I expect the East Germans had equally compelling rationales for watching the intimate lives of their people. Concerned with the welfare of people's immortal souls, the inquisitors of medieval Europe had their good reasons to scrutinize religious conformity. The only difference is what they thought sufficiently important to document. A political society records ideological deviance; a religious one, supernatural practices; an economic one, economic data. One of these days I expect we'll hear a story about an American woman who divorces her attentive husband because he was hired by a marketing firm to learn the intimate details of her consumer desires and economic practices. Either way, Big Brother is watching. And I'm sure it's always for our own good.

On Power, Anthropology, and Universities

2000 SfAA News 11(4)

The incredible structural power arrayed against unions became apparent as I tried to understand the ethnography of locals in Chicago. A multitude of laws, practices and highly paid consulting firms act as a management wall against organized labor. Even universities are not immune, as a look at any campaign to organize graduate assistants will show. Universities claim that working for them is not work, that organization interferes with mentoring relationships. If anyone is looking for a Ph.D. dissertation topic, I suggest a comparative study of mentoring relationships among universities with and without graduate assistant unions. I'd like to see some data.

We see the power of universities in other arenas as well especially agriculture. About the time martial law was declared in Poland in the 1980's, when I was at the University of Iowa, I got interested in the Farmer's Union in that state. In the archives I read newspaper and magazine articles about the "cow war" of 1931 and martial law. I went to the courthouse where the union leaders were tried and got copies of the evidence and proceedings. There was a change of venue because there could not be a fair trial in the county of the accused where everyone was a member of the union. The court records showed that all the jurors that convicted the accused union leaders were members of the Farm Bureau.

I started reading about the history of the Farm Bureau and kept finding connections to the Land Grant Institutions. About then, I dropped that line of inquiry. Someone, an anthropologist whose grandfather had been involved in the radical agrarian movement, asked me why I didn't write a book about it. I replied that it was too depressing. The story is too familiar to even be interesting. Power is arrayed against those without it to force compliance. But the unsettling part of it was that a whole propaganda machine was made to support these uses of power. Central to it were the Farm Bureau and the burgeoning sciences of agriculture that took as a doctrine, as holy as any that any theologians ever discussed, was that farms are businesses.

Now most of them may be because there are fewer and fewer family farms. The industrialized agriculture that Goldschmidt warned about fifty years ago in California is now a reality across our land and much of the rest of the world. In the control of food is real power. Monsanto can mount an educational program about genetically modified plants that is powered by a budget that could run a third world country or a university. They've even bought their own agricultural university to provide credibility.

In our studies of the swine industry, Kendall Thu and I wanted to provide accurate information for Iowa legislators. We wanted something that would stand up in a court of law, something that would stand up to the sneering agricultural economists and self-satisfied meat-science guys from the ag schools. When Kendall organized a meeting of 35 experts on air and water quality, social, economic, and health issues, everyone cautioned us that it wasn't enough to be accurate, correct, right. We had to be credible.

Circulating through informal networks, our story about the swine industry in North Carolina achieved the status of an underground classic before the Des Moines Register published some of it, and we started hearing from deans and department heads at universities and extension services throughout the Midwest, and state legislators who let us know that we lacked credibility because we'd gotten the wrong answer. As some farmers had put it, "those guys from the ag schools come and tell us that hog shit don't stink." That's the right answer. That's what was credible.

To be credible, we worked with a planning committee that included folks who knew all the right answers. Kendall undertook the challenge of getting funds and keeping all the parties involved. But we began to fear we were being absorbed into the process, becoming part of it. The price of credibility could be our independence and our ability to articulate a meaningful critique. We could see ourselves pulling our punches and developing accounts that would be credible, agreeable, acceptable, and maybe consequential. But not cogent.

We figured we could be either cogent or consequential but not both. We were echoing C. Wright Mills's essay on structural immorality in government (reprinted in *Power, Politics, and People: the Collected Essays of C. Wright Mills* New York: Oxford University Press, 1963. Edited by Irving Louis Horowitz.) He said you can stay outside of the process and understand it, or you can get involved in it and be corrupted. His example? One senator Richard M. Nixon. That was in the fifties. Due to Kendall's unfaltering diplomacy and hard work, the conference did take place, the work got published, and into the hands of the legislators in Iowa and many other states. By then we were taking seriously the challenge of understanding the channels of information and how some signals get amplified and some damped.

Here's what we found out. The largest contributor to the Republican governor's campaign fund was Iowa's largest industrial swine producer. The governor set up a shadow department of agriculture to report on swine production. It was filled with people from various commodity production groups. The governor provided funds to Iowa State University for research on swine issues. The dean of the College of Agriculture chaired the governor's livestock commission and provided "credible" research for the governor to support industrial swine production so that industry could support him. We've told that story, and a similar one from North Carolina. We learned that no amount of accurate information in the hands of policy makers made any difference up against that kind of power structure. We were operating with a false model of the political process and the place of factual information in it. Iowa State was operating in the process as something beyond the familiar mission statement of universities—to create, disseminate and preserve knowledge. They were using it as a weapon against the weak. We opted for cogency when we edited our book, *Pigs, Profits, and Rural Communities*. As of the last election, Iowa has a new governor of a different party and Iowa State has a new Dean of Agriculture. Kendall tells me that there is room for optimism.

There may be some room for optimism even in the face of industrialized agriculture. I've started looking at alternatives such as community-supported agriculture. Laura DeLind assures us that the community part is over-stated, and I think she is right. But there's still a lot left in the idea of a group of consumers contracting with a farmer to provide vegetables to them every week for more than half of the year. I noticed that one of the figures Laura cites is that there are at most 100,000 CSA members in the U.S. As I was discussing these figures with a colleague here at Penn State, I mentioned that as a percentage of the U.S. population that's about a decimal point with three zeroes in front of a 3. Not much. Then she pointed out that CSAs got started only a few years ago.

I didn't have to read far before I came across the ag economists and started laughing. It wasn't that funny. They were doing the same thing that the aggies from Ames did back in the 1920s and 30s. They were scratching their heads and wondering how a person could stay in business without imputing proper values to all the inputs—labor, rent, and so on. The problem with CSAs was that they were not proper businesses.

If CSAs continue growing at that rate, we'll have aggies telling us that Monsanto can organize CSAs more efficiently than any family farmer. Those big guys, they know how to do a business. They are credible. They're the guys from the ag schools.

When things like this happen, and when Land-Grant Universities take a hard-nosed stance against their workers organizing, we see the distance we've traveled between an ideal of universities serving the people in a democracy that the Morrill Act envisioned in 1862 and the contemporary reality of universities being tools of industry and management.

On Human Rights

2002 *SfAA News* 13(1)

The U.S. is shocked, I tell you, shocked to learn that we've been voted off the UN Human Rights Commission. Austria, France and Sweden are on the Commission along with Vietnam, Cuba and China.

We Americans discuss human rights a lot. We talk 'til we're blue in the face about the necessity for freedom of the press, freedom of speech, freedom of religion. Our Constitution guarantees us these rights and others like them. Some of us who haven't heard about the National Guard are persuaded that to maintain a well-regulated militia we still need to be armed to the teeth—as a natural human right.

Back in the 18th century, radical dissenters who were rebelling against the legitimately constituted government needed those militias and their weapons to prevent the authorities from catching and hanging or shooting them. But now we have the National Guard. And the Brits are long-gone.

Listen to a Brit:

The American Declaration of Independence is one of the most comic and preposterous documents ever penned. Yet Thomas Jefferson was not, in any technical or ordinary sense, a fool. This, however, did not prevent him and his fellows from affirming something totally absurd—namely, that views which, for 99 per cent of mankind, would have been unintelligible or at best blasphemous, heretical and subversive, were actually *self-evident*. (Gellner 1995:18, emphasis original).

Well, what do you expect of a Brit? To Americans, raised on this ideology, culture is obvious, natural, and self-evident.

When we discover that there are different systems of meaning, that people live in different ways and different worlds, that no system is self-justifying, universal or self-evident, that cultures vary and that self-evidence "is a shadow of a culture" (ibid.), the revelation is intoxicating. Culture-blind Americans are thus vulnerable to . . . hermeneutics. Our well-meaning British colleague does not advocate a prohibition of hermeneutics to protect us from ourselves because he knows that will only lead to hermeneutic speakeasies and the mafia smuggling in thick descriptions from Canada—but he does advocate voluntary restraint—a Hermeneutics Anonymous—and medical supervision for the legitimate scholarly use of hermeneutics.

In spite of that we tend to think, the American inventory of human rights is natural, universal, and self-evident. I can't be the only American anthropologist who has been called on that. While I was living with Shan peasants in the valleys of Northwestern Thailand, people were listening to the news of a presidential election in the U.S. One evening the headman and a number of villagers visited to ask whether it was true that people in my country actually believed that all people are equal. This was so foreign to their world-view that they wanted the confirmation of a credible source. Immediately I understood the problem.

Shan live in a world of beings of differential power, a world in which some are powerful and some are weak and all are arranged in a hierarchy of power from the greatest to the least. All of this is verified by the experience of life and the ideology of Buddhism. How could such basic truths of logic and practice be denied?

How can an American explain to anyone else the epistemological status of such a statement—all people are equal—in a society in which we incessantly repeat the words but shudder at the thought much less the practice of any kind of gender, racial, or economic equality. Deans, male and female, at the University of Iowa where I was a department chairman even had an explicit policy that faculty members could not receive equal merit pay raises. Any one of these administrators would have earnestly upheld the abstract assertion that all people are created equal, but they would equally vehemently insist that my colleagues could not all be equal. In this they were very much like Shan peasants. The assertion of equality comes to nothing but words and words are cheap in a society that guarantees free speech.

Rights are cheap as long as there is nothing to them. We can discuss them the livelong day. Significant rights, rights to healthcare, education, livelihood, shelter, dignity in old or at any age, these are substantive and costly.

It takes visiting Icelanders a while to comprehend that most Americans feel that they are one paycheck from the gutter, insecure in their jobs that promise only vulnerable futures in a land in which institutions have no loyalty to individuals. But Scandinavians understand it when they notice how obsessed we Americans are with our financial futures—how we watch the stock market, think about retirement programs and savings accounts. To people who are guaranteed a secure retirement, healthcare, education for their kids, housing and livelihood, this is a puzzle. Why would people choose to spend their time and energy in that way?

Our constitution and all of our talk of human rights do not guarantee any important right. The right to vote? For what? Provide the important rights—ones that provide security—and the others— those that people without security assert—are unnecessary. I think it's time we stopped blinding ourselves with talk about vacuous rights and start working on gaining real ones for everyone on this planet. We can start with our own universities and towns. That's why I'm not all that upset that the United States is no longer in the catbird seat to monitor the human rights of the rest of the planet. Austria? There may be something to worry about there. Or France. But not the ouster of the U.S.

Reference Cited

Gellner, Ernest. 1995. Anthropology and Politics: Revolutions in the Scared Grove. Cambridge. Blackwell Society for Applied Anthropology Page 5.

Single Issue Politics

2002 *SfAA News* 13(2)

"What's a tree-hugger?" my 9-year-old friend asked.

"Someone who loves Mother Earth and tries to keep the earth clean—someone who likes trees and tries to save them so we can all enjoy them and helps keep our water and air clean," her mom answered, looking daggers at me for my derisive comment.

"Well," the daughter proclaimed, "then I'm a tree-hugger."

The stakes are so high and the opponents are so mighty that the only way to influence policy is via sharply focused movements and messages that carry sufficient emotional wallop to get people to open their minds and their wallets. The policy ground is quicksand. Opponents erode the edges of any victory with legislative initiatives and amendments, media campaigns, court cases, administrative rule-making processes, appointments to boards and agencies until nothing is left to savor but the memory of a triumph in the good fight. Think of any example from the National Rifle Association's perverted concept of human rights to Monsanto's distorted concept of an educational campaign.

Policies go to those sufficiently well-endowed to be vigilant and persistent. Single issue politics is the key to hope for any less well-moneyed than corporate coalitions, even though in the process of moving policy through its complex channels single issue advocates distort realities beyond all recognition. When they are victorious they may well deform realities as badly as their enemies.

In a booming economy, shrimpers and fishers could find work in shipyards or oil and gas or construction as they were put out of work when environmentalists won fishery regulations that helped to make the Gulf of Mexico a playground for the rich. In days gone by, shrimpers might have worked in the pine forests to tap pine resin and make turpentine, tar and naval stores. Now those lands are cropped with spindly evergreens for the pulp paper industry that fouls the Gulf breezes. Those same tree-huggers might be eager allies of any fishers that remain when agricultural runoff sucks the oxygen and life from the Gulf's waters.

In Thailand, international environmental groups applaud and support the outlawing of hillside agriculture and programs to plant trees where villagers I lived with used to grow rice on swiddens. Trees are good. Cutting trees is bad. The eucalyptus they planted are for making paper in the mills of the lowland elites. They are just another crop like the evergreens of the Gulf. The two-thirds of villagers who don't have access to enough irrigated land to feed themselves can work for wages for the people who have more than enough or in the paper mills or cleaning the houses of the city elite or in a factory.

In a land where we all sell our labor, who considers the price of selling your labor rather than making your own living?

When these thoughts run through my head, I imitate the Icelandic mode of running lexical items together to make new words like "sandal-flapping-latte-sucking-animal-loving-tofu-eating-tree-hugging-liberal." When I see industrial agriculture and swine production polluting our national waters, I'm glad tree-huggers are there raising hell for the water and trees.

So, I cautioned my young friend as we put on our coats and boots to go to a Christmas tree farm to cut a tree, we'd have to be on the lookout for tree-huggers.

As we cut the tree, I thought that issues never come singly, though our politics may make it so.

Why Witchcraft Won't Go Away

2002 *SfAA News* 13(4)

Friends, anthropologists, fellow-citizens—lend me your ears. I have come to praise Marvin Harris, not bury him. The good people do is oft interred with their bones. But not Marvin Harris. He left us a valuable legacy in the exemplary clarity of his popular writings.

After thirty years his books speak to our students to challenge their imaginations and make them think hard about culture and causality. As he circles in from far away and exotic lands to our own he leads readers to consider how anthropology pertains to their own societies and their own lives.

You want to see a sacred cow? He dares us Americans. Look at your car. Consider the energy costs. Think of the industries that support it from construction to steel to oil. Understand the politics of it. Each American in 1970 used 60 times the energy of one Indian. "Automobiles and airplanes are faster than oxcarts, but they do not use energy more efficiently" (1974:32)

He promoted the idea that we can understand cultural similarities and differences and historical processes in terms of the political and economic forces that shape the material conditions of peoples' everyday lives.

He explained the witch craze of Europe as a response to the conditions of the time. Feudalism had collapsed; capitalism had not yet become established. There were revolutionary religious movements all across Europe. "One way to get rid of the troublemaking alienated poor," he tells us (1974:229) "was to enlist their aid in the Holy Wars, or Crusades, aimed at recapturing Jerusalem from Islam." Sound familiar from today's (October 11, 2002) news? But in those days, these military efforts were less well organized. They tended to backfire and become revolutionary, aimed at the rulers who set them in motion. Witches to the rescue.

Witches? "What happened?" Harris asks, not "What did people think happened?" In his straightforward way he challenges us to sort out realities from the fantasies of the various participants.

"…the poor came to believe that they were being victimized by witches and devils instead of princes and popes. … Did the price of bread go up, taxes soar, wages fall, jobs grow scarce? It was the work of witches." (1974:123).

The state wasn't responsible for the economic crisis that befell the continent. Witches were. The state would aid the church in helping to defend people against these enemies. Was a rapacious nobility to blame? No! It was witches. The church and state protected people against an "enemy who was omnipresent but difficult to detect," (1974:238).

The ruling class, Marvin Harris explained, perpetuated a witch mania to disperse and fragment people, demobilize the poor, increase their social distance, fill them with mutual suspicions, make people fearful, heighten peoples' insecurity, and to make people feel helpless and dependent on the governing classes to protect them.

In so doing, it drew the poor further and further away from confronting the ecclesiastical and secular establishment with demands for the redistribution of wealth and the leveling of rank… It was the magic bullet of society's privileged and powerful classes. That was its secret. (1974:240).

Today people worry about the efficient uses of energy, the oil business, and the relationship of big oil to big government. The stock market crashes and sends the economy into a tailspin as business empires built on bogus accounting practices collapse. In the collapse, people worry about the increasing poverty and joblessness that stalk them. Insurance companies increase co-payments for healthcare to insure their profitability. People begin to think they should be grateful for a minimum wage job as low-paying jobs replace well-paying ones. People fret over concentrations of wealth and worry about connections between barons of business and political elites. What's the solution?

Is a rapacious business/government nobility to blame? No! It must be….witches? That won't play in today's secular society. Communists? All gone. What can business and state protect people against? An "enemy who was omnipresent but difficult to detect," (1974:238).

A war on terrorism just fits the bill. Thanks, Marvin. Rest in peace.

Reference Cited

Harris, Marvin. 1974. Cows, Pigs, Wars, and Witches: The Riddles of Culture. New York: Vintage.

The Acid Test of Democracy

2004 SfAA News 15(1)

There's a T-shirt that proclaims, "Those who cast the votes decide nothing. Those who count the votes decide everything." That's attributed to Joe Stalin who could throw a convincing one person, one vote election just like the American Anthropological Association does, and win every time by controlling the nominations. Like the Bush family, he also controlled who counted the votes. Joe Stalin is the figure that came to mind when a Chicago union leader explained to me about democratic centralism. I saw the central part, but I couldn't figure out where the democratic part was.

That's what Suzan Erem and I are studying now with a grant from NSF. We continually ask, where's the democracy?

About a year ago I reported in these pages that Chicago's International Brotherhood of Teamsters Local 705, under the leadership of Jerry Zero and his slate, passed a resolution against the then-impending war in Iraq.

We saw democracy in membership meetings and stewards' meetings where anyone could speak up. We saw it at the bylaws meeting where people debated and voted on the rules that govern the union, a meeting that was raucous, but surely democratic by any measure. The members weren't letting anything happen behind their backs.

We saw democracy in the frontlines of class warfare where management sat at the bargaining tables opposite negotiating teams composed of very articulate truck drivers and negotiators. We saw it in the nominations meeting where it took two people to get a slate on the ballot—one to nominate and one to second rather than the impossible hurdles we saw at other locals. We saw it in the concern of all the reps and officers with representation and contract enforcement. "The way to get re-elected is to provide excellent service," more than one person told us. And they did. They won impossible grievances. One case was so impossible that everyone explained why it could not be won but the guy won! "Sometimes you catch lightening in a bottle," an old timer said, "and you don't question it too much…or expect it to ever happen again."

Throughout we heard about the fucking feeder drivers who drive the big rigs between UPS depots. The adjective always went before the noun, no matter who was speaking. Except feeder drivers. We met *them* at the picnic that launched the campaign to re-elect Jerry Zero and his slate for a third term. They introduced themselves as "the opposition." We went to their depots and rode with their reps. When they put up an opposition candidate, we tried to get in with them, but they weren't having anything to do with us.

We were interested in the politics of obligation that we had seen in other locals but found that something else was going on here. No obligation went with saving a guy his job or getting a good contract or anything else. It's just what a union does. It's not a favor that you need to think about repaying.

As the campaign heated up we had no compunction about pitching in to help Jerry Zero and his slate. We went to leaflet early in the morning and late at night and helped with a phone bank in between. This put us cheek by jowl with the folks we were trying to understand, on the front lines of democracy, getting out the vote.

Early one morning at the gate to one of the barns, a feeder driver who was leafleting for the opposition got in my face and hissed, "Doesn't this cross the line between objectivity and advocacy? Taking sides?"

I tried to act like a Teamster. I stood my ground nose to nose, didn't flinch, stared into his eyes and said, "We discussed dat." Indeed we had. Participant observation won. And we couldn't have learned half as much being aloof.

We polled reps. "My barns are solid," each one around the breakfast table after a leafleting reported. "So what's the point of all of this frenetic campaigning?" I wondered, often aloud. "Is it a ritual to make the staff share adversity and increase their solidarity?" Staff people were up early and stayed late every day for six weeks to get their slate elected. They paid for the campaign from their own pockets, time and energy. I put the question to an old time politico as we drove to a barn to leaflet one evening. "It's better to run scared than to run confident," he responded. And he explained in graphically expletive detail what's wrong with the fucking feeder drivers. "One point of view is that we'll beat them by a thousand votes, so bad they'll never raise their heads again."

Suzan went to Chicago for the vote count at Teamster City. I had to stay at Penn State and teach. I made it through my classes till Saturday, the day before Pearl Harbor day. I could imagine the scene at the auditorium, and tried to stay busy, but called Suzan's cell phone four times asking for news. The phone was off. She didn't get the messages. Early in the evening she called.

"We lost," she said dejectedly, "I gotta go."

I was stunned. So was everyone else. The fucking feeder drivers won.

When a Chicago reporter asked a labor studies guy what the upset meant, he said that the fact that an opposition slate could win an election meant that 705 was in fact reformed, democratic, and no longer run by the mob.

I don't think that's it. What does this tell us about democracy? I think it tells us that elections are not the acid test of democracy. Of the 20,000 members about 8,000 returned mail ballots. That's about the same 40 percent that vote in U.S. presidential elections. In a post-election survey, we heard stewards say, like the 60 percent of Americans and most American Anthropological Association members who don't vote, that it doesn't matter who wins. The American Anthropological Society has elections but to get nominated you have to make it past a gauntlet of guardians of equality that would make the old 705 mobsters or Joe Stalin blush. In that process it doesn't matter who you vote for but who gets nominated. That example shows just how easy it is for a well-organized minority to control elections.

Elections are not where democracy is built or lost. That happens at negotiating tables, in grievance hearings, in the management of collective assets, in the determination to spread the benefits of real democracy by political involvement and opposition to wars in Iraq, organizing against Bush, solidarity with other unions, the Labor Party and civic groups. It's giving working people more control of their work and their lives by getting good contracts and enforcing them. It's in not being blind to economic atrocities and being with the people in class warfare. That's democracy. The 705 elections? We don't know. We have to wait to see what they mean for 705.

"It's the Economy, Stupid"

2004 *SfAA News* 15(2)

In State College, PA, home of Penn State, people packed a whole Corning factory in containers and moved it to China. A thousand people lost jobs. Then an electronics factory closed. Our students all have parents, uncles, aunts, siblings or friends who have lost jobs to free trade.

When I wanted some help with a gadget I bought for my computer I called the number on the package and talked to a guy named George. Very pleasant, but no help. I fooled with it some more and tried again with Samantha's soothing help. George and Samantha live in Bombay. That's not Bombay, Texas, but India. Thousands more tech support and telemarketing jobs gone from the U.S.

Our students work minimum or near minimum wage jobs, or if they're lucky add tips. And we ask them to buy intro books that cost eighty bucks? They have to stretch those wages to cover rent and food. They call tech support and talk to folks in India. They see software development off-shored. They see the newspaper articles about computer science not being what it used to be in the U.S. First manufacturing leaves and now white-collar jobs are flowing out. They wonder what their college degrees will be worth by the time they finish and stretch their wages to cover an occasional bender. This is real life as they experience it…joblessness, doubt, insecurity, lack of opportunity. When people talked about leveling the playing field, I don't think they meant to make everyone poor, but that's what the kids we teach are experiencing.

I am not much of a believer in education except insofar is it's anchored in experience.

One of those high priced intro books suggests a connection between its stories and experience with a photo of some painted savages juxtaposed with one of sports fans with painted faces.

But we aren't the only ones who try to educate people, letting them know they are not alone their experiences from painted faces to the experience of kin relations. And our students aren't the only ones facing hard times.

Just before our SfAA meeting in Dallas, I was sitting in a folding chair in a hotel ballroom in Philadelphia. This fieldwork with unions seems to require more time in folding chairs than on picket lines.

In front of me were tables arranged in ranks and files for delegates from the constituent locals of the Pennsylvania AFL-CIO. Bill George, the president, was telling how he went to Miami to the WTO meeting to ask for compassion and was met with armed people tear-gassing college kids. He came to this convention to do something about it. "Bush doesn't believe America was built on the sweat and genius of working people," but on the wealth of corporations—and working people live in fear. He said labor is under attack, but the legacy of the labor movement is to get back up. Always get back up.

The president of the International Association of Fire Fighters was late because some of his members had been killed in a church fire. "The American working class has gotten a raw deal," he said. Everyone stood and clapped when he told them there were only two people who needed lay-off notices, Bush and Cheney. Rich Trumka from the national AFL-CIO, told the brothers and sisters that we're lucky to have leaders who, "Just won't quit and won't give up." He started spouting numbers the way I like to do. The number of people without healthcare, that file for bankruptcy every day, who work full time and live in poverty, of kids in substandard schools. The numbers will increase by the time you read this, so check them out. He went on to say that Bush isn't standing still—he is actively attacking unions on every front. Every person in that room had felt it in one way or another. They knew it was true. It connected with their experience. So did all the numbers.

Then we heard more numbers from the Pennsylvania Secretary of Labor. *Is this going to be on the test?* I wondered. *No, this* is *the test,* I answered.

Bill George sends the sergeant-at-arms out into the hallways to round up the delegates who had drifted off in boredom during the numbers. The band plays "Sixteen Tons." Cecil Roberts, president of the United Mine Workers from West Virginia, recites his genealogy and the ancestors who died in the mines. His language is not the same as the Pennsylvanians'. Coolness greets the foreign tones and cadences. But he isn't there to lecture. He preaches. This leadership, he tells us in rousing tones, "Is the blood of your blood, the flesh of your flesh, the soul of your soul...." People start clapping, jumping to their feet, warming up. He evokes the Pittston Coal Strike when Bill George came down to help. He tells how just after 9/11, 13 mineworkers were killed in an explosion in Alabama. More numbers. All bad. "It's time for us to take back our country! Tell them this land is my land, this land is our land... A government of the people, by the people, for the people...we ARE the people...We BUILT this nation...." More on outsourcing and job loss to free trade. Again and again delegates rise to their feet with applause and cheers. "It's time for a living wage in the U.S. of A. A living wage for all God's children. It's time the working class had what George Bush and Cheney's families have...when they get sick YOU pay for it." He evokes the memories of Gandhi, Moses, and Jesus who were mocked and how they, like Martin Luther King and John L. Lewis marched. "Ain't no George Bush-Cheney-union busting White House—no jail house, gonna turn US around."

A few days later, back at Penn State, I was one of about a dozen who attended a town meeting in a big lecture hall where representatives from the Steelworkers and the Pennsylvania Manufacturer's Association, a couple of businessmen, and a woman from the United Way all sang the same tune against free trade! They had numbers, too, in the form of charts. All diving toward the floor. I had never expected to see a union person share a podium with a guy from the Manufacturer's Association. That was disorienting enough, but then I heard one of the businessmen saying things that *I* usually say—economics is a religion, not a science; economists can model what has happened, but can't predict the future because they really don't know what they are talking about. He talked about the breaking up of local economies. By then I had dropped my pencil in shock as he said something like, "They say economies are natural, follow laws like the laws of physics. They say, 'You don't ask how many people have been hurt by the law of gravity, do you?' But economies are not natural. People make the policies that make the economies. These economists remind me of those ideologists in the former Soviet Union who were so committed to an ideology that they could not see their own system collapsing around their ears."

There was no preaching here, but a former human relations director for Corning, now retired, talked about killing the goose that lays the golden egg. The Corning factory needed boxes. Now the box factory is closed. They needed pallets and skids. Now that factory is closed. It rippled out. That giant sucking sound. This is education through experience.

The AFL-CIO leaders were clear in their message. Vote for Kerry. Defeat Bush. The Manufacturer's Association guy was less clear. I asked him point blank how he would translate his observations into political action. "I'm not going to vote for Kerry," he announced. He elaborated that the problem is bigger than Democrat-Republican. He had little faith that any Democrat could do much about it. This group advocated organizing a social movement like the civil rights movement to staunch the flow of jobs, to reign in free trade in favor of fair trade.

So what do we do? What do we do with the numbers and the experiences and what we see around us in our communities and our country and our world? I'm nearly as skeptical as the Manufacturer's Association guy. Not quite, but nearly. I'll vote Democratic, because it's the only thing I can think of to do. But when I contemplate the reason that our whole country didn't take to the streets after the last election the way people did in the former Soviet Georgia or in Taiwan when they suspected stolen elections, I can't help but think it's because it didn't matter that much who won. But now we're four years down the pike. Now, with a union-busting White House and an administration run by business insiders concentrating wealth in fewer and fewer hands like never before, it may just matter.

But there's a more profound thing that we can do if we are teachers of any kind. We can teach it as it is. We can connect our anthropology to the experience of our students and give them ways to understand it. We can let our kids know about the processes of globalization and how they affect their towns and regions, their cities and families…and their prospects for the future. We can let them know how those processes aren't natural, like weather, but products of policies. We can let them know who makes those policies and whose interests they serve. We can teach about the realities of our class system. We can let them know that what they experience as class really *is* class and not tell them it's something different. We can assign the books our colleagues have written on these subjects. We can show them how ethnography matters. We can help them understand their own social-political-economic system. We can paint the big picture for our kids just as labor leaders did for their members. After that, we have to trust them to use the knowledge well.

Why I'm Nervous

2004 *SfAA News* 15(3)

I'm scared. And I'm puzzled.

Suzan Erem and I have been studying labor unions for a while. Our book on our work in the Middle West, *Class Acts*, is coming out from Paradigm Publishers. Now, funded by an NSF grant, we are observing contract negotiations with Service Employees International Union (SEIU) 1199P in Pennsylvania.

An exhausted mediator exclaims to me in the privacy of the hallway that this kind of bargaining, where you let the whole peanut gallery in, takes a long time. Caught between immovable managers and an intent union bargaining team, he's beginning to get exasperated. I'd talked with him at other, less nerve-racking, negotiations where he could facilitate motion on both sides. He told me about the old days with steel workers.

Bargaining teams get punchy late at night after a full day of work, junk food during caucuses, and the rigors of negotiating. While management prepares their next response, union members tell stories of dementia wards, unbearable supervisors, human kindness, the foibles of husbands and lovers. They joke and banter. I sit with the smokers and listen; I join the non-smokers and listen. I follow the mediator into the lair of management to hear their thinking, but if I revealed it, they'd have to shoot me. I talk with the union organizers. The drama increases as the contract's expiration date approaches.

Suzan and I see only one small part of the union members' lives. Far from the late-night negotiations, we see a different part of their lives on this is beautiful Saturday morning after a week of chilly rain. The air is clear and the sun is shining. In the morning coolness, I work up a sweat in jeans and my SEIU purple t-shirt as I walk up hills. Today we visit the working class where they live—the small part of it that's organized by unions, anyway.

Numbered streets intersect numbered avenues as they climb a hill from all four directions. At one foot of the hill is a courthouse; at another, a school. A junior high school sits on top. Street signs say, "Emergency Snow Route Use Snow Tires or Chains." There are lots of steps and the streets are steep. A city bus rumbles through. Some sidewalks are brick; most are cement. Some are pitted with potholes, slabs of others project at angles precarious for any pedestrian. An exercise walker stays on the streets. Between the well-kept mostly two-story houses is room for walks of brick or cement. Any of these houses would bring a fortune in California, but there is no view of the Pacific, and few of them are for sale. This is Altoona, PA.

It is what some who don't believe in a class system would can a middle class neighborhood. I would call it a working class neighborhood.

Many houses and people sport some American flag motif, as many as eleven of twenty-four in one block where I counted. It's a week after Memorial Day and Ronald Reagan just died.

Here American workers make their...homes? What do you call a building where you sleep days to recover enough to return to the next night shift? Where your spouse works days and tries to keep it quiet while he or she vacuums the house on this glorious summer day? A home? Maybe. House for sure.

The birds and squirrels run and chatter in the trees and I wonder how many folks could afford these houses today with their diminished wages. Many have kids who have grown and married. I didn't ask because it wasn't on my survey, but many are at an age where they could have paid off their mortgages if they bought in their mid-twenties.

Most cars parked on the streets are no more than a few years old. One guy tinkers with his motorcycle while a neighbor across the street sits on her porch to smoke a cigarette and read a newspaper. The other folks are sleeping, gone, or working.

Suzan and I are with a Pennsylvania labor walk to ask union members how they will vote in November and what they think the important issues are. Because of the new "campaign reform" laws, unions are prohibited from using funds collected from members to talk to non-union people. Instead of organizing to talk to registered Democrats, as in days gone by, unions now organize to talk to their own, no matter their party affiliation. I find it hard to believe that 40 percent of 1199P's members could be Republicans. I wonder why any working person would support a party that systematically wars on them. I'm learning. I've been to nineteen houses. Twelve people are gone of whom four are kids who worked union jobs long enough to get on my list but now live in other places.

Of the people I've talked to, two are for Bush; two are undecided; five are for Kerry. In this swing state, Kerry wins these union houses by a squeaky one vote. And as in most elections, a sizable portion didn't get counted. Six folks said healthcare and six said "exporting jobs" are their main issues. That makes twelve, but three listed both. Who knows what the folks who weren't home think. "It's a small sample," I try to console myself.

After I finish my first neighborhood, I meet Suzan and Molly at Molly's van. Molly is a member of the Communication Workers of America who has worked at Verizon for 23 years and has lived in Altoona all her life. We were put together as a team that morning at the local labor council building where we got our maps, our forms, and leaflets.

We cruise to the school and Suzan and I climb up the slope to the next address. We are met by a yapping Yorkshire terrier puppy and a guy who is recovering from a stroke, supports Kerry, and says social security is the big issue because it's taken him forever to get his first check.

We pass a guy planting a tree between the pavement and his sidewalk. He's not on the list so I just say, "pretty tree." Across the valley we see a cemetery on the next hill. Nobody's home at the next couple of addresses so we coast down the hill to the car. Suzan and Molly drive off and I go to another area to walk.

Altoona was built as a railroad town. Once-upon-a-time, everyone who lived here except the few in management was union. When there were jobs. Before the railroads were emasculated. Before the unions were busted by Republican labor boards and policies. Before free trade sent what jobs were left to other lands with cheaper labor and fewer regulations. Now it's a hike between union houses.

I walk up a steep slope and a bunch of steps to get to a door. A man answers and I am whacked with the smell of stale cigarette smoke. He's undecided. He calls to his wife who is putting groceries away in the kitchen. She comes to the door smoking a cigarette and says she's for Bush. "Issues? Social Security, I'm getting older." Their daughter, also on my list, has moved out.

"How can I understand this?" I ask myself. I have no answer.

I climb up the stairs to the back of the next place on my list to find a crew rehabbing the upstairs. "No, nobody lives here," they told me.

I hear vacuum cleaners inside the houses I pass on the way to the next one on the list. An undecided woman answers. Her husband works night shift and is sleeping, but for sure he's a Kerry man. His issue is jobs because he's been laid off since October and just found work again.

A tall heavy-set guy with a shaven head is waxing a dark blue Volkswagen Jetta on the street. I ask directions. He points the way and explains how best to walk to avoid more hills than necessary. He's not on my list, so I don't ask any questions. "Good looking car," I say.

"I keep my cars up," he responds. "It's like therapy," he adds slapping me on the back with a laugh.

I follow his directions and see my next destination is a bit of a hike away so I pick up the pace. A few minutes later he cruises by and offers me a lift. The air conditioning feels good. I don't even know if he's a Republican. A random act of kindness.

As I get out of the car, I see a woman going from a car to the house I am looking for. "You live here?" I ask. A baby is crying inside. "It's my daughter's. I'm babysitting."

The next address on my list is annotated, "retired." The woman who answers the door is undecided. She thinks education is an issue. I can check off "healthcare," "exporting jobs," and "social security." Education's not on the list, so I write it in. "And senior issues. This Medicare deal isn't helping anyone." I write more in the small blank space for "other."

I hike back to the intersection where I said I'd meet Molly and Suzan and we drive back to the hall for lunch. It's 1:30. We fill out a survey about our work. Yes, we got enough training. Comments? Yeah. I wrote, "I'm scared because of so many undecided people and Bush people."

The organizer of the event is an SEIU staffer Suzan and I know from our work. She glances at the survey and says, "Yeah, we've got our work cut out for us."

I hear all of the issues in detail at the bargaining table, in the hallways and banter and proposals of negotiations. I don't understand how people so in need of a decent healthcare system, OSHA regulations, decent retirement, labor boards that will enforce the law, some kind of economic security, some control on corporate rapacity, and jobs cannot know which side they're on. And, at least, who is *not* on their side. Maybe it's my lack of understanding that scares me. Maybe it's that people can be enticed to support their enemies. Maybe it's my fear that if we do elect Bush, there's no limit to the depravity of our political system.

Food and eating

Microwaves

Not Broadcast

We recently had a crisis in our household. The micro-wave died. Ceased to function. How could we cook?

I am fond of thinking of our species from the time we first learned to walk, from the time we first learned of fire. I taunted a colleague with having no respect for tradition when he questioned my continual use of DOS based computer software. But when it comes to cooking, I want a microwave; tradition can take a walk.

Not that we've had a microwave all that long. Long enough for one to croak.

While people have had their eye on televisions, speculating on how the new storytelling has shaped our culture, the microwaves sneaked into our kitchens to make real changes in our households.

If you want to understand people, it's a good idea to follow the example of the mythical Norse king who kept asking the gods, "What did they eat?"

If you follow the food, everything else will fall into place. Even the stories. In some times and places, meals bring families together around the food. Microwaves liberate us to cook whatever we want whenever we want without having to think of the whole family. We don't have to coordinate schedules for more than a couple of minutes—till we can get to the microwave.

Television brings people together. They huddle in its flickering light hearing and seeing the art forms we share across the land. The microwave separates us, or liberates us, depends on how you want to see it. Everyone can fix their own food.

As television watchers tell us, it's not all in the technology, but in the content. Think of what folks are heating up. Packages of frozen food. Keep your eye on the food. Somebody plants it and grows it, somebody picks it and sends it to a processor who . . . . Now, read some of those packages. The processor sends it to another who sends it to another. Each one pulverizes, or extracts, or adds, or re-hydrates, or preserves until it comes to us in little plastic trays--all process and precious little substance.

Trace the money back down the line. Display, packaging, advertising, processing, how many times? Delivery, picking, growing, planting. The farmer gets precious little of the food buck. The poor bastard that picked the stuff even less. We're eating the product of a giant industrial machine. A machine that comes into our kitchens in the paper, or plastic, bags from the grocery stores.

This is what has turned our land upside down from the fields to the families. And it all sneaked in the back door to the kitchen while our savants were all watching television.

We got a new microwave. We can eat again.

Anticipation

Not Broadcast

You still have to wait for watermelons. You can't get them in the winter time. It's hard to find a decent peach out of season. There are pulpy spheres from California, but not real peaches, voluptuous and sweet and juicy. And you still can't find a persimmon very far from the tree.

We are surrounded by such bounty all year long that I think we've forgotten the sweetness of anticipating a once a year food.

At Thanksgiving virtually every American table groans under the weight of the turkey, dressing, cranberries, and sweet potatoes that define that meal. But you can get turkey, cranberries, and sweet potatoes any time you want to in the grocery store or a fast food chain. You don't have to wait for Thanksgiving. Does the ancient slogan, "A chicken for every pot" even make sense for a presidential race in a land of such plentiful chickens? It did when chickens were valued and anticipated Sunday fare.

It's the same for all the festive foods. We are surrounded by them all year round. When you can have any food any time of the year, there's not much to anticipate.

When I was a kid I'd send in the tops from cereal boxes with a quarter to get some magical thing. I'd imagine what it would be like, savor it for weeks while my letter made its way wherever it went, and got processed. An eternity later the vision would fade and I would begin to lose all hope. I'd begin to think my letter must have been lost. And then one day, a package would be there for me.

Delaying the gratification of desires, especially until after you're dead, may be good for accumulating capital for an industrial economy, but it's of no use in a consumer and service economy designed to cater to the motto, "I want it *my* way, *now*." That's the voice of the immature in all of us.

A whole economic system is geared up to satisfy our most immature longings.

If you have to have your own way all the time you can never know the delights of waiting. We can order things by telephone and have them in hand the next day. One of the costs is the loss of that sense of anticipation.

Some of the other things that go along with these developments seem to be overuse of credit cards, de-emphasis of concepts of taking turns and fairness, increasingly youthful sexual activity, unreasonable impatience when we have to wait in lines of people or cars, the flashes of anger we observe when people are thwarted, and the association of immaturity with power.

Anticipation, as the song says, is making me wait. A service-oriented economy doesn't do that. It institutionalizes immaturity.

Global Tomatoes

2004 *SfAA News* 15(4)

In July and early August, Suzan, her eleven-year-old daughter, Ayshe, and I traveled through Turkey to visit Suzan's relatives. Istanbul to Cappadocia to Ankara and then along the Mediterranean coast to the trading crossroads of Izmir to the end of the Silk Road from China in Bursa and back to Istanbul. I wasn't on an archaeological or historical mission, but in Istanbul it was hard to miss the crusader castles and Ottoman fortifications. We watched the continuous stream of tankers and container ships going through the Bosporus, transporting the oil and goods so necessary to sustain the current world system.

We rode buses through golden fields of wheat, most of it cut and gathered in small stacks to dry in the sun, some grain threshed in small piles in fields, some grain piled high in front of elevators, and some in already stored in sacks. As the constant stream of ruins suggests, people have been using this area for ten thousand years, ever since they discovered agriculture.

In Ankara, Suzan's cousins gave me a "village tomato." That started me thinking about how to describe the taste of sunshine and rain, of moonbeams and starlight. How can words convey the textural, olfactory, and taste sensations of a ripe tomato? The problem remains unsolved. I won't even go into the watermelons, figs, apricots, peaches, grapes or plums.

Lest you think me a hopeless Turkophile, I will admit that when I was practicing asking for red wine with a Turk who lives in State College, he tried to teach me something like, "Forget about the wine, bring me a beer," because, "Turks don't drink wine." When I was in Turkey, I found out why.

I got other tomatoes in the pensions we stayed in along the Mediterranean coast—part of the usual breakfast. The first one I bit into, I dissected to find out the difference between it and the ones in Ankara. These things had skins of leather, thick pulp from the center to the skin, little juice, and no flavor. As poor a simulation of a tomato as California peaches are of real ones. I guessed they came from the vast expanses of greenhouses we saw nearby producing vegetables for the EU. Like California peaches, you could throw them all the way to the EU and when they landed with a thud, they'd still be as good as when they were picked.

Suzan was dreading the ride along the twisty mountainous road down the peninsula to Datcha. To her relief, the road had been much leveled, widened, and barriers added on the hairpin curves. Even with gas selling for between four and six dollars a gallon, the road system was everywhere expanding and improving.

In Izmir I had tea with a guy who called Portugal on a cell phone to try to line up a gazillion electronic parts for a Turkish TV manu-facturer. "We produce 15 percent of the world's televisions," he explained. Before we had a second glass of tea, he called the factory to tell them they were out of luck. "Their bad timing of production is no emergency for me," he explained. "I think they ordered the component from China, and only asked me when the Chinese didn't deliver on time." There ensued a long discussion of electronic components and the global system, how Ottoman trade had worked in Izmir and how the same families are still powerful eighty years after the founding of the Republic.

On the way to Bursa, I saw tractors plowing and pulling wagons full of people and produce. There were fields planted more densely than in Iowa with corn and unlike Iowa, interspersed with fields of string beans, and sunflowers, olive trees, peaches and apples. Lone men walked the rows with back-pack sprayers. Groups of people were doing handwork in the fields.

All around us in the landscape, as prevalent as the goats, we saw ancient ruins—evidence of previous world systems from the Hittites to the Hellenes, from the Romans and Byzantines to the Ottomans. And still rural people produce agricultural products to send to distant cities, to fuel the world systems.

A ten thousand year record should be sufficient to suggest that the rural people here have something sustainable going on here even if the world systems don't. What does it mean?

I don't know the details of the systems I was seeing, but in sustainable systems, people who make decisions bear the costs of the bad ones and reap the benefits of good ones. The livelihood you destroy—or save—is your own. People who make decisions know the details of the work and are close to it. There's some relationship between energy, waste, and decisions. People do things slowly and deliberately. When they find something that works, they stick with it. It means counting all the costs, not transferring them to someone else by some supernatural hocus pocus like money or economics. It means being sure the real benefits outweigh the real costs. It means knowing what a cost is and what a benefit is. All of that is pretty much the opposite of any industrial system.

It probably also means knowing that a peach or a tomato that travels well doesn't taste good.

The records of these landscapes also tell us that no matter what their denizens thought, the cities and civilizations they remind us of were not sustainable and suggest that if *they* weren't, maybe none are. Maybe civilizations and cities are only good for making impressive ruins and providing work for archaeologists.

In Izmir we saw a neo-ruin in the great columns and structures of an unfinished highway interchange soaring into a park...because the people had refused to give up their water frontage to the freeway.

One by one the systems that upheld the cities collapsed. And now there's another one based on highways, oil and globalization. Tractors and chemicals. Money, economics, accounting, and the distancing of decisions from consequences.

This got me curious enough to look up some stats when I got home. Here's some of the information that I was able to find at http://www.phrasebase.com/countries/ (figures for Scandinavia are from http://www.worldworx.tv/regional%2Dinformation /):

	%GDP from:			% Labor force in:		
	AG	IND	SERV	fishing &AG	IND	SERV
Turkey	14.5	28.4	57.1	39.7	22.4	37.9
US	2	18	80	2.4	24.1	73.6
Iceland	15	21	64	17.7	12.9	59.5
Scand.	3	26	71	4	17	79

Here's some more interesting stuff:

	Consumption of			
	lowest 10%	highest 10%	Gini	GDP/capita
Turkey	2.3%	32.2%	41.5	6.7 K
US	1.8%	30.5%	40.8	36.3K
Iceland	NA	NA	NA	24.8K
Scandinavia	2%	24%	25	29K

The Gini coefficient is a measure of income maldistribution. Zero is complete equality; 100 is complete inequality. I threw in Iceland because it provides an example of a pretty reasonable country for comparison. The stats aren't exactly comparable—I put percentages of the workforce in fishing and AG together for Iceland as that's the statistic reported for the U.S.; I'm not sure whether GDP from Iceland went with Industry or Ag, and since Iceland depends heavily on fishing, I put in all of Scandinavia for balance.

In Turkey, a lot of people do agricultural work and produce a small part of the GDP, so in terms of money-magic, agriculture is less productive than industry or services. In the U.S. the sectors are about equally productive and a few people work in agriculture to produce a small part of the GDP. It looks like industry is most productive in Iceland too.

Thirteen percent of people in the U.S. live in poverty. Turkey doesn't define an official poverty rate, but some sources estimate it to be about 14 percent and 2.4 times higher in rural than urban areas, but with so many people involved in agriculture, the rates may not be very comparable. Especially, with less industrialized, less "productive" practices in monetary terms, sometimes rural people can get by with less money than urban folks because they rely less on the magic of money and more on the realities of food production. I couldn't locate poverty statistics for Scandinavia or Iceland or a Gini for Iceland.

So the bottom line looks like Turkey is growing closer to the U.S. in its maldistribution of income—but maybe the U.S. is trying to catch up with Turkey's Gini coefficient and level of poverty. It depends on how you look it, I guess. So, back to Turkey.

In Bursa we got a bus to Yalova to catch a ferry to Istanbul. Outside Bursa, first Ottoman capital, end of the Silk Road, was a sign that said "Cargill."

For sustainability, I thought, the technology transfer is going the wrong direction.

We got on the ferry just as it was leaving and burned oil on the way to Istanbul as I anticipated the taste of the tomatoes that I knew were ripening in central Pennsylvania on the Brubaker farm that provides food to the CSA I belong to in the ancient pattern of rural folks producing food for city people.

The cities and world systems never endure but the people do. I suppose there's some comfort in that thought. And a good tomato goes a long way toward soothing the feeling that this'll all just be a pile of ruins someday.

Markets, money, business and economics

Oracles

All Things Considered 1/5/1996

Part of any newspaper or news broadcast, right there with the national disgrace s and triumphs of wars, negotiations, sports, and weather, is the stock market report. It has the price of the stock of the companies that produce the stuff of a consumer and warfare economy from cigarettes to tanks. Usually there will be an article or two devoted to why the market is doing whatever it has elected to do that day and what it will be doing in the future.

Why is there a whole industry devoted to selling advice about what to do in the stock market? Buy, sell or hold? You can virtually an advice you want in all of this stuff. At any moment, some person will be celebrated as a great genius for having made a killing in recent market events. This trader must have the system figured out. A player who gets rich must be smart. So you and I should follow suit.

All we know is that the market closed at a new high or took a dive or the economy improved so the market crashed or dollars are down in Europe so the market went up. Or is it down? Does that mean buy or sell or hold? So we read the oracles, and like all oracles, they tell us whatever we want to see. Someone will always be vindicated by today's news. Old geniuses are forgotten and new ones proclaimed as the numbers roll in. This is an ancient human proclivity

We know of the precursors to the Chinese because archaeologists have found the questions that they put to their oracles inscribed in bone. The Romans read the guts of birds to know the future, and the Greeks had their oracle at Delphi. American Indians burned the shoulder bones of caribou to locate game. Like the prophecies of the I-Ching, all becomes clear only after the fact. "Oh, that's what it meant."

So, like all people who want to know the future, we have our oracles. But we've made an industry of it and some of these firms are themselves traded in the stock market. Whatever method these prophets promote, all have learned, as one of the fraternity observed, that money is to be made not by taking advice but by selling it. Like all fortune-tellers, they read patterns and project futures. Now that casino gambling is so widespread, I wonder why the news doesn't cover that. If you're really interested in the future, you might want to keep reading till you get to the horoscope section. After all, it projects futures based on well-known patterns.

Business Ethics?

All Things Considered 8/6/1996

While I was waiting for a bus I overheard this conversation:
"It's a required course?"
"Yeah, all business students gotta take it now."
"What do they teach you in a course about ethics?"
"Well, that sometimes you're going to have to do things that are wrong, but that you oughtta think about it first."
I waited for the titter or disclaimer to indicate it was a joke. There was none. That conversation has given me a lot to think about. I'm not sure what it meant to those two individuals, much less what it means for our system of education, government, and business.

There was no nuance. The lesson wasn't, "Know right from wrong and do no wrong." But was it: "Be prepared to do wrong?" Was it, "When you inevitably do wrong, you should think about it enough to feel guilty about what you've done but not sufficiently guilty not to do it?" Or could it have been: "Your own personal security with the firm is more important than your sense of right and wrong?"

I wondered how these guys would argue at a sanity hearing with a judge trying to decide whether they knew the difference between right and wrong if that knowledge did not temper their actions. I wondered at the distance between what teachers teach and what students learn. I find it difficult to believe that someone had actually taught that lesson. I would prefer to imagine that this guy had boiled his conclusion out of a more considered treatment of the subject that distinguished right from wrong and tried to inoculate the students against doing wrong, an attempt at education gone awry.

I considered the possibility that these students may, after all, have abstracted the meaningful lesson of business ethics. If you think about doing wrong things before you do them, you can be prepared for the consequences and assess the costs and benefits. You can count the cost of a possible recall of your product and see if it's worth the risk to the bottom line. You can retain or hire sufficient legal talent to defend you in court if the stakes are high enough to justify it. You can prepare and advertising campaign to claim that you didn't do it, or that if you did it wasn't wrong or wasn't your fault. You can hire lobbyists to buy sufficient political clout to change the law so that it's no longer wrong to do what you want to do.

What was more frightening, the more I thought about, was the idea that these guys would soon be in business somewhere actually putting these lessons into practice, whether it was what they'd been taught or what they'd learned. And some people say that government ought to be run like a business?

Death by the Market?

WPSU 3/14/2000

Should physicians have leave to help terminally ill patients end their own lives? Legislatures in the U.S. and abroad have supported both alternatives, and a legal and ethical debate continues along with the practice.

Why all the controversy? People kill themselves all the time without permission. It's generally against the law in this country, an idea that becomes more than usually absurd when you think about how to enforce it.

The debate became hot just about time we began to seriously industrialize health care. The unit of health care had been the individual patient. Until recently, the goal was to end suffering by restoring health, or failing that, by alleviating symptoms and pain. There was plenty of money to be made in the process. Then the unit of health care changed to the capitated annual fee payer and the goal shifted. Now those fee payers—those patients—became a source of profit for corporations just like any other commodity.

For the first time it was possible to imagine that a physician—owing loyalty first to a corporation rather than the healing arts—might consider an alternative to keeping a suffering patient alive if it hurt the bottom line. When ending suffering by ending a patient's life can be profitable, who can guarantee a pure decision that considers only the welfare of the patient? It became plausible to think of the profitability of human death.

It's still hard for you or me to think of an individual patient as a commodity like a car in the showroom or a loaf of bread on the supermarket shelf. Patients are living people just like us--individuals, not statistics. Human life is a unique gift--beyond the calculation of value. Isn't it?

In the corporate world, you and I don't do the calculations. Only the bottom line sets the terms for the reckoning of costs and benefits. That's what makes us suspicious of physician-assisted suicide. That's what fuels the debate.

For a long time we have thought ill of killing people for gain. It's one of the things we call murder. We penalize it so heavily that it's bad for business. On the other hand, if it is not directed at a particular person, that's different—even though people die. Corporations can complain that a health or safety measure interferes with profits and compute the costs of fixing it. Industrial accidents, automobile deaths, death from environmental pollution—these are not murder, though they kill more people than murder. They're business. Nobody goes to jail.

We can't quite decide where physician-assisted suicide falls between murder and business. If it's murder—we decided a long time ago that's wrong. But what if it's business?

Do we want to admit that our own lives have become commodities for corporations to use or dispose of for profit like bars of soap and loaves of bread? That's the rub. When we decide, we will know whether we are ready to die by the market as we live by the market.

Money

Not Broadcast

The treasury is changing our money, chiefly, they say, so we can more easily distinguish between the genuine and spurious. It's important to be able to tell money issued by the Treasury Department itself from something knocked off on a sophisticated copying machine.

Why? I wondered as I was waiting in line at a super-market checkout counter watching people make lightning fast transactions with credit cards, debit cards, checks, and even some money.

What is this stuff? I looked in the lined up baskets and saw food and other consumer products. All of the commotion in front of me was about moving money around in some relationship to the stuff in the baskets.

Have you ever repeated a word over and over until it sounded absurd? That's what happened to me in the line. I began to think about money. People work for it, spend it, buy things with it—it makes our whole economy work. People use it to gain elected office, or access to those with elected office. It makes our whole political system work. People use it as an indicator of worth and a gage of power. People use it as a measure of security, insecurity, and self-evaluation. It makes our whole psychology work. What is it? It doesn't even stand for anything beyond what it says itself, that it is "legal tender for all debts, public and private."

A people who orients everything from power and influence to the depths of their souls around money has to worry about whether it is genuine or spurious. Anything that central to a whole land had better be genuine.

But what is it? Beyond the agreements to accept it for all debts public and private, a silent tacit agreement we all make all the time. Is it possible it has no reality outside our heads?

How else could you do all of this? I mused, looking at the brightly lit isles full of food and stuff.

Well, I answered, thinking about things I had read about Inka, maybe by orienting a whole system around a god incarnate, a king so pure and holy that he has to marry his own sister to preserve the virtue of the blood line, organizing great public works projects by drafting workers, by taxing in kind to support the whole apparatus, and administering it all from some central place. Of course, you'd have to have some way to insure the central guy was genuine and not spurious . . . .

The reverie ended as I handed a plastic card to the person at the cash register. No, I thought, that kind of system would be preposterous because to make it work, you'd have to get all those people to agree to a fundamentally absurd idea . .

Contracting

Not Broadcast

Take one function, perform it well, sell it in the market, and save everyone who uses your services money and effort. This is called contracting. Prostitutes have made a living at it for ages. With improving communication and billing technology, sexual services can now be purchased per minute rather than per job by telephone. Restaurants and caterers contract by the job. I haven't heard of a purely phone-food deal. Pizzas still have to be delivered to be at all satisfying.

Another function that's being contracted out is cleaning. The shift to contract cleaning of rest stops on Iowa's stretch of I-80 was noticeable in the smell in the restrooms, the trash on the grounds, and their fast descent into unkemptness.

When the computer giant, Hewlett-Packard contracted out the cleaning of some of its buildings in California, Service Employees International Union said it was to avoid having to deal with organized janitors. Depriving people of benefits doesn't eliminate costs. It just shifts them to the public. And it does nothing to promote expertise, pride, and quality of work.

I never could figure out why contracting is supposed to cost less. Someone still has to do the work. Someone still has to do all the administrative jobs—getting the payroll out, being sure the supplies are on hand, matching up the people to the work. If you contract the job, you have another level of administration to pay. The only way you can save any money is to pay for less work or pay less for the same work. Using less-skilled workers is the same as paying for less work, as corporations that have cut back their experienced personnel to downsize have found out when they began to falter.

One place where people notice quality of work is in aircraft piloting and maintenance. The Interior Department has some aircraft and pilots for specialized jobs. There haven't been any fatalities from their planes crashing, but eighteen of their employees have died in charter crashes.

Someone in Congress thinks Interior can save money by contracting its areal jobs and wants them to sell their planes.

I notice the CIA has been hiring psychics. I can understand why they don't want psychics to be a line item on their budget to a Congress dedicated to scientific principles of management. But it seems to me they might be able save a little by paying for their information by the minute by using a 1-900 psychic hot-line like everyone else.

The Monet

Not Broadcast

The numbers are in on the big show of Monet's art in Chicago. Dorothy and I didn't go to the show at, though friends offered us a pair of the coveted tickets. We had seen lots of his work in other places, and every report agreed that the lines and the wait were long.

The exhibit was up for four months and broke all records. The gift shop made a million and a half bucks selling catalogues and paraphernalia. With this, 55,000 new members from the show, and ticket sales, the Art Institute is well in the black for some time to come. 950,000 people viewed the 159 works on display. That was 7,500 people per day; 940 per hour.

Dorothy once told me that museum viewers spend an average of fifteen seconds viewing each work. If the Monet viewers were average, it would have taken them about 40 minutes to see all the works—even if they looked at one of them twice. That would be 620 people per hour in the exhibit. At 940 per hour, the museum's numbers show that some visitors were inefficient and others were below average. It must have taken some of them an hour. Hence the lines.

Given the money making potential of such shows, the crumbling national support for the arts, the emphasis on tough-minded competitiveness and corporate logic that is supposed to keep the art world alive, it wouldn't surprise me to see some changes that would make for more efficient viewing next time a big art show comes to the Middle West.

I've often wondered if museum curators couldn't decrease the viewing time to, say, ten seconds and make the process more efficient. The Barnes Museum in Philadelphia used to seem to me to be ideal for efficient viewing. Every wall was packed from floor to ceiling with paintings. An efficient viewer could stand in the middle of a gallery and view hundreds of paintings by scanning one wall, turn 90 degrees three times, and be done in maybe two minutes.

There were so many Renoirs on wall that it was dripping with naked flesh. But I hear the curators of that institution are actually making it less efficient than it was by reducing the density of art per square inch of wall. Retrogressive move. Not competitive.

Chicago's Art Institute might consider a moving sidewalk like the one at O'Hare Airport to increase efficiency. They could incorporate a voice like the one at the airport to say "walk, walk" and some flashing lights to move more people through the exhibit even faster. That would teach a lot of people what art is really all about and help move the museum's bottom line toward something corporate America could respect.

Toys

Not Broadcast

Before the holiday decorations were down, the social critics were having their usual field day with toys. Barbie is a favorite subject. Her proportions are unrealistic and the young girls that play with her will feel inadequate when they find that they do not measure up to her phantasmagorical dimensions. Toy guns make kids into violent adults. Board games about shopping teach girls mall-crawling consumerism. Board games about dating inculcate precocious sexuality.

The counter-arguments are equally familiar. The guns and dolls are just games; children don't see them as adults do. Kids are still capable of enacting fantasies and can tell the difference between fantasy and reality. Barbie isn't the only model of femininity girls will meet in their lives or the only time girls will fail to embody someone else's fantastic standards. If kids didn't have guns, they'd use their fingers; if the guns didn't make shooting sounds, kids would supply them. The board game about shopping teaches anyone who plays it mathematics and logic and dating games mirror social reality.

Whatever their judgments, the reviews concluded that the toy companies won't produce toys that kids don't want and will produce toys that kids do want. Thus, the toys mirror rather than create the preoccupations and interests of the kids who play with them.

When I read these critiques I find myself nodding in agreement with both points of view—that toys create perverse mentalities and that they merely reflect social realities. I wonder, though, if both sides don't miss the point. The significant observation may be the one that all the critics and apologists seem to agree upon, that the process is market driven. Like other commodity purveyors, the toy industry works with existing dimensions of desire to exacerbate or create a hunger they promise to satiate by ownership of a unique commodity whether it be Barbie or Bambi, sexy or violent, gendered or gender neutral. This makes sense to parents who spend their lives getting money to buy the great and small objects to satiate their own adult cravings. So they purchase the toys, and the children who play with them still feel a gnawing emptiness that even possession does not fill. It is that emptiness that might be the important dimension of the toy phenomenon, because that may be what drives the kids to become adults who will hope to fill it with more adult consumer goods and work for the wherewithal to do so. Monopoly is still the best selling game.

The Opium of the Masses

SfAA News 12(2)

Karl Marx was wrong. The opium of the masses is not religion. It is opium.

I didn't have to be in the hills of central Pennsylvania long before I noticed a certain similarity with those in Northern Thailand where I'd lived with Lisu tribal people learning about how they dealt with misfortune and how they made their livings by growing rice, corn, and opium poppies. When the director of the Pennsylvania Association for Sustainable Agriculture invited me to participate on a panel on the topic of industrial swine production at their meeting last year I was happy to relate the lessons Kendall Thu and I had learned in North Carolina and Iowa. There I heard about the difficulties of small farmers in Pennsylvania and some of the ways they are responding. That put me to thinking, always a dangerous thing.

I sent PASA's director an e-mail one day and asked whether opium poppies wouldn't be as good a crop in the highlands of Pennsylvania as they are in the hills of Thailand. "Are you serious?" he asked. "Sure, I said. Look, one problem is how to make a living on small farms. National Public Radio just did a piece on the scarcity of opiates for making all of the family of opium-derived drugs from morphine to codeine. Here's a solution to both problems. If it's agronomically feasible, why not produce our own supply of opium in the U.S.? It could be an ideal crop for small farmers—the demand is proven and small farmers could make some money from it. Drug firms would have a secure supply and not have to deal with the uncertainties of world markets and distant suppliers. It should work equally well for some of the most powerful firms and least powerful farms. Opium poppies are very adaptable, so with some selective breeding, we could develop varieties suited to different conditions and even increase their opiate content. Maybe some aggies could figure out a way to mechanize the harvesting process to make it less labor intensive." He said he'd check it out.

He did. He put the question to some agronomists. They said poppies would grow here. But then he went on to say that that still didn't make it a good crop because he'd learned that the Drug Enforcement Agency had removed all the poppies from as innocuous a place as the gardens of Jefferson's own Monticello. Jefferson wasn't that much of a conformist but if DEA wouldn't let his ghost raise poppies, what were the chances for small farmers in central Pennsylvania? None at all. It's the law. The end.

There you have it. A good crop, suited to the place, suited to the interests of small farmers, a crop that fills a need of our own domestic drug industry, and it's against the law. For that reason it can't be done. This shows the poverty of American agricultural/drug/foreign policy as well as any example anyone could think of.

Expand the idea a little bit. Go beyond the modest proposition of producing legal opium for drug companies and suppose that the whole thing gets away from the DEA or whoever is enforcing it. What if there's a dark side to opium production as there is in the rest of the world—where we get our legitimate and illegitimate opiates—the opium that's in the formal economy and the stuff that's in the informal economy?

If we produced our own opium we would no longer lose valuable foreign exchange to drug lords in distant lands. We don't have to worry about corruption of the banking system as the drug money is laundered and re-introduced into our domestic economy. We don't have to police the borders because we know opium is coming from domestic sources. We don't have to worry about the corruption of public officials tempted with the speedy acquisition of great wealth. We don't have to worry that opium will play a role in corrupting our foreign policy as it did during the days of the Vietnam War when we used it as a means of rewarding our minions in Southeast Asian governments. We don't have to worry about our informal economy financing powerful and irascible drug lords in other lands.

If we wanted to be far-reaching, we could suggest legalizing heroin use and taxing it to raise revenue. That would put the Mafia out of business and save the FBI a bundle. Altogether, there are probably big enough savings in government expenditures that we could afford a handsome tax cut for everyone. As an added bonus it would remove a major source of police corruption in all big cities across our own land.

If the thought of addicts strung out on the streets of America boggles your mind, walk down any big city street as the sun sets and have your mind boggled by the realty that's already playing out.

If we wanted to be extreme, we could imagine expanding such a beneficial and practical policy to other drug crops such as coca and marijuana, already a significant cash-crop in many areas of the U.S. That could remove drugs from the foreign policy machinations of Latin America and the kind of sleazy dishonesty that took place under the "Iran-Contra" program of a previous administration.

I wouldn't want to suggest anything radical—just a good crop for small farmers in central Pennsylvania and maybe other parts of the country. I expect that's why most people would find it an impractical policy—because it favors farmers over the DEA, FBI, mafia, international drug-lords and foreign policy establishment all of whom depend on one another as much as on America's addicts, drug policy, foreign policy, agricultural policy, and small farmers in distant lands for their livings. To my mind that's a short-sighted view of the practical.

We have a new president dedicated to obliterating corruption in all its forms, devoted to saving public expenditures and committed to practical policies. He will no doubt adopt the major dimensions of this policy so we can expect to see our plant breeders in their labs and extension agents in the field . . . . I'd better quit before I say something sarcastic.

Ritual and religion

The Super Bowl

All Things Considered 1/29/1996

Football is part of the American holiday tradition. In addition of the 4th of July and Thanksgiving, our main national observance is the Super Bowl. It's purified ritual, stripped of the superfluous feast, origin myths, and fireworks. Created within living memory, this celebration, as commercial and pre-processed as the foods that accompany it, is as gripping for many as any that were invented earlier and count as tradition.

We must be a nation bereft of drama to create the demand that the entertainment industry strives to meet with such creations. At work, people put a lid on it and get on with the job. If your boss starts acting like one of the Shakespearian kings, or the prince of Denmark, it's probably time to change jobs, or bosses and no employee can risk a Falstaff or any of the other underlings. You wouldn't want your kids to emulate Romeo and Juliet.

Jealous of our privacy, the wide audience for the domestic dramas that village and tribal life offer people who are all kin is denied to us because we act them out within the protection of isolated households fearful of what relatives and neighbors would say if they saw the dirty linen. These isolated dramas are better watched on stage or screen than lived anyway.

We lack the public spectacles of the Romans, Greeks, Mayas and Aztecs. Our news comes to us in forms that lean heavily on the arts of the storyteller and blends seamlessly with fiction. Our politicians try to provide us with some decent theater now and then, but it is hard to take them seriously when most of us don't participate in our own political system even to the extent of voting.

I think the lack of real drama explains the demand for professional sports in every imaginable form. Viewers can identify with participants, debate, argue, and create their own inconsequential sub-dramas. Spectators can heighten the effect of participating in the ritual by buying tickets and attending or partake vicariously by viewing television. Either way, or both ways, there is an immense market that the sports industry strives to meet.

This denatured theatre comes to us on multiple television channels every day of the week, every hour of the day. The values of industry have already overtaken those of sport or drama. College athletics are all too often ill-disguised counterfeit professional endeavors. Take away the regional identities, local loyalties, and traditional rivalries and all that's left is a form as empty of sustenance as the junk foods that accompany it and lots of bucks for all participants to fight over, a pure market product. It is fitting that the Super Bowl is the commodity the entertainment industry offers our land as a national celebration.

On Martyrs to Business

WPSU 11/8/2001

We know what suicide attackers look like now. We've seen them in Israel for some time, and now we've seen them in our own land. We know what the Kamikaze pilots of the Second World War looked like. But we have a hard time understanding them. We cannot understand people going to a certain death with joy and the certainty that their deaths are achieving something good for themselves and for others. We can't imagine revering the names and faces of people who die, holding them up as examples for future generations, respecting their decisions and wishing to emulate their selfless generosity. Not since the Middle Ages have there been martyrs in Europe and we've never had them on this side of the Atlantic.

Maybe it's because we don't share a common religious tradition. But I think we do share a religion. We differ only on the details of where and when to worship, not really how or what to worship. Leaders of countries in stress appeal to the religious values of their citizens. Our president told us to shop. I think it was an appeal to the religion we share—business. Can you imagine martyrs for business? No. It just doesn't add up. We don't just speak of the almighty. We speak of the almighty dollar. Maybe we have no martyrs because nobody dies for business.

But we die for business every day. About 114 of us die every day in our automobiles. Our automobiles move us around and the define us as persons and as a people. We are the people addicted above all to gasoline. And for that we will and do die.

About fifty-seven of us die every day from firearms—about equal numbers in suicides and homicides and fewer in accidents. Leave aside all the talk about the right to bear arms and so on. The important thing is that making and selling firearms is a big business. More than a thousand one hundred of us every day die for cigarettes, another business we don't want to interfere with. Fifteen of us die every day in work accidents. Another fifteen from asthma from polluted air.

We like to think of death as a gamble in which we all have equal odds. We think that we can outwit death by skill and vigilance and hope that we will be spared. If we are, we live to think that those who died lacked either our skill or our luck. And they're not here to speak up for themselves. We don't revere the business-dead; we try to forget them lest we think of ourselves as the next to roll the dice of death.

Our industry pumps 2.4 billion pounds of toxic pollutants into our air every year into areas where 140 million Americans live. We look at maps of cancer and wonder why the dice are so loaded against the people who live downwind from the 300 some plants between Baton Rouge and New Orleans in the area known as Cancer Alley. Are they unskillful real estate buyers? Or just unlucky? What we know is that the chemical industry does not plan for them to die. The industries make heavy contributions to politicians and universities to propagate that view. It's just the price of business.

And so are all of these deaths. The price of business. Would we do without our cars, cigarettes, guns, and chemicals? Not likely. That's stuff to die for. And we do. But we don't celebrate it. We try to hide it. We ignore it. It's a secret that sits uneasily on the back shelf of our consciousness.

Imagine celebrating these deaths as martyrs to business. Imagine giving them meaning. We could create a myth of everlasting life after death in a paradisiacal shopping mall where the martyrs have never-ending credit cards with no monthly statements and unlimited lines of credit. Then maybe people could volunteer for it. Then we could celebrate these deaths as part of our national religion and make them meaningful.

Why I Will Vote

Not Broadcast

On Election Day I'll vote. I'll walk down to Longfellow School and see neighbors I haven't seen since the caucus. We'll exchange pleasantries about our gardens and the weather.

Many are complaining that the presidential campaign is especially boring this round. We have a Democrat who repudiates the title of liberal as if it were something terrible. He doesn't leave the Republicans much to say.

And we have a real Republican. All he can say is that he doesn't like his opponent. He can't even say that because it doesn't play well in Peoria.

We have a two party system that gives victory to whoever captures the center. Close doesn't count. Or thirty degrees off. People who just do it for a hobby or because they have an alternative vision aren't even invited to the debates. No wonder the joint appearances are boring.

That populist from Texas, John Hightower, once said that there's nothing in the middle of the road but yellow paint and dead armadillos.

More people don't vote than do. But I've always voted, even when it's been a lot of trouble to get an absentee ballot in Thailand or Iceland. I do it because, like eating Thanksgiving dinner, it's a ritual that makes me feel that I am participating in America.

I enjoy the feeling. At least until the returns come in. Most Americans don't participate in our political system even to this minimal ritualistic extent because they know better than to waste effort, even small ones.

I don't think my vote is going to change anything. I usually throw it away on some hopeless third party candidate rather than for one of the big two who are battling to be least controversial. I don't think I'm sending any messages. I'm just voting for someone who makes sense by being out of the middle of the road.

Armadillos don't make it as far north as Iowa. We have other kinds of road kill in the middle of our roads. But, when you think about it, whatever's in the middle of the road is all pretty much the same.

Invisibility

SfAA News 14(4)

Anthropology often causes us to see what would otherwise be invisible. Certain rituals do the same thing. I was recently involved in one that did just that and started me to thinking about why some people do such rituals to bring the invisible to attention and others are content to let the invisible remain well out of sight.

When Suzan Erem and I started writing about hospital workers in Chicago, we described them as invisible workers—the people you never see that keep the hospitals working by changing the air filters, cooking the food, moving the charts and patients around, keeping the elevators running and the water flowing. When you go into a hospital your eye moves to the people in white—doctors and nurses. You may deal with a clerical worker when you check in and surely when you check out, but a most of the workers you only see out of the corner of your eye moving garbage cans or food trays silently through the halls.

It is these workers and many like them in other health-care facilities such as prisons and nursing homes that Service Employees International Union District 1199/P represents in Pennsylvania. With a grant from the National Science Foundation, Suzan and I are studying the differences between more and less centralized unions. When we were invited to attend the annual meeting of workplace leaders from all over the state, we were glad of the ethnographic opportunity.

The meeting was lively and when a hurricane reached a hand inland to shut down the power at the hotel in the middle of the night, we continued without the benefit of electricity. The hotel staff even managed to lay out a hot breakfast for us that they'd prepared in the kitchen of another hotel that did have power.

There were workshops and speeches and raffles and lots of discussion. Suzan and I talked to people and took notes and urged everyone to complete the surveys we'd managed to include in their packets. We were learning how this union actively encourages its members to *be* the union. That's a far cry from allowing them to just passively buy insurance against unjust treatment on the job or loss of benefits. It requires them to be visible to their bosses.

I had sat in on negotiating sessions and seen the workers from the kitchen and housekeeping and other invisible workers negotiating against what seemed to me to be impossible odds for their next contract. I had heard them discussing with each other the possibilities of a strike and whether they had enough fuel and food laid in at their houses to weather it. All were white women. When one said to the group, "...but what do I know, I'm only a kitchen worker," the others chimed in and said, "Without us, this place couldn't function. Without us to clean and cook...."

One evening at the annual meeting, I sat with a group of African American workers. When a white waiter brought us our supper, one woman said, almost embarrassed, "I'm not used to being waited on." The waiter smiled and said, "Relax and enjoy it."

On the last evening, everyone was gathered in a large ballroom for the final dinner and a rousing speech. I sat with the workers I recognized from the negotiating team of the hospital. After supper, the president of the union announced that people would pass through the diners to collect money for a tip for the hotel workers.

In a few minutes, the president called for the hotel workers to come up front and line up and presented them with more than $900 to standing applause. Everyone knew these weren't even union workers. It didn't matter. Tears were streaming down the faces of some of the hotel workers. They had moved from being invisible workers to being the center of attention for a brief moment. Everyone they had served recognized their work and their value as workers.

That can be a moving experience.

Later, Suzan pointed out that such a gesture is common at union meetings. This raises the question of why it is so uncommon in other venues. I've never seen academics do such a thing. People may leave tips at the tables, or take up a tip from the table. But to bring the staff workers up to the front of the hall, to present them with the collection, to recognize them, for everyone to stand up and clap? That I had not seen.

And I wondered why. One answer that comes to mind is that invisible workers understand the phenomenon of invisibility. And they understand the power of being made visible if only for a brief moment...a moment of recognition that your work counts and that someone has seen it and appreciates it. That's a powerful statement.

When Suzan and I discussed why we don't see such ritual statements more often, one answer that made sense to me was that except for unions, except for other invisible workers, the people who eat in hotels, the people who eat at banquets do not think about making invisible workers visible. They are, after all, invisible.

In a ritual that so infrequently happens, we see a powerful statement of class at work in our land and we see how it permeates our culture to make the phenomenon of class as invisible as the workers who make our system work.

True Believers and Anthropologists in Fisheries Management

2006 SfAA News 17(2)

The organizers of a session on the ethnography of fisheries at the recent SfAA meeting in Vancouver invited me to be a discussant. One of the papers was by a guy who had heard a fisheries economist's talk and thought that to be as important as an economist and be in the policy loop, anthropologists should develop some over-arching theory that will help to understand everything that happens in fisheries in the same way that economists understand everything that's going on with economics.

Put that economic understanding together with biologists' understanding of how life works and you get a blueprint for fisheries, an abstract model that takes into account the payoffs and costs of fishing, the effect of fishing on the population of fish, and lets you know when you should back off the catching or when you can increase the harvest. Governments have whole bureaucracies devoted to achieving maximum sustainable yield. By U.S. law that has to be based on the best available scientific knowledge and there are committees of folks who get together to verify that the managers are using the best available scientific knowledge. This protects the managers from lawsuits because a judge in a court of law will uphold that imprimatur.

Anthropologists know a lot about many different fisheries, but it's hard to figure out where ethnography fits into this management picture. That is because we don't have any theoretical apparatus at the same level of generality as those of economists and biologists. So, this guy argued, we should develop one and then there would be a place for anthropology in fisheries management. Then we could be heard. Maybe important or powerful.

Any theory is a statement that follows from first principles or axioms, assumptions. It doesn't need to be true except in the sense that it follows the rules of logic, and then it's valid, but validity is no guarantee of truth in any empirical way. Science is the task of connecting the theories with what we can know of reality by experiment or observation. The feedback between experience and theory makes science different from religion. If our theoretical formulations don't capture the realities we observe, then we change them and try again.

It seems obvious to people who grew up in state-organized capitalist societies that any patterns in social phenomena are aggregates of decisions of self-interested individuals. From these assumptions flow the economists' tidy formulations. Can they prove it? Of course. Are they true? Joseph Stiglitz, not just a garden variety economist but a Nobel laureate economist, says that if they were true, the policies based on them would work a whole lot better than they do. What is missing, he observes, is that critical feedback loop from observation to theory. That's why he calls economics a religion rather than a science (*Globalization and its Discontents*. 2003. W.W. Norton).

The strength of ethnography is its roots in everyday practice. When ethnography and theory clash, a scientific approach must privilege ethnography over theory. This is especially so when the theory was developed as an ideological framework to justify a particular economic system as neoclassical economics was.

In spite of the request for some high level theory, the other papers in the session informed us about the details of management schemes and particular practices and systems in different parts of the world and how they worked—or didn't. That was encouraging because the theoretical formulations are likely to be wrong and misleading rather than enlightening.

These and other ethnographers have shown that the intersection of relevant economic, ecological, and political and social variables defines the relationship between policy and practice and that it is not given to any general formulation except that effective fisheries management is close to the people it affects and involves them. Co-management entails building institutions and creating structural conditions that promote and encourage local communities to manage their own resources and their own development. The goals are the same as those of political and economic democracy and result in resilient and sustainable systems. Our ethnography shows that management for adaptability and long-term system viability is local and not generalizable, that it's practical and that it can be implemented.

Why don't we see it everywhere? What's the barrier? One of them is the bureaucratic structures of economists and fisheries biologists who privilege their abstractions over realities.

So when it was my turn to make comments I said some of these things and added that it's not the job of anthropologists to learn how to speak the language of economists. Our task is to make that a dead language.

As a member of the Scientific and Statistical Committee of the South Atlantic Fisheries Management Council, I had observed abstractions in action as well-intended people gather to work out what the best scientific knowledge is and how to use it in fisheries management. I had also reviewed proposals and seen the requests for proposals that generate the research that produces the knowledge. The problem is that few of them are doing anything that could possibly result in sustainable co-management. That isn't even a goal.

Imagine a bunch of well-intended priests discussing how many epicycles and retrograde motions a planet traces as it completes its orbit, along with the sun, around the earth. They compare observations, discuss methodologies and models, and agree on what the best available science is. Give them a proposal to study planetary motion around the sun and you're a whack-job who just doesn't get it.

So when the anthropologist who was on the staff of the Council left for another job, and the Council decided to replace her with an economist, I could no longer lend my support even remotely to such a system and I resigned my seat on the committee.

Does that make economics a dead language? No, but I don't have to participate in the legitimization of systems that produce such products. I don't have to join the chorus singing in perfect harmony that this stuff makes sense or is scientific knowledge. As I wrote my letter of resignation it occurred to me that whatever stock assessments are put before the Council as the best *available* knowledge, it is never the best *possible* knowledge because the Council isn't asking the questions or funding the research that could produce it. To be the best possible knowledge the Council would ask for, support and fund research on co-management, sustainable systems, and ethnography. In the review process they wouldn't ask biologists or economists to evaluate proposals from anthropologists.

I wondered why this guy at the SfAA meeting was even talking about the necessity for an overarching theory akin to economists' models since Tom King and I edited a book that showed the fallacy of such an approach (*State and Community in Fisheries Management: Power, Policy, and Practice* 2000, Bergin and Garvey). Maybe this fellow hadn't read it. Or maybe he was a true believer from economics and didn't need to see any ethnography or real-world people in action.

Anthropologists know better than to try to convert true believers. We also know it doesn't do any good to tell people in power that they're the problem. But we don't have to join them.

Communication

Communication Problems

All Things Considered 12/27/1995

It used to be that when you saw people clutching their heads and talking to themselves, you knew they were in communication with a dimension most of us do not perceive. These days they are likely to have a cell phone in their hands. The phones suggest that they are in the same orbit with most of us, just overdoing it a bit. I think this need to be continually in touch is part of a larger pattern of over communication.

Have you noticed that if you disagree with someone, they are likely to think you didn't understand? So they say the same thing again. If they're creative, they find some different words, or use some different sentences, but often they don't. If you still disagree, they may say it more loudly or more slowly. In exasperation, they may use some aphorism like, "Watch my lips," assuming that you can read lips better than you can hear their voice. If you persist in the error of your ways, the poor person may be driven to conclude that there's been a communication breakdown.

I think a lot of people concur that if others understood us they would agree with us. The only legitimate reason for disagreement is faulty communication. It seems to me that if we were confident in our abilities to state things clearly and other people's abilities to understand us, we could get along with a lot less redundant talking and explaining. Maybe the problem is too much communication.

If I were an economist, I could make some assumptions here and make up some numbers and tell you about how much all of this extra talking costs our business world and government in lost productivity every year. I expect it would come to billions. It usually seems to when economists get involved. So it's something we should probably pay attention to.

If people disagree, it might be constructive to acknowledge that, and try to figure out how their assumptions differ and why. Repeating something over and over just convinces us that the dimwit who refused to understand and agree is stupid, or maybe deaf, or at worst that we've slipped into speaking the unknown tongue without having noticed it. Unless this has actually happened, no amount of improving communication skills will help. What will help is respecting other people and reasoning together. If there really is a communication problem, the solution is not to make it into an over communication problem, but just to keep quiet.

Misnomers

Not Broadcast

Drive through any big city and you'll see some establishments that call themselves "gentlemen's clubs." From the look of them and their advertising, I would be amazed to find among their patrons any persons of the male persuasion of any breeding or refinement that might deserve the title "gentleman." I don't imagine anyone would be astonished to find a clientele of louts.

I think we're sufficiently acclimated to the surrealism of advertising and political hyperbole that we automatically correct for such misnomers without thinking. It's a skill we perfect through consistent exercise, so it's a good thing that we have obvious examples regularly in front of us to keep us in practice.

Everyone knows that when people speak of "entitlement programs" they mean all of the interlocking connections among the rich and powerful that own and run the country. These programs insure the orderly transfer of power from one generation to the next via elite prep schools, universities, fraternities, clubs, seats on boards of directors, and marriages that guarantee its responsible use.

Everyone knows that when you mention the recipients of the "welfare system" you are talking about corporations. We all know that the role of the unemployed is to bid down the price in of labor, supply replacement workers for strikes, help bust unions, and thus maintain high profits. Nobody would think of changing something that has such a positive effect on profits except to insure that the labor reserve is better qualified by more job training programs.

Since the police rioted in Chicago in 1968 everyone has known that being charged with the crime of "assaulting an officer of the law" means that a cop beat you up. We understand that when people speak of the "justice system" they mean as much justice as you can afford and what a lawyer can get away with in a court of law, nothing that has anything to do with ideas of right and wrong.

The entertainment industry helps to keep us aware of misnomers in our daily lives. The purveyors of the television programs and movies the industry calls "adult entertainment" warn viewers that "this program contains material intended for mature audiences." We all understand that this is a sure sign that there is something that panders to the prurient and appeals to the adolescent, something of interest to the immature.

With these kinds of examples constantly before us, we keep our minds sharp so we can correct for all of the minor misnomers we happen upon in our daily lives.

Education and schools

Excellence

All Things Considered 12/27/1995

I was checking out of a hotel when the receptionist asked me, "How was the service?" There was a three-acre bed, a TV that I didn't turn on, and functioning indoor plumbing. I said it was adequate. "Adequate?" she bristled, "Not excellent?" "Whatever," I said and settled up the bill. Waiters come to you while you are eating and ask, "How's your meal?" expecting you to say something in the range from excellent to superb when you'd be glad to settle for competent, acceptable, passable, respectable or tolerable if the food is more or less properly prepared and promptly and politely delivered and they would keep your water glass full.

The worlds of commerce and industry as well as arts, humanities, and sciences are in a mad pursuit of excellence. Not competence or adequacy, but excellence. This has something to do with what teachers call "grade inflation." Everybody wants to be above average.

Think of what happens when we shift our scales of quality to the low end where "excellent" comes to mean "adequate" and "acceptable" means "intolerable." The high end gets cut off so you don't notice the CEOs of corporations who are busy downsizing their operations and beating down wages and remunerate themselves at many times the rate of the people who work for them. They are off the scale. You begin to put up with the left end of the scale as normal. It becomes acceptable that there are people with no jobs and no places to live.

And all of this is because of grade inflation gone wild; a consequence of ideas like continuous quality control, better and better in every way every day, the search for excellence. If you can't really make it better, you just say it's better. The policy demands it. Saying things are better than they are becomes part of the job. And your boss does the same thing. And so on. And so the scale shifts. It would be one thing to change the realities. But this is a rhetorical shift that just moves the scales. With this substitution of rhetoric for reality comes a cynicism about the whole idea of quality that exacerbates the inflationary process.

Maybe it's time we thought about changing our rhetorics from "pursuit of excellence" to "pursuit of adequacy" or "competence" so there would be a place for "unacceptable" at the left end of the scale and the right end would come into view. Maybe we need to keep both ends of these scales in sight and understand that what happens at one end affects what happens at the other end. Maybe it's time we forget the aggrandizing and self-congratulatory rhetoric of grade inflation and start thinking about the realities at both ends of these scales.

Fast Food for Thought

Not Broadcast

Having endured the anxiety, frustrations, and tensions of big city traffic on the way in, my friend was rushed when she stopped to get some provisions for a morning meeting she had organized. "I don't much like the food here," she said. "It doesn't have much flavor. But it is close, easy, and cheap."

I thought that her response epitomized our age of speed. We are always on the move, always in a hurry, always seeking to maximize something we call convenience to minimize the precious time we spend at any task to make more time for more tasks. Time is money so we ration it, save it, watch for its unwise use. Money is time so we have to budget it. "Close, easy, and cheap" become the criteria for an age.

While I waited for the counter person to assemble the pastries as my friend called them out by name, I thought we wouldn't walk across Europe to read a book as ancient scholars did. We'd rather turn on a TV. What a far cry that medieval outlook was from our impatience to download tracts from the World Wide Web. I thought of those bygone scholars reading, pondering, poring over texts, studying the marginal notes previous readers had left, and contemplating each turn of phrase and rhetorical subtlety.

I thought of medieval university readers reading books aloud from their podiums while students dutifully copied them word for word and how copying machines have made university lectures obsolete if printing presses and mimeograph machines had not. I thought of the contemporary scholars who deliver those lectures, all pressed for time, all in a race for tenure or fame or the next publication who scan with great speed, impatient to move to the next text and process it with equal irreverent incomprehension, more interested in the name and reputation of the author than any subtlety of argument, dialectical nicety, of concern for fact or such a conjectural matter as truth.

I thought that this scholarship doesn't have much flavor but it's close, easy, and cheap. It's a scholarship suited to a modern age when no one has time for subtlety or reflection let alone walking across a continent to learn a thing or two.

Maybe universities will one day have drive-up windows for enlightenment. Or maybe we will drop the idea that enlightenment or education is supposed to be part of the process, like the idea that taste is supposed to be part of food, and will, like the Wizard of Oz simply sell diplomas to those who are on the fast track to certification and make the process even more efficient.

My friend nudged me out of my reverie as she paid for her box of pastries and we rushed to the meeting.

Debaters

Not Broadcast

Our library was overrun by a swarm of adolescents.

They were walking at forced march pace between the shelves of bound periodicals. There was a press of them around each copying machine. They had invaded every computer terminal. Full of nervous energy, their eyes were glazed, as though they were about to enter a trance, or were in the early stages of one. Early in July, the only tan these kids showed was the pallor of being indoors too long.

I was unsettled by the noise—the sheer hustle and bustle—of all of those people, the crowding, and the subdued chattering tones around the copying machines and in the corridors. I was more unsettled by the image of larvae. I felt like one of those science fiction heroes who comes across a cave full of larval aliens who, if allowed to mature, will eat the human species for breakfast. It bothered me.

I asked a librarian what was going on. "Debaters." she said. "It happens every year. I think it's a public health problem."

That explained it but left me with the unsettled feeling. What bothered me was the realization that these were larval lawyers.

When I told a friend about this at dinner, she told me that she had been on a debate team, and the topic she had been assigned, and the position. "How can you develop any passion for a position you are assigned?" I asked. She explained that it's a matter of learning the techniques of forensics and how to win.

That was the crux of my unease. Where in this forensic process is the search for truth? Or beauty? Having heard these debates on WSUI, our NPR station, I have been appalled at the rapid fire marginally intelligible shrill voices, devoid of all humor and modesty, shrieking authority after authority, trading opinions of heavy hitters like baseball cards, but never asking why they were doing it. Never asking what the truths of the matter were.

I'm sure a lot of lawyering is devoted to making things work and avoiding adversarial relations, but when things come to loggerheads, the lawyer's job is to win. It doesn't matter for whom or why or what the truth of the matter is. Justice depends on how much you can afford as the old saying goes. And so for lobbying and politicking and too many other things in our society.

That's what bothered me, the idea of putting winning over truth, competition over cooperation, and of promoting that as a sport. And these swarms of larval lawyers were in our library feeding. No wonder I felt uneasy.

Kites

Not Broadcast

My sister told me one of her daughters' teachers had called to check the improbable story she was telling of a summer's afternoon flying kites down on the Gulf of Mexico with her uncle, the university professor. One of the kites we flew that day was more tail than kite, a dragon's small head with the long body trailing behind rippling and whipping through the gulf breezes as the Chinese wind-beast came alive to frolic in its own element. We had other kites with pictures of Spiderman and a pirate on them. The pirate flew too far out over the water and too high up, tugged demandingly, broke the string and got away from us—we clapped and laughed to celebrate its liberation.

Perhaps one of the reasons my niece's teacher was incredulous is that flying kites is useless activity—it accomplishes nothing. It is its own thing.

Some of the old Chinese philosophers extolled the useless. When someone asked one of them about a gnarled old tree, he explained that it was only because the tree was so useless that it had lived so long. Had it been straight and true it would have long since been made into boxes, furniture, or chop sticks, and people would not be able to enjoy talking in its shade. He continued that we don't use the parts of the path our feet are not on, but we wouldn't want to do without such useless things. I think of the narrow range of plants and animals we use in the agriculture of our planet and imagine these guys might have understood the wisdom of keeping the ones we don't use around even if they are useless.

There is no objective to flying a kite. It is subversive of an economic system geared not only to accomplishing things, but doing them efficiently. One idea of freedom is not having anything to accomplish. Flying kites is being free. I enjoy the connection to the wind, being the earth-bound part of a wind dragon riding the breezes, and marveling at a soaring piece of plastic suddenly come to life.

Maybe people can accomplish things by flying kites. Ben Franklin used one to discover electricity and the Wright brothers used them to inspire their flying machines. There are fancy and expensive kites for people who take it seriously and make it a sport or a profession to do intricate stunts and amazing tricks. I fear that if they keep it up, it may become a way to accomplish something. They could give flying kites a good name so it won't be subversive.

Elementary school teachers would find it a worthy thing for a grownup to do with his sister's kids. Then it would be something useful, and like a straight tree cut down for lumber, no longer a refuge. Then it wouldn't be fun.

Everyday matters

Water

All Things Considered 1/2/1996

It's a constant effort to control the water that runs through our house. Sometimes it's a dripping faucet. Sometimes it's the singing of a toilet with a stuck valve or the intermittent nearly but not quite random melody of a flapper that hasn't seated itself properly. At the wet seasons of the year it can be water infiltrating into the basement or insinuating itself a drop at a time through some vulnerable point in the roof. Sometimes I think of the Corps of Engineers facing these problems on a national scale as they try to control all of the water that flows through the country on its way to the seas and that puts my problems with water into a more manageable context.

There's a little town here in Iowa that decided, after being flooded several times, most recently in the great flood of 1993, that they would move off the flood plain and up onto a nearby bluff. They contacted government agencies from the county to the federal; they discussed and planned and had meetings and voted and formed committees, made maps and filled in forms. After two years of this they gave up and decided just to disband the town. It wasn't that their plan was impractical—it simply proved impossible to implement through the layers of government. They might as well have tried to control the water—a hopeless task.

Old Chinese philosophers used water as a metaphor for slow moving but certain and eternal processes. The highest good, they said, is like water. It benefits all things but is without strife. It stays in lowly places that people dislike. It is effective in its actions. Water is formless. You can grasp it but not hold it. What happens if you confront it? It is elusive and evasive. It is continuous and unceasing. It reverts to nothingness. It is self-sufficient and unchanging. It never claims greatness, though its works are great. It does nothing, but everything is done. Be quiet, they advised, and be like water. To understand and emulate these ways, they said, was enlightened.

When you look at it that way, you can see all of human existence as a minor transitory obstruction in the middle of that hydrological cycle we learned about in school. Water falls from the heavens in rain, flows into the streams and to the rivers and to the seas where it evaporates and gets taken up into the atmosphere where it becomes clouds and precipitates again. Our bodies are short detours for water. My house fits between the rain and the Mississippi River.

Those old Chinese guys may not have been rocket scientists, but they sure understood water. That's what I think of when I hear the toilet running and resolve to take the lid off the tank and check that valve one of these days.

Weather

All Things Considered 2/5/1996

Traveling through Iowa's winters is an iffy thing. I bought plane tickets to Texas in a fall sale. I enjoyed the mild weather there and talked about my good luck in going through Chicago and missing the storm that paralyzed St. Louis. As my departure drew closer, I consulted the newspaper and television weather reports. Would I wind up stuck for hours on a runway while they repeatedly deiced the wings waiting for a chance to take off? Would flights out of or into Chicago be canceled? It really didn't matter. I had my ticket and my friend who would pick me up at the airport could ascertain the status of the flight with a phone call to the airline.

Whenever I talk to my father-in-law on the phone we exchange weather reports. He tells me of continental patterns and how they are affecting coastal Texas and I tell him what I see out the window. Conversations with others are less detailed, but weather reports are part of the formula long-distance telephone conversation between the opening "hello" and the closing "goodbye." Face to face, people exchange anticipations and experiences about weather if nothing else. I've even heard people argue about their hopes for future weather. Rain would be good. No, it would be bad.

People who live close to the sea have learned to hightail it for the interior when a hurricane is coming, and Middle Westerners hit the basements when the tornado warnings sound. The weather forecast might make a difference in whether a farmer applies a chemical today or tomorrow, the route of a trucker, the plans of a sailor or pilot, but most of the time most of us just fret about it. Since we all just have to accept whatever weather we get. I wonder why we are so preoccupied with predicting, knowing, and talking about something we can do so little about.

For one thing, it's part of our pervasive pattern of anticipating the future rather than enjoying the present. Capitalism rests on the logic of enduring extant miseries of work for the promise of future rewards—deferred gratification. Communism promises a working class utopia as the reward for present agonies. In this the religions that predict salvation or a messiah are similar to both. Equally reliant on the promise of the future is the most frequently told lie in our land: "The check is in the mail."

The stoic sum up their stance with the saying that there's no bad weather, just inappropriate clothing or gear. But they are unlikely purveyors of big philosophies or weather forecasts. As it turned out, I spent more than an hour on the runway, waiting not for the weather but for the adhesive on a replaced windshield to dry and my friend didn't call, but dutifully waited for my belated arrival.

Bumper Stickers

All Things Considered 4/23/1996

Any time you're in a car, you're surrounded by a profusion of slogans to applaud or abhor. I enjoy reading bumper stickers. After I've pondered the slogan and guessed what it might mean, I have a fleeting feeling of identification or disjunction with the person whose car is displaying it.

This is most obvious with those that name candidates for contested political positions. If it isn't the person I favor, I conclude the driver is a jerk, perhaps crazy, at least unbalanced. If the sticker names someone I like, then the driver must be a sane, reasonable, and responsible individual such as myself.

Some stickers specify political or religious positions, philosophies, outlooks or worldviews. I admire whoever boils down complex and intricately related ideas to a handful of syllables—a discipline as demanding as haiku. "Save the whales," classifies the driver as among those who are against despoiling the planet and opposed to those wish the worst. "Think globally, act locally," might occur with it. Those that proclaim the necessity to arm bears, taunt people who advertise their membership in the cult of firearms with battle cries about the right to bear arms. The answer is the one about prying my gun from cold dead fingers.

There are old classics like, "Question authority." A friend said his response is, "Says who?" Some are enigmatic, if wise such as, "Assume nothing." I wonder why I am made the beneficiary of this advice, sagacious though it may be, and I am always glad to be among the aware rather than the oblivious whether I agree or not.

Some, like the popular and ambiguous, "Don't mess with Texas," issued as a macho proclamation against litter, evoke nationalistic identities or antipathies. I like the one from Wisconsin that says, "Honk if you love cheeses," urging an action to indicate your identification with the sentiment to let the driver know that you're a kindred spirit.

I don't think a bumper sticker ever convinced anyone of anything. Has anyone ever changed a position on a political issue, a philosophical stance, or a candidate because of a bumper sticker? Did anyone quit watching television and become a library regular because of seeing the sticker that urges, "Fight prime time, read a book?" or disarm upon reading, "Commit random acts of beauty?"

These badges of identity have no practical impact. The industrial equivalents of tribal totems show the world what we are and what we are not, distinguish "us" from "them," provide a sense of belonging to some indefinitely large clan who, unknown to each other, share some sentiment. They express the hope that we are not alone.

Honk if you believe in bumper stickers.

Being Busy

All Things Considered 8/29/1996

A friend from Thailand once wrote and said that he hoped I was busy. In some times and places, that would be a curse. We're all too busy, always complaining of so much to do and so little time to do it. I wondered why he would wish busyness on me instead of leisure or whether it was a linguistic mistake, perhaps some kind of cultural misunderstanding on my part or his. It finally dawned on me that he had articulated something about our society that is so close that I hadn't seen it, something that seemed odd because we don't articulate it except to complain about it. From his vantage point he could see that we complain of busyness to emphasize our importance. Far from cursing me, he was wishing importance and significance for me.

Being too busy to do anything means that you're important. Today's pecking order is determined by who will wait for whom. You know people are important when they are so busy that they can't get to their appointments on time.

Some folks are so busy that they can no longer just do one thing at a time. Multi-tasking, as they say in the computer business. People take work with them wherever they go so they can remain busy. Hotels have fax-modem hook-ups. You see people with laptop computers on airplanes. And lots of people have cell phones in their cars or briefcases. I heard a voice resonating in a men's room. It was coming from a stall. The voice said, "What number would that be?" and was replaced by the high pitched beeps of a dialing cell phone. Now that's multi-tasking. That's a busy person. That must have been someone important.

We're not the only ones that have raised being busy to the pinnacles of prestige. Ancient Chinese kings had complex courts full of busy and important people and lots of intrigue. There's a story of a king who invited a philosopher, famous for his greet wisdom, to join his court and use his insight on the human condition to care for the whole land. When the king's ministers found the philosopher, he continued fishing and told them he had heard their king venerated an ancient turtle shell, dead for thousands of years. He asked whether the turtle was better off being important and famous, wrapped up in a box and venerated or dragging its tail in the mud. When the ministers said it would be better off dragging its tail in the mud, the philosopher sent them away and said he'd drag his tail in the mud too.

So, while my friend had given me an important insight into our society and wished me well according to our own values, my mind turned to the old Chinese philosopher dragging his tail in the mud, sufficiently occupied with his fishing.

Aggressive Cars and Drivers

WPSU 6/12/2000

You're peacefully minding your own business when a car abruptly starts blasting away with its horn. Nobody is anywhere near the thing, and it's sounding off like the end of the world. That's a breach of the peace. That's aggression. When cars act hostile, there's usually a driver involved.

I was cruising down Interstate 80 with the control set at about 68 miles an hour when I pulled into the left lane to crawl around a car that was going just a little slower. A low slung white muscle car materialized in my mirror. It was right on my bumper, headlights flashing on and off. This was the aggressive driver I had been hearing about in the news. I went around the guy on my right and pulled over to let the maniac by. Both lanes were full up ahead; he wasn't going anywhere. But, I thought, maybe that's not the point.

In one of the tribal groups anthropologists have studied the men get into chest pounding duels. One guy plants his feet firmly while the other winds up and hits him with everything he's got right in the middle of the chest. Then they trade. If they get irritated, they escalate to pounding each other on the head with poles the diameter of baseball bats. These guys don't have to get anywhere; they're just being assertive, forceful, intense as part of a woman-devaluing macho warrior complex that supports killing some of their girl children to keep the population down to a level that their hunting and gardens can support.

Antagonism isn't always so violent. Eskimo rivals duke it out with songs until public opinion lines up so persuasively behind one side or another that the losers know they can't win a fight much less a feud. It's a way to crank down hostility.

Aggressive drivers have traded cars for the poles or fists and we have our honking duels. Somebody cuts in front or turns left from a right hand lane and we let them have it with our horn. The offending driver may answer and we get a duel going.

We've all had bad days. We've all been in a hurry and been impatient. We've all been stupid enough to feel invulnerable. Maybe we've entered horn duels and added our blasts to the outraged bellows of the drivers we've offended. However perverse these duels, however dangerous the aggressive drivers, they do something for some person. They're a personal form of expression we can understand and forgive.

But it's hard to forgive the same kind of aggression from a machine. You can give the road to an aggressive driver, but it's hard to escape a car blasting its alarm at nobody. That's pure aggression— nothing personal, no greater social or ecological reason, just aggression. No wonder it's so irritating when cars start sounding off on their own.

Drug of Choice

WPSU 8/11/2000

Drugs have been in the news a lot lately. When I think of drugs, I think of ruthless cartels in distant places in league with secretive branches of governments to bring consciousness-altering substances to our streets with the help of sinister gangs of domestic criminals.

When I think of drugs, I think of substances that give a person a sensation of being more powerful, effective, and intelligent than in ordinary life. I think of a feeling of moving effortlessly through the environment so the landscape seems like it's whizzing by in front of the eyes. I think of blurry colors and strange noises. I think of being removed from the ordinary travails of reality to some other-worldly realm.

In other words, when I think of drugs, I think of cars. If it weren't for my car, I wouldn't be involved with gangs of unsavory foreigners and domestic gangsters and government officials to get gasoline.

Without gasoline, I would not be able to drive and I'm sure I'd go into withdrawal at least as severe as when I quit smoking.

Addicts live for the next fix. They don't care what they have to do to get it. If they don't get it they suffer horrible withdrawal. At best they will be terminally annoying to themselves and everyone around them. Addicts can't quit. That's the way I was.

Quitting tobacco was bad enough. I don't think I can really imagine the worst of it. Withdrawing from other drugs can be much worse. But, now that I'm over demon nicotine I don't think much about drugs unless I'm pulling into a gas station for a fix. And then I realize that I still have a long way to go before I kick the monkey on my back.

You're probably in the same fix. But it's not just you and me. Think of what it would take to break our society-wide addiction to cars and gasoline. Think of living in a country where people walk and ride bikes, trains, busses, and trolleys. No cars, parking lots, highways, interstates, car alarms. No automobile industry. No fuel industry. No oil spills. Not as many jobs for air pollution control people. A whole society in the throes of gasoline withdrawal. Not a pretty sight.

So, now that gasoline is more than two bucks a gallon in some places, instead of feeling ripped off, I just think of it as getting a fix of my drug of choice and supporting a social addiction.

That makes everything feel better.

And that's what drugs are for.

Tibet in Iowa

Not Broadcast

We hear more about Tibet now than we did before the Chinese took over that land. The news of the Tibetan women at the recent women's conference in China was not very bright. Now and then the Dali Lama gives a speech or an interview. Surely the Chinese are not the first foreigners to meddle in Tibetan politics and religion, but before they moved in, and refugees began moving out, our images of Tibet were shrouded in the same mysterious haze that hid Shangri-La.

I've never been to Tibet, so I don't really know what it looks like. My images of it come from travel books I read when I was a kid, with sepia toned photos Lhasa and the lamasery of the Dali Lama, row upon row of parallel tiers built on top of a mountain.

On my way to work I frequently walk through a park. The path turns into a stairway at the end, and from that spot, until a while ago, I could see house roofs marching up the opposite slope to several large brick buildings in various earthen tones at the top. One is marked with parallel rows of square windows. Atop it are several small towers with hip roofs, and one large roof whose angle breaks in the middle like a barn roof.

On a foggy day when the mist is hiding the creek in the valley, hanging in the bare trees, and enveloping the houses, I could see in that vista the mysteries of timeless Tibet.

I admired the view from that bluff for years. I once tried to describe it to a friend who knew the place, but failed. I resolved to send her a photograph of that landscape so she could see the uncanny resemblance as I saw it. I walked to the bluff with my camera, composed the photo, snapped the shutter, and congratulated myself for capturing the view on film.

When I saw the print there was no hint of Tibet. By some magic my vision had been purged somewhere in all of the harsh chemical processes of photography leaving only a dreary Middle Western town—a hillside covered with telephone poles, electric wires, transformers high in the air, cars parked on the road below, television antennas soaring above the roofs, and dirty snow turning black in the gutters—the hollow meaningless view my friend had seen.

The next time I passed that spot, I stopped to think about it. I could only see the Tibetan vista by consciously editing much of the reality. In that confrontation with reality, I lost my mysterious foggy timeless view of Tibet. Now, conscious of the realties, I have to work pretty hard to conjure up any image beyond the starkness of the wires and poles. I never did send the photo.

Time

Not Broadcast

We face the beginning of a new year, and with it, the task of making a myth of the old one in the incessant reviews, assessments, and evaluations, attempts to pin it down, name it, characterize it, make it mean something.

With the parties, gifts, kisses, funny hats, songs and religious services, we have done the sacred and secular rituals of marking a collective end and beginning as we do individually every year with our birthday observances.

We make a fetish of time. An astronomer put it into perspective for me over dinner one evening when he said that the sun would go nova in a hundred million years. The end.

The ancient Maya had astronomers, too, and obsessed with beginnings and ends, they devised elaborate calendarical systems for keeping track of time. Equally obsessed with time, we make much of collective or personal beginnings and ends which we await with apprehension or confidence about what happens after the new beginnings they herald.

We give mythological origin stories scientific meaning with our quest for understanding the first moments of the cosmos and our incessant search for our progenitors in the fossil record and our own DNA. Cold War stories of the nuclear end and the nightmare-making political dramas that went with them are being replaced by visions of a poisoned planet unfit for human habitation and visions of the end of our species in a whimper rather than a bang.

Many have prophesied the end of the world much sooner than the astronomer I broke bread with, and so far all have been wrong.

The new beginning rekindles the sense of hope, control, and choice that our resolutions express. That sense of confidence may dim with our endurance of the inexorable immediateness of daily life that we track with our watches, clocks, and calendars, but the anticipation of the new beginning after the end keeps its spark alive. And so we categorize and name the past periods—years, decades, generations, centuries—to help guide us through an ever-present now to the anticipated new beginnings.

The Maya civilization perished. I sometimes wonder how the intensifying agricultural and political system with its warfare was for those Maya kings and commoners as they approached that point of no return when their social order collapsed. I wonder whether they had any sense that the end they predicted and celebrated was written by their own practices. I wonder whether any anticipated that while the civilization would perish, the people and languages would endure.

Mice

Not Broadcast

I've read that the stories of alligators in the sewer systems of big cities are urban myths, but when we were in Boston the thing that amazed me the most was not visiting all the historical sites where a bunch of guys did things that would get them arrested today as surely as it did more than two hundred years ago but the mice in the subway. Here is one of the monuments to industry and engineering—those thundering trains running through tunnels underneath a huge city, but when the trains rumble off, little brown mice swarm out of everywhere and start bouncing in the gravel between the rails. In a few minutes they sense the vibrations of the next train and hightail it into their hiding places to wait for the next lull. Fascinated, I would watch the mice and forget about the trains and getting wherever Dorothy and I had decided to go.

One time Dorothy consulted an exterminator about the ants that invade our house on occasion. After he examined the place he said that after all the ants were there first and the house had been built in their place, and though it had been there some seventy years, we could expect the ants to try to reclaim it once in a while. He said there wasn't anything to do about it as long as we insisted on keeping the house there.

The building where my office is has termites in it. The story is that the termites were there first. After the university built a building in their area some decades ago, they slowly reclaimed it and began to spread out. Years later, they have crossed the street and reached my building.

I find these as hopeful signs. They suggest that no matter how hard we try, we won't be able to displace other creatures entirely.

Even in the built environments of cities, the insects reassert their eminent domain, the mice lay claim to the subways, the seagulls and bears feed at the landfills.

The forest reclaimed the great ancient civilizations of Mesoamerica and Cambodia, and if I didn't mow our yard, I am sure it would soon take our place too. As it is, the corners inside the fence get more and more rounded as the summer progresses and the jungle moves in.

All of this makes me think that sooner or later most of the wounds we have inflicted on the planet to make our living on it with agriculture and industry will heal over. Sometimes I wonder what Boston and the other big cities will look like when they're grown over and how long it might take.

Unique or Uniform

Not Broadcast

Just as surely as every descendant of human ancestors re-invents the art of the bipedal locomotion that our Australopithecine progenitors pioneered, each new generation originates its own forms of disaffection, withdrawal, and uniqueness. In recent decades some have rejected as de-humanizing the plethora of numbers that characterize us—telephone numbers, ZIP codes, personal identification numbers, license plate numbers, social security numbers, credit card numbers. Capturing this sense of outrage, the hero of the 1960s television series, *The Prisoner,* opens each episode by asserting, "I am not a number. I am a free man."

As an expression of their shared singularity, the alienated of every age, exhausted with the hopelessness of inhumane numbers and conformity to incomprehensible molds they did not create, institute their own distinctive dress, music, dance and slang form beatniks to punks, from hoods to gangstas. These badges of individuality are preserved in drama, literature and film.

The mark of genius in a writer is to capture the categories so the dialogue seems familiar. We feel so strongly that we have been there before and spoken those words; that we know the characters as we know ourselves. We see ourselves because the authors dip their dialogue from the limited number of conversations and categories in the familiar streams of discourse. A well-read acquaintance says that if you think you've had an original idea it means you haven't read enough.

I came in on one of my own conversations recently when I found myself eating rice and vegetables with disposable wooden chopsticks from a Styrofoam tray in a nearly deserted Chinese hole-in-the-wall restaurant and nodding in agreement with a person I was overhearing at another table. I had played his role in the same conversation not long before. If I had read the dialogue in a book or seen it in a play or television show I would have considered the author a genius.

The writers who define convention by making up forms for bureaucrats invite us to put ourselves into pigeon-holes whenever we fill in the blanks that demand information on our age, gender, ethnicity, and all the numbers from phone to zip. Each puts us in a category. Except our social security number. That is ours alone.

When we get dressed, we fill in the same blanks. Which power suit will you wear today? Or blue jeans? Or punk garb? When we open our mouths to speak, we fill in the same blanks. When I think about these things, I am glad I have a Social Security number. That may be the one thing that we all share, and the one thing that makes each of us unique.

A Ray of Hope

2005 *SfAA News* 16(3)

"He walks the walk." That's how Suzan introduced Jack Heyman, a longshoreman from Oakland that we met in Liverpool at the ten-year anniversary of a dockers' action there that sparked the organization of longshoremen's locals around the world for mutual support. Jack was the guy who got the Charleston longshoremen in touch with this network of activist dockers in 2000 when 5 of them had been charged with felonies after an altercation over the use of non-union labor on the docks.

A motto of the ILWU is "An injury to one is an injury to all." The California locals of the ILWU raised money and supported the Charleston local even when its own International Longshoremen's Association and the AFL-CIO did not. Some say it was the support of the international dockers and their threat to shut down world shipping if the Charleston longshoremen saw the inside of a courtroom that got them off eighteen months later.

Jack and his wife were visiting friends in Harrisburg and going to a wedding in Philadelphia. In between, they came to State College to show a film on the ILWU's anti-war movement and one event in which the Oakland Police had over reacted. Suzan and I were at the Portland SfAA meeting the day the war in Iraq broke out. We joined other protesters in a Portland park where we met an ILWU friend of ours who had organized the workers at Powell's Bookstore. She complained that though her local had come out against the war and was represented at the action, the "woosey-assed Longshoremen had not." They came around, though. And Jack was in State College to tell that story. His visit was sponsored by the State College Peace Center, on whose board I sit.

Jack had been a student at Penn State in the 60s. He visited the place where he burned his draft card and other places he hadn't seen in 40 or more years. He still works on the docks driving a lift truck that moves containers around. And he walks the walk. He is at every demonstration. He organizes for peace marches. He organizes support for fellow dockers. He works with the ILWU.

When he spoke after the film, he talked about class war. One of the students asked where he could sign up to fight in the class war. "They don't pass out sign-up sheets for that," he said.

***

One of the members of the State College Peace Center has been Marjorie Smith. We last saw her at a play a couple of weeks ago. She and her husband, Reed had walked to the play from their residence at a Quaker assisted living facility. She was 86 and had suffered a fall, so she was using a walker and the walk back up the hill was a bit strenuous. Then we heard she had bone cancer that had metastasized.

Then we heard she had died. Today we went to her memorial at the assisted living facility.

There were about two hundred people there. Many were fellow residents. Many were her family and friends from all over the country. In the Quaker fashion, people spoke when they were moved. In turn friends, relatives, co-congregationalists, and co-workers spoke of this woman.

One spoke of Quaker queries that measure the life as people lead it to what they say. "Was thee faithful?" is one such query. Last week, he continued, Marjorie was at the peace vigil and did her shift at the food bank.

One daughter said Marjorie said just before she died that everyone has to go sometime, but the important thing is to live life to its fullest to the end.

Another person told a Bible story about Jesus who said that when he was naked he had been clothed; when he was hungry he had been fed. The disciples said they hadn't done these things. Jesus said whoever has done these the things for the least of people has done them for me.

A person from the Housing Appeals Board told how Marjorie calculated family budgets and indicated when people needed more help than they were getting. Another person said she was always apologizing for what she had not done.

A guy stood and spoke about Quaker axioms: let your life speak; see what you can do and how Marjorie was a pen pal to a guy on death row. All of his family had forsworn him but she believed that god was in all of us, that there was hope for redemption and reconciliation. She believed it. She practiced it.

One woman spoke of riding a bus to Washington for a demonstration against the war in Iraq. The Peace Center chartered the bus to take young people, university students and old people from the assisted living facility to Washington.

Another said that Marjorie paddled upstream. If one can do it, two can do it. Take strength and continue to work for peace was her motto.

***

One of these activists was a unionist to the bone. The other was a pacifist Quaker through and through. Their paths almost crossed in a little town in central Pennsylvania. Every day we do our little bits to make a better world. Maybe we attend a peace vigil or organize with the peace movement or to help reshape our electoral system. Most of the time it seems to make no difference. Most of the time it seems to be going nowhere. But we keep on doing it. And it's people like these two who give us the vision and the strength to do that.

It seems to me that we anthropologists should be telling these stories. We can be telling about the realities we see in our research as well as the remedies we can imagine. We should at least describe the class war. And we should do whatever we can to prosecute the war on behalf of our working class brothers and sisters. I'm not for romanticizing anything, and I'm not for telling propaganda stories that make people into heroes. But when we find sparks of hope, such as the radicalization of the leadership of the Charleston Longshoremen and the fight they have waged, and the international organization of dockers, then I think we should tell the stories truthfully so that others can share the hope. That's what Suzan and I are doing in our research on the Charleston Longshoremen, and that's what we'll do in our forthcoming book on that topic from Monthly Review Press.

Anthropology and Anthropologists

The Problem of Class

*2001 SfAA News.*12(1)

There is but one truly serious ethnographic problem, and that is class. I paraphrase Camus' opening line of *The Myth of Sisyphus*. All of the other things we discuss and debate from gender to literary stylings; from ritual to choice of mates; from conceptualization to commerce are derivative. No longer is there refuge for people outside a global system of information, culture, commerce, capital, labor, and affect, all of which mutually affect the others; all of which are determined by class.

One percent of the people in the U.S. control 48 per-cent of its wealth. The next 19 percent of the people control 46 percent of the wealth. The bottom 80 percent of the people control 6 percent of the wealth (Longworth 1998:201). Our theoretical stylings must start and end with these stark observations. Postmodern fashionability demands nuance, shading, shadows, moving from the clear light of day into the recesses of the less visible. We need fewer distinctions, not more so we can see the phenomenon more clearly rather than obscure it. We need a less nuanced approach to class.

When Jay Gould said he could hire half of the working class to kill the other half of the working class, he was speaking in the unnuanced rhetoric of guns in the hands of Pinkertons he hired. The contemporary approach, as Ehrenreich puts it (*Fear of Falling*), is to hire half of the working class to manage the other half of the working class on behalf of the employing class. Anthropologists are part of that structure. We too eagerly join with sociologists to speak of SES, socioeconomic status, or to assert that in the United States there is no class, only status. A generation of anthropologists has criticized a previous one for cooperation with the colonial enterprise while it has systematically obfuscated facts and issues of class at home and abroad.

The specter that haunted Europe, that frightful hobgoblin that stalked through Europe, as the first English translation of the Communist Manifesto put it (Wheen 1999:124), has been laid to rest and now the demands of the manifesto look curiously like something from a platform of an acceptable American political party respectably engaged in electoral politics and the American Communist Party had only half the card carrying membership of the American Anthropological Association when their long-time octogenarian leader Gus Hall died in the year 2000. Did we notice the specter? We chronicle nuances of resistance to hegemony without talking about a ruling class. We play with consequences and dare not discuss causes.

What happened to the working class that was so clearly visible to the Industrial Workers of the World that they could unambiguously state in the preamble to their constitution that there are but two classes—the employing class and the working class and they have nothing in common? Jay Gould furnished part of the answer. He and the employing class hired the guns. That's no joke. Consider the alternatives for class consciousness. One is discussion. In the last century Peter Kropotkin pointed out the pitfalls of the right to free speech. In Great Britain revolutionists, persecuted and chased from Europe, could speak as openly as they pleased, publish what they wanted, discuss as openly as they desired as long as they did not do anything untoward. In Tsarist Russia to even think or speak in subversive tones demanded organization into paranoid secret societies. The cost of freedom of speech was organization.

The observation is still appropriate. When the rage of impotence moves people to arms they are met with sure and swift and overwhelming violence from any one of a number of government agencies from Alcohol, Firearms and Tobacco to the Coast Guard to the National Guard or a local Special Weapons and Tactics Team likely trained if not armed by the Department of Defense. It seems almost every agency of government has its own goon squad. For those agencies that do not maintain their own means of violence there is the all-purpose Federal Bureau of Investigation. The examples are all too frequent in the news from Ruby Ridge to Waco to either example of Wounded Knee to the latest worker gone postal or whack-o with a gun taking as many others as possible with him to the next life.

What Scott observed of Indonesian peasants is true of other stratified societies—not only are people not fooled by ruling class symbolic or ritual proclamations but they also know from hard won experience that head-on resistance only results in tragedy. It may be that every generation in every land must pay a price in blood to learn that lesson but what the peasants taught the Yale scholar remains is true.

The safer alternative is to remain within the law and try to organize for common purposes. Some countries such as the Scandinavian ones demand it. But even this element of corporatist states is weakening under the hammer of global economics as manufacturing moves its well-paying jobs to the cheap labor markets of the third world to achieve greater profits for shareholders, save on their tax bill, undercut the tax base, and threaten the social contract that has underwritten class co-operation on mutually agreed terms. Other lands, such as the United States, incorporate into law charters for the employing class to systematically prevent such cooperation and destroy whatever gains the working class may threaten to make through organization. The Taft-Hartley amendments to the Wagner Act are examples. As Miriam Wells points out, local and national administrative interpretation of the law is another avenue. The third avenue is the inevitable and tragically predictable internal collapse of organized labor under the weight of its own political necessities (D&E) and personal proclivities (C.W. Mills).

Democratic societies provide the option of victory through their electoral processes. Economist John Kenneth Galbraith (1992) documents how this system works only for those for whom it works. Most of that lowest 80 percent of the population of the U.S. is so ill served by the political system that it is a waste of their time and effort to participate in it even to the extent of voting. The 40 percent of the population who either are well served by the political system or who can come to think of themselves as possibly served by it, participate in the process and continually reinvent it to serve their interests—those of the employing class and that part of the working class that serves them.

As Galbraith points out, all that's left is for the employing class to hire some academics to proclaim that they do not even exist to make the sham complete. This explains our unwillingness to address clearly issues of class. We are implicated in the process of obscurantism. Why else does the American Anthropological Association see in two-worker households that sometimes don't even manage to stay above the level of poverty a working middle class instead of the working class? Why else do anthropologists endlessly discuss nuances of their own north-eastern suburban high school days? Why else do we avoid the issue of class and obscure it so thoroughly? It's time we quit it.

References Cited

Camus, Albert. 1955. The Myth of Sisyphus and Other Essays. New York Vintage Books.

Galbraith, John Kenneth. 1992. The Culture of Contentment. Boston Houghton Mifflin Company.

Longworth, Richard C. 1998. Global Squeeze the Coming Crisis for First-World Nations. Chicago Contemporary Books.

Wheen, Francis. 1999. Karl Marx. London Fourth Estate.

Why the Idea of Social Capital is a Bad Idea

2002 *SfAA News* 13(3)

Over the past few years there's been a lot of buzz about social capital. I have no quarrel with the idea that social connections have economic value. That may be what that often cited quote from Polanyi means—the economy is embedded in social relations. My quarrel is in calling that "social capital." It's a bad idea because it plays a kind of conceptual trick on us to make classes disappear, to make it appear that everyone has access to resources in a classless social order.

Because of the relative prestige economists enjoy in policy-making arenas, those who wish to be heard are often tempted to assume their rhetorical forms, "to speak their language," or to the fashionable, "to appropriate their tropes." Rather than asking economists to put their feet on the ethnographic ground to understand human relations in human terms, some think they can gain more prestige in conference halls if not in factories, fields, and workshops by pouring those realities into the mold of economists' metaphors. One such mold is the concept of "social capital."

If everyone has social relations, then everyone has social capital. This metaphor tells us that everyone controls capital. That's the sleight of hand that makes classes disappear. That's why this metaphor conceals more than it reveals. If we all control capital, then we can't distinguish classes based on who controls it and who does not. Classes become invisible. They disappear into a cloud of metaphoric thinking. Maybe there are differences in income, prestige, occupation, education, but these are things anyone can aspire to, available to all as freely as uncut forests in a long fallow swidden system that knows no concept of land ownership.

> Capital is wealth used to create more wealth as part of a system of production in which all the components are market commodities. One of these is labor, which creates more than the value of its cost because the system continually increases productivity through technological innovations. In Eric Wolf's words from *Europe and the People without History* (1997:78):

>Wealth . . . is not capital until it controls means of production, buys labor power, and puts it to work, continuously expanding surpluses by intensifying productivity through an ever rising curve of technological inputs.

Merchants may profit by selling the things people make, but unless their wealth organizes the process of production in this way, it is not capital. So, Wolf goes on (1997:79), there is no merchant capital. There may be mercantile wealth, but it is not capital. Capital is a component of one kind of political-economic system in which it functions to define the rights of its owners to the value that labor creates. Capital does not exist apart from the social and political system that defines and enforces it. It is wealth that has a specific function in an economic system. Some people have it and many do not. That's why there are classes. Some people use their wealth to organize production and the rest work for them.

This is commonplace to anthropologists who are accustomed to understanding the life-ways and economies of people who are organized in many different ways. Without this comparison with other systems, capital seems as natural and inevitable to people inside a capitalist system as forest spirits are to swiddening folk.

In an article about social capital in *Business Week*, Karen Pennar (1997) says that, "The new research shows that the nature of social relationships in different places can influence schooling, jobs and earnings . . . as much as talent and initiative do." The research of anthropologist Katherine Newman (1988, 1993, 2000) shows that the concept that talent and initiative determine success is a dimension of middle class ideology, not a sociological datum. She shows how this self-serving ideology can become tragically self-destructive. She also shows that many talented people with great initiative are structurally disadvantaged. Their choices, their talents, their initiative make no difference. Decades ago in his *Power Elite* C. Wright Mills pointed out that access to resources powerfully determines the kinds of social relations people can have. Katherine Newman's latest book, *No Shame in My Game* makes the same point from the perspective of those without access to resources. It may be that "the web of social relationships . . . affects economic growth" (Pennar 1997:154). But that does not make them capital. It makes them social relations.

Extensions of the metaphor lead to absurdities such as "bad social capital," social relations that incorporate prejudice or encourage criminal behavior (Pennar 1997:154). "Good" and "bad" social capital depend on where we are in the system. As a means of maintaining economic flows into structurally disadvantaged neighborhoods and the subsistence of individuals, gangs may be positive. People in the neighborhoods threatened by theft, violence, and drug-dealing might see gangs as negative.

What about the view from the system as a whole? Comparative studies of political systems (Fried 1967) show that in stratified social orders, those characterized by differential access to resources, without which there could be no capitalism or capital, there is no system-wide advantage, no shared system-wide point of view. Advantages have to be assessed in terms of position within the system with respect to access to resources. Those with privileged access can benefit by measures that are deleterious to those without. That is why poverty exists along with wealth in such social and political orders.

These observations seem so simple as to not require statement, but we must state them in the face of such metaphors as "social capital" to return us to a more realistic view of social, political, and economic systems, a view in which we can see rather than hide classes and differential access to resources.

References Cited

Fried, Morton. 1967. The Evolution of Political Society: an Essay in Political Anthropology. New York Random House

Mills, C. Wright. 1959. The Power Elite. New York Oxford University Press.

Newman, Katherine S. 1988. Falling from Grace: the Experience of Downward Mobility in the American Middle Class. New York Free Press.
1993. Declining Fortunes The Withering of the American Dream. New York Basic Books.
2000. No Shame in My Game: the Working Poor in the Inner City. New York Vintage Books.

Pennar, Karen. 1997. The Ties that Lead to Prosperity. Business Week. December 15:153-155.

Wolf, Eric. 1997. Europe and the People without History (With a new preface). Berkeley University of California Press.

SfAA and Public Policy

2005 *SfAA News* 16(1)

This morning, some whack-job from the Hoover Institute was on NPR saying that since all prescription drugs have some side effects, you and your doctor should be free to decide which ones you want to risk taking. The FDA has no business controlling that part of your life by judging the risks and benefits of drugs.

Heard about Social Security Reform? It only gets rid of the "social" part and the "security" part so that we invest in the stock market to make brokers rich. The "social" part is supposed to mean people helping each other—while I have an income, I contribute some of it to support those who don't. The "security" part means that if I don't have an income because I'm disabled or retired, I can count on getting an income from the system. I earn that right by paying in while I do have an income. It has nothing to do with stocks or brokers.

I suppose one of these genius whackos is busy in a right-wing think tank coming up with some way to justify saying that it's your choice where you work and OSHA shouldn't meddle with businesses that don't care to invest in workplace safety. It's your right to breathe particulate matter if you choose to live in Atlanta or Los Angeles and the EPA shouldn't interfere with your right to elect slow suicide.

But somehow it's not a woman's right to decide whether she wants to carry a fertilized egg to term. The government can decide that one. If you're in a reserve unit that's called up, it's not your choice whether to go to Iraq and violate that commandment of that jealous god of that Old Testament that ordered people not to kill. So the government can make you violate your religious tenets.

That's the thing with whack-jobs; they aren't bothered by such hobgoblins of small minds as consistency.

And that's the thing about their think-tanks. The brokers, war mongers, and drug companies that benefit from this insane chatter pay these people to think up these absurdities and repeat them until they seem obvious to people. People lose that fine sense of the absurd that gives life spice and come to think of themselves as strange if the absurd does *not* seem obvious. Jules Henry wrote about that in his book, *Culture against Man.*

What he didn't write about was how those absurdities become public policy or how people come to vote absurdly. People work harder than ever before for less and less. Everywhere they turn, they lose. Healthcare. Pensions. Security. Education. Potholes. Schools. Jobs. So they get angry. They know there are some bastards out there making their lives miserable. Liberals. And they vote against them. And it gets worse and worse and they get madder and madder and vote more and more against those frigging liberals. That's the thesis of Thomas Frank's book, *What's the Matter with Kansas? How Conservatives Won the Heart of America*. The Democrats dropped the ball when they took economics out of politics.

Anthropologist Dimitra Doukas points out that this right wing barrage on reason is no new phenomenon. In her book, *Worked Over: The Corporate Sabotage of an American Community,* she dates it to more than a hundred years ago when trusts re-organized as corporations justified their piracy by promoting the gospel of wealth—that wealth generates wealth—in opposition to the prevailing gospel of work—that work generates wealth. They endowed university chairs and sponsored university professors who would spread their gospel via the religion-as-science doctrines of economics. They sponsored a cultural revolution. If you're at a university, see who bought your department of economics, check who built the buildings. Here at Penn State, people and corporations buy whole colleges and collect individual professors as well. Most universities are the same.

Here I keep hearing that song, *Send in the Clowns*, but there are too many syllables in "anthropologists" to fit where "clowns" should go.

But where are we?

Where are the anthropologists in the formation of public policy? Nowhere to be seen.

A bankruptcy judge just decided that U.S. Air can violate its contract with the flight attendants' union and delete their contract because the corporation's obligation to honor contracts with workers comes low on the list. The policy this proclaims to corporations? Declare bankruptcy, scrape off the unions that represent your workers, and continue with non-organized workers. Work them more and pay them less…I'm not predicting the future here, I'm reciting the past. We've seen the exact same tactic used by coal mining companies in Pennsylvania that now pay low wages to non-union workers. Thanks to some bankruptcy judge, coalminers dying of black lung and other ailments have lost the health insurance and pensions their union negotiated for them decades ago.

So workers get angry and vote for the politicians the corporations are buying anyway.

Neat. It doesn't get any better than that.

Or Congress takes seriously proposals to "reform" social security.

Or a grassroots movement organizes to oppose abortions.

Or OSHA doesn't get enough funds to enforce job safety rules.

Or FDA changes its rules about approving drugs.

Or a conservative judge says you don't have to honor your contracts with unions.

And where are we?

Well, whatever you want to say about anything else the American Anthropological Association has done lately, they've at least put a little bit of their money behind a Public Policy Center. In addition, AAA sections including the Biological Anthropology Section, Association of Senior Anthropologists, Central States Anthropological Society, and National Association of Practicing Anthropologists all kicked in. The 5k from AAA and the contributions from the sections don't amount to much compared to the coffers of irrationality, but it's a start.

And it's a damned sight more than the Big Fat 0 that our own SfAA board put behind it.

Want to hear a voice of reason? Well, if not reason, anthropology? Then help the SfAA leadership see the necessity of supporting a Policy Center. The committee working on this policy center has spent years answering every question, and foreseeing every wrinkle, writing plans for every contingency, even making an administrative setup so that the SfAA doesn't lose its identity in the process. They've crossed every 't' and dotted every 'i.' Now it's time for the SfAA to put up.

Shoot, if each member ponied up a buck a year, that would do it. If we decided to forego one big reception at our annual meeting, we could make a meaningful contribution to the seed money the Policy Center needs to get started.

So let's all think about what we value and help our SfAA leadership see the sweet light of reason—let's all spend a little effort educating our board members and do something to gain a voice for anthropology in the discussions of public policy that affect us all.

Society for Applied Anthropology Policy Paper on Employee Free Choice Act

Unpublished

One way to shut people up is to lower the boom on anyone who speaks out. Graham Spanier, President of Penn State has announced that he will press the maximum charges against those 31 students who sat in in the public spaces of the administration's office building known as Old Main. Of course this sends a chilling message throughout the academic community—students and faculty alike. Radical right wing activist David Horowitz knows the power of corporate funding to silence dissent via legislative action and demands on university administrations to silence anyone who does not toe his corporate line. He sponsors advertisements in the Penn State student newspaper that say that the Muslim Student Association is in league with terrorists. These are all of a piece with the Patriot Act of 2001 which sent a chill wave of fear across the land when our legislators passed and then reauthorized it in 2006.

It's a pity that such actions can and do have the power to induce such reticence among academics and especially among anthropologists. It's more than a little disappointing that such political influences can emasculate the SfAA Board of Directors to the point that they fear speaking out on behalf of sound public policy. The SfAA statement of purpose and vision says that, "The Society for Applied Anthropology aspires to promote the integration of anthropological perspectives and methods in solving human problems throughout the world; to advocate for fair and just public policy based upon sound research…." I haven't seen this purpose and vision in action since the Patriot Act passed.

For more than a decade I've been working with Suzan Erem on labor unions and reporting our findings to colleagues at SfAA meetings and other venues. In fact, I've not written much for the pages of the *Newsletter* lately because I've been involved in a research project with longshoremen in Charleston, South Carolina. The book on the topic that Suzan and I published, *On the Global Waterfront: The Fight to Free the Charleston 5* came out in January from Monthly Review Press. In the meantime the anti-union movement gained strength under the umbrella of silence and inaction induced by the chilling effects the Patriot Act and other such actions great and small meant to intimidate any who speak against the complete corporate take-over of our land. To any who remember it or have read about it, this must be reminiscent of the McCarthyism of the mid-20th century.

One example has been the explosive growth of anti-union consultants that management can hire to bust unions. Karen Brodkin and Cynthia Strathmann have documented how these operatives work in California. Others have documented the rise and tactics of this industry. Here's one example.

Under current law, when a majority of employees select a union to be their bargaining agent by signing union cards, the union may call for an election under the rules of the National Labor Relations Board, established by the Wagner Act of 1935 that first granted American workers the right to organize. Notice that a majority of employees must have already selected the union as their bargaining agent. The law requires a second election. During the time between the scheduling of the election and the holding of the election, management consultants may use all manner of dirty tricks to intimidate workers so they will vote against the union and be left without representation. Of course the overriding chill of national, regional and local actions aids and abets these corporate hirelings in their task.

The remedy? The way to restore democracy in this small arena? Change the law. That's what the Employee Free Choice Act (EFCA) was meant to do. Edward Kennedy (D-MA) introduced S.1041 on March 29, 2007. The legislation would eliminate the requirement of the second election and it would increase penalties for violating existing law. It passed the Senate but failed in the House with the promise of a presidential veto. This much was predictable. It is also predictable that after the November elections EFCA will be introduced again with a better chance of passing both houses and winning a presidential signature.

What's the appropriate role for anthropologists and the SfAA? It seems to me it is to speak out in support of this legislation. We've done it before. In 1998, based on "results of detailed scientific research in many U.S. agricultural locations" the SfAA called on legislators to not include the " 'Agricultural Job-Opportunity Benefits and Security Act of 1998' in the Commerce, Justice, and State Department Appropriations bill" (The documents I cite can be found at the SfAA website under "committees" "special committees" "public policy" "SfAA Policy Statements" with various extensions such as, "guest workers.") The same year, the SfAA submitted testimony that it "is opposed to S. 1691 and other measures that have the effect of further compromising the sovereignty of American Indian tribes" (immunity).

In 1999, the Society advocated, "Because of the complex issues involved in these questions of data access and confidentiality, the SfAA strongly recommends that OMB utilize a process of negotiated rulemaking to allow all affected parties to participate in the revisions of Circular A-110," "Uniform Administrative Requirements for Grants and Agreements with Institutions of Higher Education, Hospitals, and Other Non-Profit Organizations." In November, 2001, SfAA offered detailed "Comments on World Bank draft Operational Policies O.P. 4.10 and Bank Procedures B.P. 4.10, concerning indigenous peoples" (worldbank).

That was just days after George W. Bush signed the Patriot Act on October 26, 2001. After that, silence. Until I submitted a policy statement that detailed the ethnographic data in support of EFCA. To see some of the content in the original statement, check the American Anthropological Association website, Issues & News, Public Policy/Advocacy, Policy Brief # 1. The SfAA Public Committee required a different format but I submitted about the same information, if in somewhat different form. The wheels turned and the process processed until at long last, out came a Board certified Policy Statement removing virtually all of the content of the original and concluding "Therefore, the Society for Applied Anthropology supports allowing employees to form unions, without interference from management."

That's almost as effective and politically courageous as the SfAA Board ratifying the human right to be bipedal. Given the history of our Society in taking rather more effective and detailed policy stances before the Patriot Act, I think that our board has followed many others who have felt the chilling effects of the Patriot Act akin to those of the McCarthy period which we now see for the oppression that it was. I think that anthropologists should exhibit more courage than that, especially if they put themselves in positions of leadership of organizations such as ours, one of whose purposes is to "to advocate for fair and just public policy based upon sound research..." rather than to cower in subservient and acquiescent fear of corporations and the right-wing.

Reflections on the Absolute

1987 *Anthropology and Humanism Quarterly* 12

In the summer of 1981 I went to Iceland to study the mysteries of fishing boat skippers that some Icelanders had reported. Before, I had studied shamans in Southeast Asia (Durrenberger 1975a, 1975b, 1976a, 1976b, 1980a, 1980b, 1981). By all reports Icelandic skippers were similar. How did their dreams, hunches, and quasi-shamanic intuitions lead them to their prey?

Gísli Pálsson had studied Icelandic fishing up close. We worked together that summer, as we have continued to do since. We discussed the mysteries of the skippers and what the mysterious quality might be how it might work. Gísli had lots of numbers. We wanted to find out how strong this "skipper effect" was. We reasoned, like Acheson (1977), it could be no stronger than the unexplained variance in catch after mundane factors such as boat size and number of fishing trips had been taken into account.

We were disappointed when our first results showed that only 10 to 12 percent of the variance in catch could be attributed to everything else in the cosmos that might affect catching fish, including weather, and the mysterious abilities of skippers. It felt like we had done ourselves out of an intriguing question. We began to examine the patterns we had found in Gísli's numbers to see whether they were general. Using historical records, we projected our tables back to the days of rowing boats, before 1920. I spent more time with the computer. The same story came out, year by year, port by port. We noticed some other patterns in the numbers and began to explore them. The patterns began to tell parts of a story. After much discussion, we concluded we may have been asking the wrong question. We began to ask about the relationships between the patterns the numbers showed us and how people thought about such things, how they represented realities to themselves and others.

The question assumed we knew the reality. People think there is a skipper effect. They are wrong. We asked why they think that.

We were looking at outcomes of behavior, or conditions, the sizes of boats, the power of engines, the numbers of radios and sonars, the numbers of fishing trips, the catches. There was no intentionality in the numbers, only consequences. The thoughts and feelings of the actors, those fishermen and skippers who routinely risked life, limb, and fortune on the North Atlantic in the winter fishery were not in the tables. There were obituaries, notices of ships lost to storms and high seas, men lost overboard or in ship-board accidents, but these did not come into our computations. Nor did our tables reflect the grief of widows, the hopes of sons, the disappointments of skippers with no boats, the anger at rejected attempts to obtain credit, the frustrations with government policy. The tables passed over the years of the Second World War with no intimation that, per capita, the casualties suffered to the sea were as high or higher than the combat losses of the warring nations. The tables showed us a reality irrespective of the actors' thoughts or feelings.

It reminded me of what Von Berralnaffey (1962) had written about Japanese prints. The artists knew about perspective, experimented with it, and then did not use it. They used parallel perspective. The perspective lines do not converge. There is no point of view. There is no observer. Whatever you see in the print is as it is. The Japanese removed the observer to represent the absolute. Europeans struggled with perspective to define the position of an observer, to represent reality as a particular person sees it. This European humanistic reality depended on an observer did not exist apart from an individual. But if we took this stance and accepted what many observers knew to be true, we had to deny the reality of the patterns of the numbers, and argue that somehow the skipper effect was stronger than the numbers showed it to be.

Humanists respect the observer, make him or her central, empathize with him. We put ourselves in the others shoes and respect other ways of seeing. Humanistic anthropology shows how the world looks through other eyes. It shows how actions make sense from other perspectives. It shows us other vantage points.

It was exciting to sit at the computer and watch patterns emerge in the numbers, to see bits of a story falling into place, to be puzzled by questions and stay up late into the night pondering them. It reminded me of Japanese haiku.

From Japan:

on the dead branch a crow settles—
autumn evening.
(Basho, translated by Akrnakjian 1979, 48).

The peasant hoes on.
The person who asked the way
Is now out of sight.
(Busan, translated by Buchanan 1973, 64).

A stark sliver of reality slices into the consciousness for a moment to disrupt the usual way of looking. It goes under, over, or around cultural constructs to confront, if only for a fleeting moment, that which is as it is. A confrontation with the absolute. One loses perspective as in a Japanese print.

From America:

Moonlit sleet
In the holes of my
Harmonica
(by David Lloyd, in Van den Heuvel 1974, 77).

Sunset dying
on the end of a rusty
beer can. . . .
(by Gary Botham in Van den Heuvel 1974, 47).

I read Icelandic sagas. They tell little of what people felt. They describe what a person could see and hear. There are no Shakespearian tragic flaws, but a fate that people inevitably act out, even if they deny it at the time. One can bring all of one's cunning, skill, and strength to bear to change it, as Njal does, in his saga, but it comes to nothing. The patterns are played out as they are laid down. Gísli kills his sister's suitors in Norway and estranges his brother. Later in Iceland, Thorkel, Gísli's brother, has his blood-brother and brother-in-law, Thorgrim, kill Gísli's blood brother and brother-in-law, Vestein, because Thorkel thinks his wife is in love with Vestein. To avenge the killing, Gísli kills Thorgrim, his sister's husband and brother's friend. Thordis, the sister of Gísli and Thorkel, marries Thorgrim's brother, Bork, and reveals to him that Gísli killed his brother, her late husband, for whom she seeks revenge. Vestien's sons kill Thorkel. Bork engineers the killing of Gísli to avenge his brother and his wife's dead husband. Thordis tries to kill the man who killed Gísli, to avenge her dead brother. At the end of the saga, Gísli, Thorkel, Thorgrim, and Vestein, these brothers, blood brothers, brothers-in-law, have all fallen in a repetition-ion of the pattern laid down long ago in Norway before the family came to Iceland.

Crunching numbers felt like looking at the absolute and trying to find a haiku to express it, like looking at a Japanese print with parallel perspective, like reading a saga. The numbers had been laid down by peoples' actions, represented the absoluteness of a haiku. So many tons of carrying capacity, so many trips, so many tons of fish (Durrenberger and Pálsson 1982, 1983, 1985; Pálsson and Durrenberger 1982, 1983). Camus (1955) finds the absurd in the contradictions between reality and representations of reality, between the observer and what he observes. To be human is to attempt to represent reality in spite of the impossibility of the task. The alternative to such a stark confrontation of contradiction is suicide, either killing the self or killing the intellect by a leap of faith.

Humanists seem to devalue attempts to grapple with that which is as it is. They are content to describe representations of reality (Barth 1966; Heath 1976), the myriad points of view and to agonize over whether they have got them quite right and whether it matters to have things right. Some do not wish to accept the patterns as they are laid down (Gatewood 1984; McNabb 1985; Thorlindsson in press). Some, in keeping with the fashion of narcissism in an age of self, despair and attempt autobiography as the only knowable reality, and then, like liberals flagellating themselves on the way co Armageddon, agonize over whether they have got that quite right and whether it matters (for various views see Fabian 1983, 87; Dumont 1978, 13; Dwyer 1982; Marcus and Fischer 1986, 42). One has a feeling they cannot quite give up agony for a leap of faith. Reflexive images bounce infinitely among the mirrors of the self (Ruby 1982; Leeds 1985). They despair at the prospect of apprehending the absolute.

The arrogance of the pretense to know reality or describe it troubles them more than the arrogance of occupying center stage with self-constructed images of themselves. If one discards scientific approaches on this basis, then just as clearly must one discard the absoluteness of haiku and Japanese prints. The problem is not simply one of Western science.

Numbers do not make science. To count is not necessarily to know. One can warp numbers just as easily as genealogies, create categories to match expectations and count such created entities. One can play numbers without scientific thought just as one can engage in scientific inquiry without numbers. Neither science nor haiku defines reality. Both assume an absolute.

People construct representations of that which is as it is. Anthropologists construct representations of representations. To stop there is to leave the job unfinished. To admit and describe the myriad points of view is one thing, to enshrine it as the only way of knowing is another, and to withdraw to autobiography and pure reflexivity is to abdicate. To give up on knowing is to admit defeat at the task of being human, a leap into the self and the myriad points of view about it instead of a leap to faith.

Many ways of knowing assume an absolute, independent of observers, independent of points of view, that which is as it is, whether it is knowable or not. To discard science as way of constructing representations of reality is similar to the abdication of being scientistic and creating a discipline composed of methodology with no thought, numbers that tell no story. It may be contradictory to maintain both a humanistic and a scientific stance. Contradiction—absurdity, as Camus says—is the lot of humanity. It is better to face contradiction with good grace than to deny it or to abdicate. There is no arrogance to the assumption that there is an absolute, only to supposition that one has reached its final description. To give up the assumption is to give up the interesting questions of anthropology.

The anonymous sagamen who set down the sagas of Iceland in the 13th century tell us that "short is the life of excess." Moderation, balance, staying within the limits is valued. Should we not look for the middle road between arrogance and the exploration of our own personalities and get about the job of doing anthropology? Echoing voices of the East, Siu (1957, 127) says that if a person wants anything, he must admit something of the opposite. Excesses bring sad consequences, as in the stretching of a bow beyond its full.

References Cited

Acheson, J. M. 1977. Technical skills and fishing success in the Maine lobster industry. In *Material culture: Styles, organization and dynamics of technology,* ed. Lechtman Merrill and R. S. Merrill, pp. 113-38. St. Paul, MN: West Publishing.

Akmakjian, Hiag. 1979. *Snow falling from a bamboo leaf: The art of haiku.* Santa Barbara, CA: Capra Press.

Barth, Fredrik. 1966. *Models of social organization.* Occasional Paper No. 23. London: Royal Anthropological Institute of Great Britain and Ireland.

Buchanan, Daniel C. 1973. *One hundred famous haiku.* San Francisco, CA: Japan Publications.

Bertalnaffey, L. von. 1962. An essay on the relativity of categories. *General Systems* 7:71-83.

Camus, A. 1955. *The myth of Sisyphus and other essays,* trans. Justin O'Brien. New York. NY: Vintage.

Dumont, Jean-Paul. 1978. *The headman and I: Ambiguity and ambivalence in the fieldworking experience.* Austin, TX: University of Texas Press.

Durrenberger, E. Paul. 1975a. Lisu occult roles. *Bijdragen Tot de Taal-, Land-en Volkenkunde* 131:138-205.

Durrenberger, E. Paul. 1975b. Lisu shamans and some general questions. *Journal of the Steward Anthropological Society* 7: 1-20.

Durrenberger, E. Paul. 1976a. Lisu curing: A case history. *Bulletin of the History of Medicine* 50 356- 71.

Durrenberger, E. Paul. 1976b. A Lisu shamanistic seance. *Journal of the Siam Society* 64:151-60.

Durrenberger, E. Paul. 1980a. Belie and the logic of Lisu spirits. *Bijdragen tot de taal-, Land-en Volkenkunde* 136:21-40.

Durrenberger, E. Paul. 1980b. Annual non-Buddhist religious observances of Maehongson Shan. *Journal of the Siam Society* 68:48-56.

Durrenberger, E. Paul. 1981. The Southeast Asian context of Theravada Buddhism. Anthropology 5:45- 62.

Durrenberger, E. Paul and Gísli Pálsson. 1982. Policy, processors, and boats: Fishing in modern Iceland. *Central Issues in Anthropology* 4:31-47.

Durrenberger, E. Paul, and Gísli Pálsson. 1983. Riddles of herring and rhetorics of success. *Journal of Anthropological Research* 39:323-35.

Durrenberger, E. Paul, and Gísli Pálsson. 1985. Peasants, entrepreneurs and companies: The evolution of Icelandic fishing. *Ethnos* 50:103-22.

Dwyer, Kevin. 1982. *Moroccan dialogues: Anthropology in question.* Baltimore: The Johns Hopkins University Press.

Fabian, Johannes. 1983. *Time and the other: How anthropology makes its object.* New York: Columbia University Press.

Gatewood, J. B. 1984. Is the "skipper effect" really a false ideology. *American Ethnologist* 11:378-79.

Heath, A. F. 1976. Decision making and transactional theory. Transaction and meaning, ed. B. Kapferer, 25-40. Philadelphia, PA: Institute for the Study of Human Issues.

Heuvel, Cor van den. 1974. *The haiku anthology: English language haiku by contemporary American and Canadian poets.* Garden City, NJ: Anchor.

Johnston, G., trans. 1963. *Saga of Gísli .* Toronto: University of Toronto Press.

Leeds, Anthony. 1985. Review of Jay Ruby, *A Crack in the Mirror.* *American Anthropologist* 87:465-67.

McNabb, S. L. 1985. A final comment on measurement of the "skipper effect." *American Ethnologist* 12:543-44.

Pálsson, Gísli , and E. P. Durrenberger. 1982. To dream of fish: the causes of Icelandic skippers' fishing success. *journal of Anthropological Research* 38:227-42.

Pálsson, Gísli , and E. P. Durrenberger. 1983. Icelandic foremen and skippers: The structure and evolution of a folk model. American Ethnologist 10:511-28.

Ruby, Jay, ed. 1982. *A Crack in the Mirror: Reflexive Perspectives in Anthropology.* Philadelphia, PA: University of Pennsylvania Press.

Siu, R. G. H. 1957. *The Tao of Science.* Cambridge, MA: MIT Press.

Thorlindsson, Thorolfur. In press. Ad vera eda latast: Er aflaskipsrjorinn adeins godsaga? In Afmaelisrit helgad Brodda Johannessyni srjotugum. Reykjavik.

Sitting Buddha in a Mississippi Golf Course:
Constructing Anthropology in Exotic and Familiar Settings

1991 *Anthropology and
Humanism Quarterly* 16

Heat waves shimmered on the asphalt. To my left, tractors rearranged trucked-in white sand to smooth the beach along the Mississippi sound, beyond which the barrier islands mark the inward edge of the Gulf of Mexico. To my right were motels, seafood restaurants, bars, and shops that sold string bikinis and tourist paraphernalia. I was heading to Bayou Caddy to talk to shrimpers and thinking about how to construct the object of anthropology.

Every time I drove west from Biloxi on the coastal highway I saw a Buddha as big as a house in a phantasmagoric mini-golf course. It conjured images of Thailand, where I had lived among Buddhist Shan, and Iceland, where I had played golf. Though I thought a lot about theoretical matters in Thailand, defining the subject matter of anthropology was never very problematic amidst many dimensions of alienness. It had been more of a puzzle in Iceland, and even more in Biloxi. As the people I tried to understand were closer to my experience, it was more difficult to conceptualize them anthropologically.

Many historians, anthropologists, and literary scholars ask what are they to study and how to do it. Some suppose that ethnography must or may be fiction, or that it is some sort of game of fashion, prestige, and hierarchy in which it does not really matter, in which anthropologists trade self-serving postmodern smiles of irony with one another, uttering only ambiguously audible subtexts sotto voce in passing. Some hint that external realities are irrelevant and that "a preoccupation with self-reflexivity and style may be an index of privileged estheticism. For if one does not have to worry about the exclusion or true representation of one's experience, one is freer to undermine ways of telling, to focus on form over content" (Clifford 1986:21).

Every day I would drive east or west along the coast to a shrimping port to talk to shrimpers, buyers, processors, social workers, dock or factory workers, or others involved in the fishing industry. I interviewed people I had never met and might never meet again. Every evening I returned home to an apartment overlooking the municipal boat harbor from which I could keep up with the activities of one group of shrimp boats. It had the usual hot and cold running water, television, electric stove, air conditioner, and electric dishwasher.

In south Alabama was a village of Cambodian refugees who worked processing crab. In their Buddhist temple my wife, Dorothy, and I had recently participated in ceremonies which were familiar from similar observances in northern Thailand. I spoke to the monk in a mixture of Northern Thai and Shan. The red earth, the food, the people, and dress were all familiar from Southeast Asia. Only the cars, house architecture, and pine trees seemed incongruous. After the ceremony and feast we drove home to watch the news on TV, have a hot shower, and sleep in our own bed.

Nearby is Bayou la Batre, a shrimping port, in which half or more of the shrimpers are Vietnamese, mostly Catholic. Killing time while waiting for a Vietnamese who worked for Catholic Social Services to join us for lunch, a sociologist and I stood side by side contemplating a map of Southeast Asia. My companion asked, "Where was it you were interviewing in Thailand?" The contrast between "interviewing" and "fieldwork" was so great that I laughed involuntarily and said, "I wasn't interviewing, I was doing fieldwork."

In the evenings, cassette recordings of American country and western music dominated the two streets of Thailand's northwestern province capitol of Maehongson. It was such "contamination" which made the tropics so sad for Levi-Strauss in *Tristes Tropiques* and shattered his illusions of pristine primitivity and purity. I had briefly entertained the idea of moving to a village remote from such influences, away from the expanding road system, but concluded that the reality of the place was one of commerce, radios, roads, and cash cropping as well as opium trading, revolutionary armies, bandits, and warlords and various manifestations of government power. There was no escaping modernity even had I elected to try.

Some months after we moved to a Shan village, we came into town to have supper in a street side restaurant with a visiting Oxford anthropologist and an international development bureaucrat from New Zealand. The Oxford man held that anthropology was a discourse among books. The bureaucrat maintained that it should be a discourse between anthropologists and the people with whom they live. It all seemed very abstract to me, mired as I was in considerations of how much rice people eat, how much land they had planted, how many days they worked at what tasks, why they sacrificed to the spirits, and why they offered food to monks.

Everything was strange at first. The smells, colors, sounds, and textures of life were different from those we were used to. There was no electricity. Dorothy and I chopped wood for our cooking fires, cooked and ate local food-rice with whatever else we could find. As we made friends, people offered us prized dishes of rooster testicles, frogs, snails-local delicacies foreign to our experience and tastes. Dorothy hauled water into our house in buckets on a carrying stick, woman's work. The road into the village was only good until the rains came. We bathed in a spring-fed pool by the road.

The people whose house we shared and our neighbors worried about what might be wrong if we were not sufficiently sociable and social. Was someone angry? Sick? Sad? Missing distant kinsmen? I could not go home at night. There was no day's work. I was always "on duty." I was not in control of my daily schedule or anything else. I responded to events as they happened. There was little opportunity for withdrawal except the physical withdrawal beyond the province to Chiangmai.

Life in the Shan village was easy compared to a highland Lisu village in Chiangmai province where there were no roads and we bathed in a shallow, cold creek near the village. We hauled water in large bamboo sections from the same creek to our bamboo house. People offered us chopped leopard, roasted monkey arm, lizard, raw pork, monkey blood for vitality. If Lisu wanted privacy, they went to the middle of the village where they could see everyone and keep the conversation among themselves. If one not privy to the matter approached, they changed the subject. Everything that happened in houses was public. We had little privacy.

My sense of wonder and my questions developed from this exposure to the exotic. What is that man doing? A spirit is riding him. What spirits are there? How do they ride people? What people do they ride? Why do they ride people? What is this woman doing? Making medicines with the help of a spirit. What spirit helps her? The more mundane questions were about how much work it takes to produce so much rice, how much rice a person eats, and how to find out reliable answers to such questions. None of my own cultural assumptions was any good at providing answers. When I relied on them, my answers were wrong.

We became accustomed to Lisu shamans' evening shouts announcing the presence of their lineage spirits to help people with their misfortunes. We came to see the logic whereby Shan and Thai say people ride airplanes rather than fly. We came to understand the logic whereby spirits help and hurt people (Durrenberger 1980, 1989a), the logic of tattoos and amulets to protect people (Tannenbaum 1987), of sacrifices for spirits (Durrenberger and Tannenbaum 1983), of power, protection, and unseen beings (Tannenbaum and Durrenberger 1988).

This Lisu village, a long walk from the last road, was still firmly tied into the international market. People wore clothes of Japanese cloth, used Taiwanese batteries and flashlights, sold their opium to traders who sold it to others until it reached Europe and the United States.

When we accommodate as well as we can to the exotic conditions of our field work we are still not living in the lives of the people whom we are studying. Their daily lives are devoted to their livings, their families, their life concerns whether they be the swiddens, irrigated fields, farm, fishing boat, monastery, or university. We spend our time working with them, celebrating with them, grieving with them, talking to them, taking notes about them, trying to understand them. But to take notes about people and to try to understand them is not to be doing what they are doing. We do not, as Geertz put it, achieve communion.

Nowadays as many anthropologists work in familiar settings as work in exotic ones. There is none of the shock of the exotic when we walk into a hospital, a regional fisheries policy meeting, a fish processing plant, an Iowa farm. The situations, dialects, and manners may be un-familiar, but not exotic. They are within the range of our imaginations and real or vicarious experiences. Most of our assumptions work pretty well. We can go home after a day's work. We are not always "on duty," day and night, day in and day out, as we are in alien settings. We can determine what to do and when.

The challenge is not to make the exotic familiar, but to make the familiar sufficiently foreign so that we may begin to ask questions about it, rather than simply assume that that is the way things are and always have been. I found it disturbingly easy to work in coastal

Mississippi and Alabama. With Americans, there was none of the filtering of language I had experienced in Iceland and Thailand. Informants' words went too easily into my brain. I did not have to ponder their meanings.

A participant in a Lisu legal case had once said to the other side, "You scratch my back and I'll scratch yours." I spent days thinking about the phrase, trying to plumb its deeper significance and meanings, trying to unpack its symbolic load. Finally it dawned on me, after discussing it at length with several informants, that it meant just the same thing to them as it did to me. That did not happen in Mississippi and Alabama. Among Lisu or Shan I could help in the fields when

I felt like it to learn as much as I cared to about the details of agricultural practice. My job as a participant observer was made possible by the availability of an observer role granted me by the Shan concepts of hierarchy, and their willingness to accept me. In Iceland I had to make a place for myself, a locally accepted role, by work. That meant a lot more participation and a lot less observation. Every morning I would get up and join the farmer in the barn to help with the milking. We talked about common lands, sheep management, government farm policy, how to expand the barn, the progress of hay making, stories about other people in the area, raising foxes for skins, the cooperatives, and golf. We listened to the news and the weather report on the radio, and then would come the music: an American country and western or rock and roll selection or a cut from The Raw and the Cooked or another album by the Fine Young Cannibals. The milking finished, I would shovel the dung, take the cows to their pasture, and walk back to the house through the drizzle or chilly summer sunshine to drink coffee and eat the breakfast Dorothy had been preparing while the woman of the farm had been feeding the foxes.

Then we would start the day's work of turning hay in the fields to dry it; collecting hay and pitching it into the barn; cutting grass to fill the silo; repairing machinery; herding and shearing sheep; butchering a fat, old, lazy horse for food; casting cement for an extension to the barn; riding out on horses to check pastures; sodding the golf course; taking sheep to the commons; or whatever work was in season. We broke for lunch and a rest, then worked until tea time about 4:30. In the evening I would fetch the cows, and we would milk again before supper.

When a relative of the friend who had established the connection that put Dorothy and me on the farm dropped by for coffee and pastries one evening, everyone knew he had come "to see if you are still alive," as the farm family put it. In the farmer's wife's retired parents' house we talked as we drank coffee at the kitchen table and the younger couple stood by the drain board. Our visitor asked, "Have you met many people in the countryside?" I paused as I worked over the question and framed an answer. "No, but I have met a lot of cows." That raised a laugh, reassured all that things were working out, and later on began the story that I was more cow-ologist than anthropologist. I was surprised the first afternoon on the farm when, after mending some fences and eating lunch, the farmer asked if I would play a game of golf. "I don't play golf," I answered. "I'll teach you," he said, and he tried his best.

The farmer's brother-in-law, who had been working the farm with him, had developed an allergy to hay and moved to the Westman Islands to work in the fishing industry. Short of labor, the farmer cut back sheep production, leaving an extra pasture, which he then converted to a golf course for his amusement and as a source of future income. Back in Reykjavik, when a friend asked how it was going on the farm, I said I had taken up the anthropology of golf instead of economic anthropology.

I didn't do any formal interviewing. I conversed: "Let's have a game of golf." "But it's blowing a gale and sleeting." "If we wait for good weather, we'll never be able to play golf." Dualistic models buzzing in my head, I inquired about the names of tractors. "The word for tractor is feminine, isn't it?" I asked, giving the properly pure Icelandic word devoid of any Latin influences. "Yes." "But the name of this one is Lili?" "Yes." "And that is masculine?" "Yes." "Why does a feminine tractor have a masculine name?" I asked, waiting for the missing piece of the structuralist puzzle to fall into place. "That is a tractor,: my friend said, using the borrowed Latinate word, just about like the English "tractor," degenerate and disparaged by the standards of Icelandic purists. "And that is masculine."

At another farm in the north, facing a pile of telephone pole-sized drift logs I was to convert into fence posts with a very dull bow saw, a wedge, and a hammer, I felt like a character in a folk story who had been given an impossible task in return for the kingdom or the hand of the princess. By and by I created a pile of fence posts and was rewarded with the task of shoveling out the winter's accumulation of matted straw and manure from a large sheep barn. During the dark, musty silences while I filled the wheelbarrow with dung I reflected on Sperber's *On Anthropological Knowledge* (1985) and anthropology (Durrenberger 1989b). There were few cows and no milking machine. On this farm the passion was opera and choral singing.

Icelandic farmers do not live in villages. The same style of participant observation of farm life in Iceland as among Shan and Lisu was impossible. Most Icelanders live in Reykjavik and adjacent municipalities or in the fishing villages around the coast. In Rekjavik, I heard much talk about farm surpluses and the expenditure of public funds to support subsidies and export schemes. Some believe that it is absolutely irrational to preserve farms in Iceland but others maintain a romanticism that centers on the purity of rural language and thought (Palsson 1989).

Some anthropological analyses of things Icelandic seemed like Levi-Strauss's hypermodern intellectual "infernal culture machine" of the universal savage mind, projections of an ill-fitting alien system (Geertz 1973:350-359). They failed to match or even characterize accurately what I saw and heard in Iceland. When an Icelander (Einarsson 1990) suggested that the conclusions of these writings were overdetermined by the anthropologist's conceptual structures and underdetermined by evidence, I was relieved at the feeling of consensual validation. When the anthropologist responded that natives have no right to challenge anthropologists, I recalled an American historian's assessment that the anthropologist's models were rather forced: "At times they seem to be generated not from the data but from preconceptions, with selection of data arranged so as not to embarrass the construct" (Miller 1986:185). When I read and reflected on these exchanges in connection with my musings on the construction of anthropology, it seemed all the more evident that those things we can see and hear and experience must be central to our enterprise.

My own cultural assumptions about things worked better in Iceland than they did among Shan or Lisu in Thailand, but still, not all that well. The challenge was to keep up with my work and still have energy left over to reflect on other matters. I had to try to balance the sense of the exotic against mundane realities. Most of the time I had to keep my mind on my job, whether it was golf or tractor driving, though I did cause more than my share of on-farm disasters by ineptitude.

Whenever I began to wax romantic, my Icelandic friends and acquaintances were cynical, honest, skeptical, sarcastic, and gently humorous enough to plant my feet back on the ground in quick order. Still, I had to try to distance myself enough to see contrasts that would evoke questions but not over-exoticize my experience into the realms of a dualistic never-never land, to let my observation of Icelandic life take precedence over my own cultural assumptions and theoretical constructs about anthropology and history.

To understand the dynamics of coastal Alabama's fishing industry, I lined up numbers for some decades and saw the ski slope curves that defined different periods, different systems. To understand why and how these systems developed, I needed local details of past events I could only get by reading, a step away in time, space, and context from the people and events, an exercise in history rather than ethnography, a trip to the archives rather than the field.

I sat in a darkened corner of a library, my head half-way inside a box illuminated from above to form white on black or black on white words on a shining white table in front of my eyes. As I located particular facts about the fishing industry, in my peripheral vision I watched the life of the United States and much of the rest of the world flash by on reel after reel of the Mobile Register and other local newspapers.

It is the 1870s and a yellow fever epidemic spreads from New Orleans to an enlarging circle of towns up the Mississippi River, east and west. Within weeks the fever is killing people in Mobile. People await the salvation of the first frost; they know it will bring relief and stop the random dying. There were other yellow fever epidemics. The response was quite different from that to the later epidemic of infantile paralysis, as polio was known, or the more recent AIDS, both fairly minor in their impact compared with yellow fever.

It is 1890 and the Republicans are being blamed for fighting an unjust war against the Indians. The white settlers, soldiers, and merchants are bringing trouble to the Indians. Withdraw the soldiers. Stop the war on the Indians. Stop the Republicans.

In 1915 the news is of Europe and the Near East. European Jews want Palestine and many are going there. The French and Germans kill many of themselves for a few yards of land. French blue devils armed with revolvers and gas masks jump into German trenches and kill all they can reach in suicidal berserk rages before they are killed. Germans methodically tunnel into French trenches to blow them up. Turks kill Armenians. Waves of Armenian refugees come to the United States. There is a stench of death about the microfilm reader. I read an editorial against lynching. Twenty-seven whites and 52 blacks have been lynched in the United States, North and South alike; night riders ride against socialist organizers of tenant farmers in Arkansas and Missouri.

In 1931, Huey Long of Louisiana is under attack by a paramilitary group called the square dealers. They arm and attack the capitol. He calls out the National Guard. The Farm Holiday association in Des Moines, Iowa, supports Huey Long. The newspaper calls him Dictator Long. He is assassinated. His killer is riddled with bullets from guardsmen. Not much of the assassin's body remains for his relatives to claim. The governor of South Carolina calls out the National Guard to control the Highway Department. There are strikes. There are problems of homelessness, unemployment, poverty, racism. There are editorials against lynching. A husband kills a wife, a wife kills a husband, a child kills a parent, a parent kills a child, a woman kills her lover's wife, a man kills his lover's husband. It is all in the family.

In 1935 Hitler says he wants peace and discriminates systematically against Catholics and Jews. I know the outcome, just as I knew how the torpedoing of the Lusitania in 1915 was going to turn out, even though Wilson said he wanted to be neutral. Now, in 1935, there is a double feeling of deja vu, a horrible sense of death, the stench of destruction as Hitler promises peace and drives out the Jews. The Jews want Palestine and many are going there.

In Alabama there is an inquiry into the race of a school child, because schools are separated by race and people are not quite sure to which race this child belongs. The Germans segregate Jews. In the United States there is homelessness, unemployment, poverty, depression.

FDR has a program and the Republicans are trying to kill it. They do not like this talk of full employment, of socialized medicine, of an end to homelessness, the New Deal. A husband kills a wife, a wife kills a husband, a child kills a parent, a parent kills a son. . . .

In 1945 the Germans are caving in. Americans advance across Europe and I wonder why the Germans did not throw it in earlier. I wonder why the Americans did not nuke them. The story shifted to Midway, Wake, Guam, Okinawa, the nuke. It was a relief when it finally came. In the United States the familial killings continue unabated.

I feel queasy as I put another reel on the microfilm reader. I know it never stops. The next reel holds more of the same. The war finishes, there is a problem of thousands of AWOL Americans in Paris, of crime waves in New York, in the USSR, in Italy, in London. What will be done with the GIs when they come home?

The French do not yield Indochina. Chiang and Mao seem to have an agreement. The British are in Indonesia to restore the Dutch. The Soviets are in Korea. I know how those stories turn out. The Jews want Palestine and they introduce terrorism as a political tool to get it. Thousands are arrested, burned, killed, wounded, shot. In the United States there is a constant bagpipe-like drone of domestic violence and terror over a hundred years. This is the constant that flashes across the screen in front of my eyes. This and unemployment, homelessness, poverty.

I wonder why we are such amnesiacs. Why do we not think of the '30s as a period of martial law? Why do we not think of the military repression of our union movement? Why do people think terror is something new in Middle-Eastern politics? Why do people think domestic violence, homelessness, unemployment are new things? I begin thinking abstract thoughts about political economy and connections to ideology, constructions of history, meaning and history, culture and process.

I decide I need some flesh-and-blood reality. I get up about four in the morning and drive to Bayou Coden, Alabama, to meet some oyster catchers. The old man is up. We drink coffee. His wife's name is tattooed across his chest and arms. He tells me about the Bible, politics, and pollution. His adult son comes in. We drink coffee. Another son joins us. The brothers and I go to the bay as the sun comes up and motor out to the reef where we join a fleet of oyster catchers already at work. We talk to them. I hear much of politics, conservation, oyster catching. The brothers tong for oysters. I cull, think, listen, ask, take a hand at tonging.

We go in early because the two brothers have to go to court in Mobile. Their brother was killed last year. He was at a party and someone slipped him an overdose of a drug in a drink. He died in his sleep. The second brother has said almost nothing all day. The first explains that he was close to the baby, the brother who died, the one they have to testify about. These are the people the newspaper stories were about.

Dorothy's sister has two silver goblets inscribed to John E. Fisher presented by the Mobile Baymen's society in 1853. This Fisher was the second husband of Dorothy's father's mother's mother, Permelia Sproul, who, at the age of 15, had married a lawyer named Wiggins and moved to Mobile. After he died, she married her husband's associate, Fisher.

She also has an old photograph of a Confederate soldier and one earring with a note in Dorothy's grandmother's writing that said it had been given to Permelia by her daughter's husband when he went to Mexico to sell cotton for the Confederacy. These, the goblets, and Dorothy's grandmother's reminiscences about the wonders of a Mobile the ancestress had never seen, a civilized town compared to the wilds of Texas where she grew up, inspired Dorothy's curiosity. Who was Permelia, who were Wiggins and Fisher, who were their children?

Dorothy began to find out, and in the process found that they could not have been "just like us." They came to a frontier to establish plantations and to build towns. The social, political, and economic systems were as different from what we are accustomed to as are Shan and Lisu systems.

From the records of tax transactions and legal cases Dorothy discovered the discrepancies between family stories, handed down from Permelia's daughter to Dorothy's grandmother, to her and her father. She systematically compared the remnants of those lives with the stories about them as she began to construct an understanding of the finances, economy, culture, marriages, losses, and travels of her ancestors.

The difference in time was as palpable as the difference in place when we were in Thailand, but the major difference was in how we experienced the differences. We went home from the libraries, court houses, and archives to have baths, eat meals prepared on electric stoves, from machine-washed dishes. We did not see any of these people we read about die. We did not see Permelia's reaction when she learned that her son had died at the second battle of Manassas. We did not hear her response to her daughter's going to the frontier in Texas.

Her $5000 Confederate War Bond decorates Dorothy's father's den, its coupons still intact and unredeemed.

It was all intellectual, vicarious, not experiential. We asked similar questions about cultural, political, economic structures of Shan and Lisu and Icelanders, but we experienced the realities in different ways.

Given the short time I could spend in coastal Mississippi and the complexity of the issues, I decided not to try to understand the shrimping industry by means of participant observation because, like Icelandic farmers, shrimpers were not concentrated in villages. All were familiar with questionnaires and surveys. They had been surveyed before by the Bureau of Labor Statistics, by the Internal Revenue Service, by the National Marine Fisheries Service. I could use the "survey instrument," a recognized cultural artifact, as a means to initiate conversations as well as to get statistical data.

At Bayou Caddy I approach a shrimper as he leaves a boat.
"Is this your boat?" I ask. "No, mine is across the bayou over there." I tell him what I am doing and ask if he will answer some questions. With some reluctance he agrees. He is reserved until he learns I am not a marine biologist. He becomes more loquacious as I depart from the interview schedule to follow up his comments. Soon he is telling me his story in great detail and I am writing it down. Then he invites me aboard the boat he had been leaving; he says it is his boat, but he had been suspicious of me. He revises some of the answers to the first questions.

I came to expect this response of reserve and suspicion. As people learned and came to believe I was not a government agent or biologist, they opened up. But I could not do this on a community-wide level. I had to repeat the experience with each of the more than 200 shrimpers, dealers, processors, bureaucrats, and others in the shrimp industry I talked with.

I gathered not only systematic data on a sample of people in the industry, but also elicited stories, biographies, political and economic analyses, folk knowledge, and assessments of scientific knowledge and policy based on it.

I could not talk to more than a few fishermen or processors before hearing about how deeply Biloxi was connected into the international system. Most shrimp processed and consumed in the United States comes from China and Latin America, where it is raised in ponds. This determines the market for locally caught shrimp. I wondered whether, if Levi-Strauss were Chinese, he would lament the "contamination" of Mississippi with Chinese shrimp and Chinese restaurants.

In doing fieldwork among Lisu and Shan I did a fair amount of repetitive and routine survey work and collected data with questionnaires (Durrenberger 1976, 1978, 1979, 1984b; Durrenberger and Tannenbaum 1983). Like the historical work, the survey process lacks the connectedness of everyday life. Because it can be divorced from everyday life, it often is. When I visited fisheries bureaucrats concerned with shrimping, some would ask how things were going with the shrimpers. They were not anthropologists and ethnography was not their job, but they knew as well as anyone and better than most that the systems that regulate fisheries should understand fishermen as well as they understand fish. It is up to us to insist on a relevant anthropology, rather than to shape anthropology after the cultural forms most familiar to agencies of regulation in order to merely ratify policy (Durrenberger 1990).

It is lucky that "Anthropologists are forever being tempted . . . out of libraries and lecture halls . . . into 'the field'" (Geertz 1973:359). As long as we do fieldwork and keep in touch with social, economic, and political realities instead of constructing anthropology as the study of anthropologists, books about other books, we will continue to contribute to understandings of the human condition.

Sometimes the abstract defleshed analyses boiled out of experience, observations, and numbers—Levi-Strauss's intellectualist abstractions, Geertz's involuted interpretations, Wolf's global history, Sahlin's practical reason, various statistical assertions and conclusions, and each's reading of the other-wavered like the shimmering heat waves on the hot Mississippi asphalt, and beyond the mirages of our stories I sensed the absurd, Camus's contradiction of living in a reality we can never fully understand, though we continue to try (Durrenberger 1984a, 1987). I think it is from an appreciation of this that we derive our sense of the unity of the species, our sense of common humanity, whether it be closer to Levi-Strauss's or Wolf's, and it is perhaps in spite of this that we continue to do fieldwork and tell stories because we are, after all, anthropologists and that is our job, though we do it in different ways. A sitting Buddha in a Mississippi mini-golf course may contribute to someone's enlightenment.

Acknowledgments. This article was largely inspired by conversations with Nicola Tannenbaum. I thank the editor and anonymous reviewer for their comments on an earlier draft.

References Cited

Clifford, James.1986. Introduction: Partial Truths. In Writing Culture: The Poetics and Politics of Ethnography. James Clifford and George Marcus, eds. Pp. 1-26. Berkeley: University of California Press.

Durrenberger, E. Paul.1976. The Economy of a Lisu Village. American Ethnologist 3:633-644.

1978. Agricultural Production and Household Budgets in a Shan Peasant Village in Northwestern Thailand: A Quantitative Description. Southeast Asian Studies Series No. 49. Athens: University of Ohio Press.

1979. Rice production in a Lisu village. Journal of Southeast Asian Studies 10:139-145.

1980. Belief and the logic of Lisu spirits. Bijdragen tot de taal-, Land- en Volkenkunde 136:21-40.

1984a. Icelandic Saga Heroes: The Anthropology of Natural Existentialists. Anthropology and Humanism Quarterly 9:3-8.

1984b. Operationalizing Chayanov. In Chayanov, Peasants, and Economic Anthropology. E. Paul Durrenberger, ed. Pp. 39-50. New York: Academic Press.

1987 Reflections on the Absolute. Anthropology and Humanism Quarterly 12:38-41.

1989a. Lisu Religion. DeKalb, IL: Northern Illinois University Center for Southeast Asian Studies.

1989b. Sperber Revisited: That Darned Dorze Dragon. Review of On Anthropological Knowledge by Dan Sperber. Anthropology and Humanism Quarterly 14:77-78.

1990 Policy, Power, and Science: The Implementation of Turtle Excluder Device Regulations in the U.S. Gulf of Mexico Shrimp Fishery. Maritime Anthropological Studies 3(1):69-86.

Durrenberger, E. Paul, and Nicola Tannenbaum. 1983. A Diachronic Analysis of Shan Cropping Systems. Ethnos 48:177-194.

Einarsson, Niels. 1990. From the Native's Point of View: Some Comments on the Anthropology of Iceland. Antropologiska Studier 46/47:69-77.

Geertz, Clifford. 1973. The Interpretation of Cultures. New York: Basic Books.

Miller, William I. 1986. Review of Culture and History in Medieval Iceland , by Kirsten Hastrup. Scandinavian Studies 58:183-186.

Palsson, Gísli. 1989. Language and Society: The Ethnolinguistics of Icelanders. In The Anthropology of Iceland. E. Paul Durrenberger and Gisli Palsson, eds. Pp. 121-139. Iowa City: University of Iowa Press.

Sperber Dan. 1985. On Anthropological Knowledge. Cambridge: Cambridge University Press.

Tannenbaum, Nicola. 1987. Tattoos: Invulnerability and Power in Shan Cosmology. American Ethnologist 14:693-711.

Tannenbaum, Nicola, and E. Paul Durrenberger. 1988. Control, Change, and Suffering: The Messages of Shan Buddhist Sermons. Mankind 18:121-132.

A Shower of Rain: Marshall Sahlins's *Stone Age Economics*
Twenty-five Years Later

1998 *Culture and Agriculture* 20 (2/3)

When Richard Wilk and Stephen Gudeman invited me to contribute to a session they were organizing for the 1997 meeting of the American Anthropological Association in Washington, D.C., to mark the 25th anniversary of the publication of Marshall Sahlins's *Stone Age Economics,* I was delighted. I had just moved from the University of Iowa where I was chair of the Anthropology department to Penn State. As a member of the AAA's Scientific Communications Committee that oversees the publication of the *American Anthropologist,* I had heard and participated in debates that caused me to wonder why "Scientific" was in the committee title. My two years on the AAA executive committee as president of the Culture and Agriculture section raised similar questions. This was a chance to focus some of my reflections on the distance between my hopes for a scientific anthropology and what I had been hearing in these venues and at meetings of the AAA. To those of us interested in systems of food production and distribution, the issues Sahlins discussed are as relevant today as they were then as we continue to struggle for ways to understand households and larger political-economic systems that contain them. We still grapple with the issues that lie between methodological individualism and Durkheimian social facts. We still face problems of asking our questions so that we can answer them in terms of observations and measurements that others can repeat, check, elaborate upon, and theorize about. Work that Kendall Thu and I were doing on the industrialization of swine production in Iowa led us to seek out Walter Goldschmidt, and Kendall organized a session at the same meetings to honor his many contributions to our understanding of the politics and dynamics of systems of food production and distribution. We called on Goldschmidt to write a conclusion to a book we edited on industrial swine production (1998). Seeing Goldschmidt grapple with these issues and problems over more than five decades has given me inspiration and hope. But that is another story. Here is the story of my involvement with Sahlins's book.

The twenty-five years since the publication of Marshall Sahlins's *Stone Age Economics* are the same twenty-five years I spent at the

University of Iowa before I came to Penn State. I have spent a fair amount of that time working on issues that came directly and indirectly from that book, issues that have to do with how economic systems work and how we can understand them. Feeling pressure from formal economics, which embodies "the wisdom of native bourgeoisie categories" and "flourishes as ideology at home and ethnocentrism abroad,'" Sahlins said he was a participant in a discipline that considers itself a science (xiii) and would be content to rest the case on the essays he presented in that volume. In 1972, anthropology may have considered itself a science. That's what I thought. Today many would deny the virtues of scientific enterprise. But let me back up a few years and tell the story from where I come into it, if not from beginning.

In 1969 I found myself in a village of highland Lisu in northern Thailand. I was there to study what they did when they suffered misfortunes, but I knew that whatever it was, it would somehow be related to their economic system. The problem was that I could not see an economic system. All I could see was people who lived in a couple of dozen households with other people and horses and chickens and pigs. I could see people working in their swidden fields to produce rice and opium, people selling opium or bartering it to Karen workers for their labor, people eating rice, people buying goods in lowland markets, killing pigs and chickens for sacrifices, distilling liquor, and sponsoring feasts.

Before I settled into one village for more than a year, I traveled to others, asking how everyone was related to everyone else, how much land they cultivated and how much they had harvested. When I settled into a village, I followed Malinowski's example and set out to map the village and take a census of the households. In addition to the questions I had asked in other villages, I asked how much livestock they had, how many pigs and chickens they had killed during the past year, and how much money and opium they had spent. I had no idea how reliable any of this data might be.

I decided to measure to the best of my ability the things I could see, even though I could not see an economic system. I made a schedule of questions and began to ask the people of each household each week what they had been doing, what resources they had used, and what they had gained. I cross checked the answers from each household with my own observations. This weekly survey took on a life of its own, becoming its own onerous obligation from one week to the next. It kept up like a demanding and sometimes oppressive bagpipe drone throughout the ups and downs life in the village. It kept going during the celebrations for New Year, through weddings, divorces, contentious legal cases, a killing and its compensation. Every week, the same questions. But not always the same answers. I was lucky that a geographer from New Zealand, Graham Keene, was studying land use in the Thai highlands and spent some time in the village to measure all of the fields. I weighed harvests and measured the amount of rice people ate so that I would have some independent way of assessing consumption rates as well as how much they harvested and how much land they used.

In 1970, I returned to the University of Illinois where I was a graduate student to write a dissertation on Lisu curing. Fortunately, I listened to the sagacious advice of my advisor, F. K. Lehman, who warned me that it would be too much to try to tackle the description of the economic system and how it related to curing. So in 1971 I turned in my dissertation and got a job at Antioch College. I managed to return to the economy of this Lisu village in a paper in which I situated the village in a wider regional and global economic network that made available labor, rice, and markets for opium. At that distance, I began to see an economic system, but I could not discern its details, let alone see how it might relate to anything else.

The next year I went to the University of Iowa and Marshall Sahlins's *Stone Age Economics* came out. I had been searching for some theoretical framework that would help me understand the numbers I had so laboriously collected and tabulated. As a graduate student, I had read the formalists who seemed to me to want to convert everyone into a capitalist firm. I had read the substantivists who insisted that the economy was embedded in social relations. Neither was of any use to me. I wanted to be able to think of the economic as something related to what people actually do—in terms of the days they spend working and the amounts of rice they harvest and eat—and to be able to see how it relates to other spheres of life such as religion, world view, and politics.

Sahlins offered a solution. He cited Chayanov and stated his rule—that there should be a direct relationship between the number of consumers each worker has to support and the amount of work that person does. More dependents to support means more work. Sahlins's reading of Chayanov was that each worker's work load should increase as the number of people dependent on the worker increased. Locate each household of a village on a graph, first along a horizontal line that specifies the ratio of consumers to workers, then along another vertical axis that specifies how hard people work. We see that there should be a straight line from a minimum where each worker supports only himself or herself to the heavy work demands of whatever the maximum dependency ratio might be.

Sahlins wanted to measure how social systems were related to how much each worker works. Return to the graph and locate each household on the vertical axis that indicates labor according to how much each worker *actually* works. We construct the line that best fits the points and compute its difference from our expectations. We thus compare what households actually produce with what the Chayanov line predicts they should produce. The extent that the two lines are dissimilar is the measure of the economic consequences of the socio-political system. The deviations of the actual allocations of labor from the expected allocations are a measure of the "economic coefficient of a given social system." The location of the points relative to the Chayanov line shows who bears those costs.

Sahlins argued we could construct a profile for the amount of work we should expect each worker to do with "a few statistical data not difficult to collect in the field" 103). Whatever else Sahlins was right about, he was wrong about the data being easy to collect in the field. I suspect that is why there is so little of it, even today. I came to appreciate detailed tables.

I took some courses on computer programming and learned to write my own programs in FORTRAN. With the help of a graduate assistant, I managed to get all of the Lisu material coded and entered as a computerized data set. Instead of relying on proxy measures for many variables, I had actual measures so I could check assumptions about the relations of days of work to areas of land and of both to harvests. In 1974 in the first volume of the new journal, *American Ethnologist,* Martin Evans published a note on how to measure and assess Sahlins's social profile of domestic production. He discussed how to determine whether the line of expected effort is significantly different from the empirical line we derive from measurements and observations. I found this very promising and worked out a computer program to do just that. This was anthropology as it should be—the relation of theory to ethnographic observation, the testing of abstract ideas against concrete data, the use of theory to enlighten observation, and a cumulative enterprise that could continue to build on the work of colleagues involved with similar issues and offer new insights. Our journals have since either sacrificed or transcended those goals in their quest for the cutting edge rather than building the foundation of observation, theory, and reason that makes a science.

One of the things I found by comparing my measures of harvests and Graham Keene's measures of land areas with Lisu estimates was that their estimates were highly correlated to our measures. That gave me some faith in the data I had collected from other villages. With that faith, I returned to Sahlins and for each village computed the Chayanov line, which climbs at a constant rate with increases in the number of dependents each worker supports. When I compared these with the empirical lines, the lines that best fit what the households actually produce, I found that each village was quite different from the others.

Here was the same region, the same culture, the same political and social institutions in several villages, but very different empirical lines. Why? I concluded that the answer was ecological. In constructing these profiles, I was only looking at rice cultivation and not the full subsistence pattern, which included opium production as an important element. As a village stayed in an area longer, the people exhausted its capacity to produce rice by swidden agriculture, and turned increasingly to the more sustainable opium production to supply the wherewithal to purchase rice from the lowlands. I needed a more realistic conceptualization of household production, something beyond the amount of rice they produced. I think it was Nikki Tannenbaum who told me that Iowa rides the crest of the wave of the past. In a retrograde movement consistent with this tradition I went backward from Sahlins to Chayanov. I got the translation of Chayanov's writings, worked out the algebra of the intersection of the curves of drudgery and usefulness that he discussed as the determinants that put the ceiling on domestic production, and computed how much each Lisu household should produce if what they did was consistent with Chayanov's logic. I could then compare these production targets with each household's actual days of labor or the area of land they used or the amount of rice and opium they produced. Rather than assume a relationship between area cultivated, effort, and harvest, I could examine them. With visions of a comparative economic anthropology based on operationalized concepts and observable data, I published this program in *Behavior Science Research* in 1976.

I found it a promising idea that household production units, unlike firms, determine their level of production by the balance of the drudgery of labor and the usefulness of what they produce. Chayanov argued that many factors determine where that balance lies—among them the ratio of consumers to workers, taxes, debts, distances to markets, rents, interest rates, productivity of soils, and many others. I quickly concluded that the dependency ratio was but one among many factors, at least in Chayanov's writing. I developed a number of ideas about household production and Chayanov and how to operationalize his theoretical ideas. About this time, in the early 1970s, Nicola Tannenbaum began to work with me first as a graduate assistant and then as a colleague.

I needed quantitative data to test and develop the theoretical ideas Nikki and I were developing, but I could find no other published data that were comparable in detail to the Lisu material. Some authors aggregated data in ways that made it tantalizingly suggestive, but not useful. There were some data available in the gray literature—one dissertation, one agency report. To test hypotheses I had developed and further develop what seemed to me a promising economic theory, I returned to Thailand in 1976 to study the economic system of a lowland Shan village in an area I had first visited in 1967 with F. K. Lehman. Nikki joined me in the field toward the end of that study.

Still hopeful that anthropology could be cumulative, I organized a session devoted to Chayanov for a meeting of the Central States Anthropological Society in 1979. In 1984, I was able to publish the papers that people presented there as *Chayanov, Peasants, and Economic Anthropology*. Hoping to correct the lack of published detail, I also published the Shan data in all of its detail in 1978. In 1979 Nikki followed me to the same Shan village. Her research strategy and problem were quite different from mine, but she collected the same kinds of data I had, so we had comparable material on the same households for two points in time as well as corresponding data for two different social orders—the egalitarian Lisu and the stratified Shan.

I took Sahlins at his word when he wrote (102) that 'to avoid a sustained discourse on generalities, to give some promise of applicability and verification, it is necessary first to attempt some measure of the impact of concrete social systems upon domestic production." Having operationalized Chayanov's production targets, it is possible to ask what affects them *besides* the ratio of consumers to workers. The investigation of this issue reveals the economic consequences of any social or political system by showing just what the consequences are and how people bear them in their work.

Nikki came back to Iowa and wrote her dissertation, and then we put our heads and data sets together to see what we could make of the differences in time and place. Those deliberations came out in 1990 as *Analytical Perspectives on Shan Agriculture and Village Economics.* Those familiar with the work will recognize our debt to Sahlins's conceptualizations of the economic relationships between different ways to organize production and different social orders and modes of exchange. We were able to show the implications of the different sociopolitical orders of Shan and Lisu for household production as well as ideology. We could see and specify the relations among production, exchange, political system, and ideology.

In the meantime, I had gotten involved in things Icelandic, among them the tradition of medieval sagas, native accounts of events over a period of some four centuries between the settlement of that island and its incorporation into Norwegian hegemony in the latter part of the 13th century. Here I could not collect any more detailed data on households than the historical tradition preserved, but the Chayanovian view offered an interesting way of interpreting the initial migration from Norway to Iceland that is consistent with the native accounts. A Norwegian chieftain, Harald, put together a successful coalition of chieftains to act as an aristocracy in a kingdom to replace the group of chieftains each of whom had about equal power and prestige. The demands of membership in the kingdom on the remaining chieftains so negatively affected their two household curves—drudgery and usefulness—that it made sense for them to risk life in the new land rather than pay the price to stay in the old. Put another way, these chieftains were not willing to bear the costs of the new social system. Here we can see an economic system in action.

I first went to Iceland in 1981 chiefly to study fisheries. In 1987 I went to the northern end of the Gulf of Mexico to study the fishing industries of Alabama and Mississippi. I was not able to develop the same kind of detailed data for shrimpers as I had for Shan and Lisu, but I did manage to get some measures of their household compositions and sources of income. So far, my explorations of Chayanov and household economies had been my attempt to contribute to a scientifically based economic anthropology; a set of ideas about economic, social, and cultural systems that we could test and develop empirically. I thought economic anthropology could help us understand such things as how Lisu remain egalitarian and how the stratification of Shan affects the daily working lives of the people. King Harald was long dead, and I am pretty sure he would not have listened to any policy suggestions I or any other anthropologist might have made.

But the analysis of the data on Mississippi shrimpers offered a means of critiquing current fisheries policy, which is based on the assumption that the people who own and operate fishing boats act like firms. Because they are classical household production units, they do not act like firms, and the main consequence is not that policy makers have questioned the philosophical or empirical bases of their policy, but that they have concluded that fishermen are at least sometimes irrational, if not absolutely crazy. This makes for bad policy and worse social relations between managers and fishermen. This brings us back to Chayanov, who contrasted the apparently irrational behavior of peasant farmers with expectations based on the assumption that they should act like firms. And this in turn brings us back to Marshall Sahlins and *Stone Age Economics.*

I agree with those who have said that Sahlins might have written more concisely. But *Stone Age Economics* does not exhibit the convoluted writing and obfuscatory rhetoric that some have come to accept as sure markers of brilliance in the writing if not the conceptualization of culture, or should one say, with appropriately placed winks and twitches, cultures. The brilliance of Sahlins's work is in its promise of a quantifiable and comparative economic anthropology, an economic anthropology that can move beyond the overly theorized maximizers of the formalists and the hyper relativism of the substantivists to conceptualize economies as social processes with political causes as well as consequences for world views, religions, and policies. This work kept history and the evolution of political and economic forms in the realm of anthropological investigation.

In 1972, Sahlins wrote that his goal was "merely to perpetuate the possibility of an anthropological economics by a few concrete examples." That he did. That was the gift of *Stone Age Economics*. I hope that my work in this field over the past twenty-five years has been something of a return for that gift. With this kind of investment in a scientific economic anthropology, I have to hope that some still agree that anthropology is a science. Looking toward formalists and neoclassical economists, Sahlins likened himself to early physicists and astronomers who worked in the shadow of dogma. He was writing a year before another collection of essays heralded a winking, blinking, and twitching hermeneutics which some have worked into another dogma. He did not expect flexibility of any dogma, but he did hope the gods would at least be just. Doubting that anthropology, this "tissue of metaphors,'" was a science, he commended his work to the gods because anthropology had "shown as little capacity for agreement on the empirical adequacy of a theory as on its logical sufficiency." In *Stone Age Economics* Sahlins was right about many things. Pessimistic about the possibilities of a scientific anthropology, he said that we "cultivate our gardens, waiting to see if the gods will shower rain or, like those of certain New Guinea tribes, just urinate upon us" (xiv).

References Cited

Durrenberger, E. Paul. 1971. Ethnography of Lisu Curing. Ph.D. Dissertation. University of Illinois, Champaign-Urbana.
1974. The Regional Context of the Economy of a Lisu Village in Northern Thailand. Southeast Asia 3:569-75
1974. The Economy of a Lisu Village. American Ethnologist 3: 633-44.
1978. Agricultural Production and Household Budgets in a Shan Peasant Village in Northern Thailand: A Quantitative Description. Ohio University Center for International Studies Southeast Asia Series no. 49.
1979. Chayanov's Analysis in Economic Anthropology. Journal of Anthropological Research 36:133-48.
1981. The Economy of a Shan Village. Ethnos 46:64-79.
1984. Chayanov, Peasants, and Economic Anthropology. Academic Press, San Francisco.
1992. The Dynamics of Medieval Iceland. University of Iowa Press, Iowa City.
1996. Gulf Coast Soundings: People and Policy in the Mississippi Shrimp Industry. University Press of Kansas, Lawrence.
Durrenberger, E. Paul and Nicola Tannenbaum.1990. Analytical Perspectives on Shan Agriculture and Village Economics. Yale University Southeast Asia Studies Monograph Series 37, New Haven.
Geerlz, Clifford. 1973. The Interpretation of Cultures. Basic Books, New York
Sahlins, Marshall. 1972. Stone Age Economics. Aldine, Chicago.
Thu, Kendall M. and E. Paul Durrenberger (editors). 1998. Pigs, Profits, and Rural Communities. State University of New York Press, Albany.

Cultural Anthropology in a Nutshell

1998 *Teaching
Anthropology.*

It's quite a challenge to try to sum up cultural anthropology in 12 minutes. And it's quite an honor to be asked to try. At these meetings there's a lot of noise in the meeting rooms as well as the halls and lobbies. If there were anything new in the cries that anthropology is dissolving, they might be worth listening to, but, as Miles Richardson pointed out in 1975, it's an old pattern. People have been predicting the end of anthropology since the AAA was founded. By now they've achieved the status of the warnings of the boy who cried wolf.

Richardson wanted to figure out why we anthropologists vilify ourselves so much because "the accusations that anthropologists hurl at each other contrast so sharply with the image of the anthropologist as a sympathetic spokesman for the small, the weak, and the forgotten." (1975:519-520). Nobody before or since has better said what it is to be an anthropologist.

About ten years later, Stanley Barrett (1984:6) argued that the crisis of self-doubt, anxiety and introspection that faced anthropology and still does is due to the failure of anthropological theory to advance. It just keeps going in circles because it can't cope with complexity and contradictions.

I think Melford Spiro (1993) was right a couple of years ago when he said that what is true about post modernism is not new and what is new is not true. The post modem critique that science is interpretive, that we do write, that we are creatures of our time and culture--these are as old as Malinowski and Marx and still worth heeding.

So I'm not going to even try to analyze the static-the noise-in the discipline. Sometimes it's hard to see a pattern in all the noise. A lot of good stuff is going on in anthropology and that's what I want to focus on today. Let me try to show you one pattern that I see.

Roy Rappaport (1993) entitled his Distinguished Lecture to the General Anthropology Division four years ago here in San Francisco, "The Anthropology of Trouble." He pointed out that by understanding problems in our own local areas in the United States, we can not only bring anthropological insights to bear on relevant issues. We can also challenge our own paradigmatic assumptions and practices with new and more complex phenomena of national and international relationships that embrace the localities and communities anthropologists have customarily described and analyzed.

Many of us anthropologists study the details of food production around the planet. After all, many of us are persuaded that if you want to understand people, it's a good idea to follow the example of the mythical Norse king who kept asking the gods, "What did they eat?" If you follow the food, everything else will fall into place by and by.

To translate this to our longstanding concern with food production, we expand our vantage points from the farmers and fishermen to the policies that play more important roles in shaping their daily lives than any decision they will ever make. When we adjust our focus this way, we begin to ask where the policies come from, who makes them, and by what process, as well as how those policies affect the everyday lives of food producers, consumers, and administrators. We begin to ask what the underlying assumptions are, who supplies them, and how they came to have those forms; questions about the history and politics of knowledge and culture. Anthropologists who have been studying fisheries and fisheries policy have been very active in such endeavors (Durrenberger 1992, 1996; Finlayson 1994).

These days, if you follow the food in our own land, it leads you right into a factory of some kind. A recent book (Garrity-Blake 1994) about fishing in the southern part of the U.S. is entitled *The Fish Factory*. Much of our food is produced in factory-like conditions. And the inputs to food production systems come from factories. So there are factories at each end of the food production endeavor.

Cultural anthropologists are turning our attention to factories to see what is going on in them and the societies that support them. Frank Dubinskas discussed how the specialization and hierarchy characteristic of American manufacturing moved from being a management doctrine to being "natural." He also outlined alternatives from other lands and the role of culture in understanding these systems. Let me read you his concluding comments (1995: 113): "If anthropologists have a strong desire to aid in the reformation of American society, new opportunities abound to deploy our empirical tools and our holistic and synthetic approaches. With a critical stance toward our culture and society, we can create new knowledge and apply it to changing social relationships at the heart of American economic life."

This is one of seven challenging papers in a book entitled *Diagnosing America: Anthropology and Public Engagement* edited by Shepard Forman. Now listen to what Jim Peacock said in the same volume: "The American Dream dims for many as the spirit of capitalism is transformed into a system teetering between irresponsible speculators and stultifying bureaucracy" (Peacock 1994:31). He continues (ibid:42): "We are trained to describe the particularities of diverse cultures, and it is our responsibility to do this because nobody else does it very much at all, and those who do, do not do it as well as we."

MacLennan takes on the issue of democratic participation and points out the weaknesses of culturalist models as well as those that are overly structural. The culturalists do not ask whether there are political or social structures that make it difficult for citizens to engage their political system, or whether there are dominating ideologies that divert attention away from democratic concerns. MacLennan (1994:S9) advocates not blaming victims, but inquiring into the absence of participation and moving beyond the citizen to the political system for explanation. Thus, we can identify institutional barriers that discourage and even prohibit political participation.

More structural approaches locate the obstacles to participation in the structure and history of power arrangements that are embodied in technologies, administrative powers of government and domination of experts, and shift the blame away from culture or laziness. Their weakness is that they suggest that the only effective participation is through formal political institutions. They raise the question of the role human action in a democratic society (ibid:60). MacLennan (ibid:61) suggests that we look at the forms of participation, as well as access to and barriers to democratic participation.

So, anthropologists who study fishing and farming are looking well beyond the boats and farms to the processes and structures that formulate the policy in terms of which food producers work. Others are looking at the factories at each end of the food production system, and others are looking at forms of political participation in the U.S.

Is all of this just another pitch for applied anthropology, the fifth field? What does this have to do with cultural anthropology? If it's going to be cultural anthropology, shouldn't there be some theory in there somewhere? And shouldn't it be mostly unintelligible?

The answer to that last question is, no. If it's unintelligible, throw it away.

This is a pitch for applied anthropology, but an applied anthropology that moves away from government agencies and their funds towards an anthropology of relevance. Understandable, clear and coherent theoretical trends in anthropology are moving in the same direction. In fact, think that this kind of anthropology of contemporary issues in the U.S. and other complex social orders can best inform that theoretical work. Cultural anthropologists like to try to figure out how people think. That's what our obsession with culture comes down to. That's why we like those bizarre examples that show the range of possibilities for thought and broaden the alternatives for our students.

Jean Lave wants to understand the kind of thought a lot of people associate with some son of "pure thought," mathematics. She wants to figure out how people make use of quantity in everyday life, how people compute outside class and examination rooms (1988:67). She emphasizes the relational interdependency of agent and world, activity, meaning, cognition, learning and knowing of people in social relations engaged in activity in and with a practical world. She suggests that there is no pure computation, no Archimedean platform. Computation is situational, dependent on people's goals, objectives, constraints in other areas of their lives and in the arena of their action.

Where does the brain start? Where is culture? Uncomfortable with the concept of culture, she suggests an idea of cognition centered on persons acting in settings to solve problems, as "seamlessly distributed across persons, activity and setting" (1988 171). Mind, culture, and history are interrelated and mutually constitute each other, a conclusion congenial to Ortner's (1984) synthetic review of anthropological theory since the 60's.

I want to mention a couple of other works in the area of theory. Stanley R. Barrett (*Anthropology: A Student s Guide to Theory and Method,* 1996) argues that throughout the period of postmodern critique, conventional approaches to anthropology have continued to thrive. They just haven't made a lot of noise. He calls these "no-name anthropology'" (178). The hallmark of this kind of anthropology is fieldwork, treating data as something more than investigators' arbitrary interpretations, talking to people in interviews, and offering generalizations to identify causes and correlations. In short, conventional ethnography (1996:179). He sees this as a good thing insofar as it keeps fieldwork alive during a period '"when so much of the literature is choked with agonizing discussions of meta-theory and meta-method" (1996-180). In case you think this is new, compare it with what Paul Radin wrote in 1933, (cxvii), "Discussions on theory and methodology. . . . are only too frequently a substitute for real work."

Most of us who actually do anthropology fit in the theoretical spectrum at the "no-name" end that just gets the work done and doesn't shout, prance, holler or gesticulate and make noise.

In an earlier book (1984), Barrett argued that anthropological theory is not cumulative because it assumes that the social world is highly structured and amenable to measurement while it is in fact contradictory, complex and chaotic. Anthropology hasn't been able to cope with this complexity (1984:3).

Reviewing the massive literature on contradiction, Barrett (1984) argues that social and cultural life is not only contradictory, it is messily contradictory, a world of "cluttered contradictions" as he calls them that are, "at times messy, lopsided, loosely integrated, ambiguously located, and devoid of ultimate rational design." He recognizes that this view makes drive logicians crazy and makes, "the philosophical hair of French rationalism stand on end" (150), but that it is closer to the character of social life than tidy systems. This does not mean that we must surrender to chaotic thought, but poses the challenge of comprehending chaos as a phenomenon. Bart Kosko (1993) has reviewed some of the systematic ways of thinking about contradictions.

Barrett (1984: 151) also suggests that because differential power always contains the capacity for immorality, the loci of differential power should be subjects of serious research.

All of the oppositions—individual/social, cultural/ structural, psychological/cultural—become dimensions of the same thing—people making up their cultures as they go along, doing the best they can with what they have. Culture becomes a set of creations through time rather than a code that determines action. Structure becomes something people change through action.

Barrett (1984:201-202) identifies the elements of an emerging synthesis as the dialectical relations between culture and structure; the process of the production of culture from the dialectic of the mental with the material; a concern with the interplay of the individual and the social; an emphasis on choice, manipulation, power, contradiction, complexity and dynamic rather than static analysis; a tolerance for disorder and open- ended conceptual schemes; and the explanation of expressions of inequality.

So, this is the pattern I see in cultural anthropology: a recognition of complexity that we encounter as we do our "no-name" anthropology in our attempts to understand the workings of our own society as well as other complex social formations. We recognize that wherever we are, one of our topics is differential power, because it contains the capacity for immorality. It doesn't matter where we see these inequalities—in gender relations, race relations, on the factory floor, in the policy process, in our universities and colleges. We aren't ashamed to call it immorality. We aren't shy to try to change it whenever we can. And we want to bring our understandings of this contradictory complexity to a revitalized anthropology that can not only understand humankind, but also serve our species well.

This kind of anthropology is at the same time practical, political, theoretical, relevant and interesting. I can do no better than to go back to Miles Richardson (1975:530-531) and repeat what he said 20 years and more ago: "If the anthropologist does not tell the human myth, then who will? Who will record these things and more? Who will search for the human secret? Who will tell the human myth? Who will, damn it, who will?"

References Cited

Barrett, Stanley R. 1984. The Rebirth of Anthropological Theory. Toronto. University of Toronto Press.

1996. Anthropology: A student 's Guide to Theory and Method. Toronto. University of Toronto Press.

Dubinskas, Frank A. 1994. The Heartbeat of Productivity: Hierarchy and Transformation in American Work Relations. In Diagnosing American: Anthropology and Public Engagement. Shepard Forman, editor. Ann Arbor: The University of Michigan Press, pages 75-120.

Durrenberger, E. Paul. 1992. It's All Politics: South Alabama's Seafood Industry. Champaign: University of Illinois Press.

1996. Gulf Coast Soundings: People and Policy in the Mississippi Shrimp Industry. Lawrence: University Press of Kansas.

Finlayson, A.C. 1994. Fishing for Truth: A Sociological Analysis of Northern Cod Stock Assessments from 1977-1990. St. John's: Institute of Social and Economic Research, Memorial University of Newfoundland, Social and Economic Studies No. 52.

Ganity-Blake, Barbara J. 1994. The Fish Factory: Work and Meaning for Black and White Fishermen of the American Menhaden Industry. Knoxville. The University of Tennessee Press.

Kosko, Ban. 1993. Fuzzy Thinking: The New Science of Fuzzy Logic. New York. Hyperion.

Lave, Jean. 1988. Cognition in Practice: Mind, Mathematics, and Culture in Everyday Life. Cambridge. Cambridge University Press.

Ortner, Sherry. 1984. Theory in Anthropology Since the Sixties. Comparative Studies in Society and History 26(1): 126-166.

MacLennan, Carol. 1994. Democratic Participation A View from Anthropology. In Diagnosing American: Anthropology and Public Engagement. Shepard Forman, editor. Ann Arbor. The University of Michigan Press. Pages 51-74.

Peacock, James L. 1994. American Cultural Values: Disorders and Challenges. In Diagnosing American: Anthropology and Public Engagement Shepard Forman, editor. Ann Arbor. The University of Michigan Press. Pages 23-50.

Radin, Paul. 1966. (1933): The Method and Theory of Ethnology: An Essay in Criticism. New York. Basic Books.

Rappaport, Roy. 1993. The Anthropology of Trouble. Distinguished Lecture in General Anthropology 1992. American Anthropologist 95 (2):295-303.

Richardson, Miles. 1975. Anthropologist--The Myth Teller. American Ethnologist 2 (3):517-496.

Spiro, Melford E. 1993. What is New About "Postmodern Subjectivity"? Paper presented at the AAA symposium, Postmodemism and Psychological Anthropology.

Review Essay:
The Cutting Edge and the History of Anthropology

1999 *American Anthropologist* 101(2)

The Craft of Inquiry: Theories, Methods, Evidence. *Robert R. Alford.* New York: Oxford University Press, 1998. 168 pp.

A History of Anthropological Theory. *Paul Erickson* with *Liam D. Murphy.* Calgary, Alberta: Broadview Press, 1998. 254 pp.

An Introduction to Theory in Anthropology. *Robert Layton.* New York: Cambridge University Press, 1997. 242 pp.

These three books are welcome additions to the history of anthropological theory. These days it's hard to know how to structure a course of study in anthropology. We see the Department of Cultural and Social Anthropology at Stanford, having separated itself from scientific approaches, advertising for an "eminent Sociocultural Anthro whose work is at the cutting edge of the theoretical & methodological developments in the discipline." There are so many voices clamoring for recognition as the cutting edge that we have to appreciate the weightiness of this quest and wonder how we would prepare our students to answer such ads in twenty or thirty years, when they become eminent. Do we organize courses on the fashionable topics we hear about discourse, text, identity, how to read French theorists so our students may be able to at least identify the cutting edge, even if they cannot aspire to be on it because by the time they finish our courses the cutting edge will have cut and having cut moved on leaving them stranded on the shore of outmoded unfashionability and perhaps political incorrectness? Are there methods associated with cutting edge theories that *you* and *I* and our students can hope to *do?* If *we* could do them would they be cutting edge? Can we teach them? Or shall we aspire to ground our students in some of the fundamental principles of our discipline so that they have some means of thinking critically about the human condition? Are there fundamental principles we can hope to show our students?

Or shall we despair when some figure sitting on a newly discovered cutting edge reveals to us, as happens once in every generation or so, that science is a cultural artifact, and an imperfect one at that, and simply ground our students in the finer points of academic politics and power play so that they can survive the kinds of academic battles in which our colleagues at Stanford and elsewhere are embroiled? I am perhaps overly fond of quoting a colleague in comparative literature whose mantra is, "if you think you have a new idea it means you haven't read enough." Perhaps if people read and understood more rather than less of the history of anthropology they would understand that point better and be better able to deal with the cutting edge when it comes at their throats.

Here we have three foreigners helping us out—one from Canada, one from Britain, and one from Sociology. And we can use the help. Erickson based his *A History of Anthropological Theory* on his more than twenty years of experience teaching the subject at Saint Mary's University and incorporates sections by one of his former students, Liam D. Murphy. A "dialogue with the ancestors" rather than "one dead guy a week" (p. 15), the book has many points to recommend it. It focuses on American Anthropology and provides good coverage of schools, including some that often receive short shrift, for instance, the culture and personality movement. The work is accessible and clearly written throughout, a stylistic approach that can serve as a good example for our future colleagues to emulate. The discussion of approaches is balanced and introduces readers to the main points of each along with a list of references for further reading. The authors provide a plausible answer to that troubling question that some of our students ask, "What is postmodernism?" when no one will stand up to claim the honor of being one, knowing one, or knowing what it means. They tell us it shares a perspective that emphasizes the subjectivity of experience and the impossibility of any one form of authoritative knowledge (p. 140). Not that those issues haven't been around for a long time, but for those who haven't read about them before, they have been on one cutting edge that's now getting a bit rusty as the discipline moves on.

The book is designed for ready reference with a glossary of terms and wide margins that contain main concepts as index points to show the way—terms such as *epistemology, French rationalism, British empiricism, comparative method, bourgeoisie, positivism, dialectical materialism, vulgar materialists, informant, adhesions, psychodynamic, restricted exchange, cognitive anthropology, thermodynamic law, adaptation, Midwestern taxonomic method, new archaeology, ethos, processual archaeology, post-processualists, false consciousness, human biogram, inclusive fitness, liminal, communitas, semiotic, world system, colonial encounter, poststructural, authoritative knowledge, ideology, hegemony, invented tradition, practice, doxa, habitus, deconstruction,* and *solipsism.* So they won't think they're on the cutting edge in a couple of decades when they reinvent the concepts they label, our students need to know most of these words.

I found two mistakes. The first is on page 118 where Erickson discusses Julian Steward and his students and the University of Illinois. Most of the people he mentions did not study at the University of Illinois, though they were Steward's students. The second is on page 141 where he misstates Thomas Kuhn's point saying "new paradigms are not necessarily superior to old ones; paradigms are merely different and incommensurable." Kuhn was very clear that he thought that new paradigms are superior to previous ones and that there is progress in science—that he is not a relativist, as this passage would suggest. In fact, in chapter 13 of *The Structure of Scientific Revolutions,* entitled "Progress through Revolutions," he contrasts science to other endeavors as uniquely progressive and discusses the differences and reasons for it at length, a position Kuhn reiterates in his postscript to the second edition when he says, "Later scientific theories are better than earlier ones for solving puzzles" (Kuhn 1970:206). Are they therefore better representations of nature? A closer approximation to truth? Without some way of knowing truth independent of theory, there is no way to tell, says Kuhn (pp. 206-207). This is not relativism, it is just that the ontological question is not answerable. There is no final analysis. That realization drives some to despair, some to postmodernism, some to philosophy, and some to keep working on trying to know the world as well as we can.

Erickson's time line starts with Homer and moves to Vergil to Herodotus, some more Greeks, and then on through the Middle Ages, the Renaissance, the Voyages of Discovery, and the Scientific Revolution. He suggests that whether we consider anthropology to be a branch of science, humanism, or religion depends on how we think about the relationships among nature, people, and god. Science treats nature as primary and encompasses people and god, humanism treats people as primary, and religion treats god as primary. Having developed the historical context for questions about human origins, human diversity, and how the world works, he reminds us that even the cutting-edge questions are ones that have been with us for ages, and that there have been a variety of answers to them, mostly reworkings of previous answers.

So if you want a good statement of what anthropology is, this is a good book. I think it will be useful in a wide range of courses. Robert Layton, from the University of Durham, is less inclusive and focuses on current debates and the way theories have impinged upon them. Layton is also to be congratulated for writing a good book, accessible, readable, and free of pretense and jargon. He moves us expeditiously through Herodotus and Tacitus to get us to the modem questions, ones formulated during the Enlightenment along with ways to answer them, and the concept of social systems, by page 3. We move from Hobbes to Rousseau to Smith to Compte to Spencer in the next five pages with great efficiency. Then come Marx and Durkheim and chapters on functionalism, structuralism, interactionalism, marxist anthropology, socioecology, and postmodernism. He shows how structuralism and functionalism both developed from Durkheim's notions and embeds a brief discussion of cognitive anthropology in the discussion of structuralism. Not all would agree that Marshall Sahlins's *Stone Age Economics* is a Marxist analysis (p. 95).

"Postmodernism means different things to different people. This is, in fact, the central irony of a word which is used to dispute the possibility of any grand theory of human behavior" (p. 185). Unlike some of his more insular British colleagues, Layton recognizes and discusses American contributions to anthropology. He uses a number of ethnographic examples to good effect throughout the book to show how different approaches provide complementary or competing interpretations of the same ethnographic material.

Layton fills in detail of argument and evidence for major approaches that Erickson discusses and for which he provides a richer historical context. Layton provides depth to complement Erickson's breadth. Thus, I think the two books would work very well together in a course on the history of anthropological theory. Both discuss Durkheim, Weber, and Marx, and that is where Alford's book is very useful indeed to bring the discussion up-to-date. At the outset, Layton (p. 1) defines anthropology as "the study of people" and social anthropology as "the study of human society" and says that social anthropology can be described as "comparative sociology." The British have been saying that for ages, and it solves the problem of trying to distinguish between sociology and anthropology.

These days, especially with so much anthropological work being done in the first world and the former socialist republics, our students are warranted when they ask what the difference between sociology and anthropology might be. I usually answer with Stephen Tyler's (1969:12) quip that the question of whether cows on a scale from 1 to 5 are more or less like gods is only meaningful to people in societies with cows, gods, and sociologists. Tyler was making a point about the differences in ethnographic description and sample survey research and the wealth of tacit and unexamined assumptions that inform the questions on surveys. Sometimes I say that many sociologists have become so intrigued with the mechanics of statistics that they are busily inventing mathematical and quantitative methods and have forgotten that they started out asking questions about how societies work. Sometimes I assert that what distinguishes anthropology from all other disciplines is that we are holistic, comparative, and ethnographic.

With the publication of Robert R. Alford's new book I think I will quit trying to make any distinction and assign his book as an example of how we anthropologists ought to proceed. The last line of the book, the punch line, is that the "'soul' of sociology lies in its location at the intersection between the humanities and the sciences, between historiography and systematic theory, combining art, science, and craft" (p. 133). Sociology graduate students, like ours, are "squeezed between alienating and demoralizing forces" (p.132) as postmodernists promote despair in their proclamations that we can know nothing or generalize anything sufficiently to guide action while global competitive forces promote individualistic "rational choice" and individual interest ideologies to fit the demands of bureaucratic policy research at the cost of structural and historical explanations (p. 132). Unlike psychology and economics, Alford tells us, sociology challenges common assumptions about the operation of social life. Because sociology unmasks power and privilege there are active efforts to delegitimize its findings. Economics, he tells us, has become transfixed by theoretical assumptions of rational choice that blind its practitioners to the relations between concepts and the phenomena we want to understand while political science has become a direct ally of policy makers. When sociologists see structures as over-determining action, they cannot see strategic interactions as problematic—there is no agency; when they see every action as socially constructed and negotiated, they cannot recognize structural determination—systems and configurations of power disappear. It won't do to define away the problem of agency with the assumption that every factual assertion is a matter of taste, interpretation, bias, or standpoint because, "the point of research is to *learn* [italics in original] something new, not to reproduce your own consciousness in the results" (p. 108). Alford counsels students to avoid equally flights into empiricism or theoreticism by moving back and forth between the two to connect theory to evidence to develop coherent arguments that recognize historical processes, symbolic meanings, and multivariate relations. This, he argues, is the way to construct valid explanations of the workings of society.

He discusses specific works of three founding figures that anthropologists also claim: Durkheim, Weber, and Marx, all of whom assumed that there are empirical regularities in human behavior, perceptions, and experience that they could explain. Alford shows how each foregrounded one dimension—a structure of multivariate relations that defines patterns of structural relations (Durkheim), a texture of meanings that define cultures (Weber), or historical processes (Marx)—while relying on the other two as background. He analyzes other more recent sociological classics to appraise how their authors use these three approaches. The analyses of sociological works provide students with excellent examples of critical readings as well as sound advice on how to embark on and engage in research that combines multivariate, interpretive, and historical analyses in the most fruitful way for the particular problem the student has selected. The book may disappoint some anthropologists because it is comparative, holistic, and very self-consciously ethnographic, because its advice will be as valuable to those of us who work in societies without sociologists as those with them—in short because, while it provides useful answers for questions about how to do anthropological research, it makes it hard to answer that troubling question about the difference between sociology and anthropology. Anthropologists who teach courses about anthropological theory or method will welcome this book as a useful guide for their students even if it makes it more difficult to answer their question about what differentiates sociology and anthropology. At least students will know the differences between psychology, political science, economics, and sociology.

If we want to know where the cutting edge is, we can wait and see what the Department of Cultural and Social Anthropology at Stanford does. Meanwhile, if our students read these books, they will learn that there are fundamental principles to anthropology, what they are, how they relate to one another, how they relate to ethnographic and historical observations to which they can contribute, and how to use them in fashioning their own understandings. They will learn that if they use different modes of interpretation, they can broaden their understandings, and they will learn to think critically. Maybe that's where the cutting edge of anthropology and anthropological theory is. If it isn't, then maybe we ought to be moving it there. Maybe we should see that it stays there while we show our students how anthropologists and sociologists have been understanding the human condition, how we are doing it, and how they can continue that tradition and contribute to it.

References Cited

Kuhn, Thomas. 1970. The Structure of Scientific Revolutions. 2nd edition. Chicago: University of Chicago Press.
Tyler, Stephen A. 1969. Introduction. In Cognitive Anthropology. Pp. 1-23. New York: Holt, Rinehart and Winston.

Anthropology that Makes a Difference

2006 *Central States
Anthropological Society Bulletin* 41 (2)

I teach a course called "Comparative Social Organization-Writing." I start off with Marvin Harris's *Cows, Pigs, Wars and Witches*. I want the students to understand the differences between their dreamwork and the realities of their lives. I also want to show them that anthropologists can talk about complex matters in ways that anyone can understand. The students like the writing. But they don't always like what he's saying. Especially the parts about Jesus, the urban guerilla.

We read other books, but to keep Harris on their minds, I stole a slogan from the religious folks. When they were saying WWJD, "What would Jesus do?" I copped "What Would Marvin Harris Do?" Or WWMHD? One day, a student asked a question about how anthropologists would understand 9-11. I asked, "WWMHD?" There was a long silence. Finally one daring individual raised a hand. "Write another book?" I laughed out loud. But the student was right.

Just before we came here, my wife, Suzan and I sent our publisher the last bits of the revised version of our new introductory anthropology textbook, *Anthropology Unbound: A Field Guide to the 21st Century*. Last time it was my turn to teach the intro course at Penn State, all the texts cost $80 or more. I used a ten dollar alternative. The rip-off text books annoyed me. I said to the owner of Paradigm Publishing that what this country needs is a good ten buck intro book. He said, "Your write it and I'll publish it." Can writing another anthropology book be anthropology that makes a difference? I think so. I hope so.

And I'll tell you why.

In 1993 Kendall Thu and I were driving around North Carolina to learn about industrial swine production that some people were advocating for Iowa. The people we talked with were frustrated and angry. They asked their government agencies from the municipal to the county to the state to help them with the ever present and oppressive stench hog manure. Aggies called it "nutrient." And said it didn't stink. They were hoping for a victory of vocabulary over reality. At all levels the response of government was intimidation and repression.

The chief difference between white and black residents was that black ones were not surprised or shocked at the responses.

I was asking myself how a couple of anthropologists could think about all this stuff.

The only thing I could think of was Walter Goldschmidt's book about industrial agriculture, *As You Sow*. It was about his research comparing industrial agriculture and family farms in California in the 40s. We got it from the library and studied it. Anthropologists hadn't done much with it, but rural sociologists had turned it into an academic industry about the "Goldschmidt Hypothesis." We read all their stuff. They said Goldschmidt hypothesized that industrial agriculture made rural life worse.

Kendall and I got together lots of data from all the censuses and ag censuses of Iowa and did a bunch of statistical tests. We found that in counties with fewer and larger farms, more people were using food stamps. In counties with more and smaller the farms, fewer people used food stamps. We also found that the welfare of people depended on the number of farms in the county, not the number of pigs. That was in line with the "Goldschmidt Hypothesis." But we didn't feel like we understood what was going on. It was still out of focus. We had numbers and tables but no real understanding. Through the next couple of years we drove around Iowa talking to farmers and groups of farmers to get a better sense of what was going on.

Kendall invited Goldschmidt, then in his 80s, to join us in Iowa. He went to Iowa State to set the aggies straight. There is no "Goldschmidt hypothesis." But there is a "Goldschmidt finding." It's so well substantiated that it's not a conjecture, speculation or theory— it's a fact. Industrial agriculture is bad for rural people.

In a small town café, a farmer nearing retirement years who was facing ruin said, "Sometimes I feel like we're five years too late." Walter said, "Son, you're fifty years too late."

Goldschmidt's book wasn't published until 1978 because agribusiness and the Department of Agriculture tried to suppress it. He didn't prove that social participation, democratic institutions, equitable distribution of income and high standards of living are good. What he did show is that those values are American and that industrial agriculture undermines them (p 470).

Kendall and I went on to document the relationships between government agencies, the ag colleges, and industrial swine producers in North Carolina and in Iowa.

Roy Rappaport also wrote about pigs. In New Guinea they played an important role in keeping people in balance with their environment. People's actions sent signals through the system that regulated the number of pigs and other ecological variables. Too many disputes because of pigs invading gardens? Too many women complaining of too much work? People have to work harder because productivity is down because of shorter fallow periods? Kill the pigs and have a feast. Signals, responses, ecological regulation.

Goldschmidt's study was an ecological signal in the 40's akin to any of the contributing factors to the pig rituals that Rappaport talked about. Goldschmidt's study was suppressed instead of amplified. It became academic instead of policy because agribusiness was calling the shots in the Dept. of Agriculture.

Kendall and I saw the political systems in Iowa and North Carolina amplifying some signals and muting others. Aggies were there to tell everyone that more pigs were better and that nutrient didn't stink. Farmers and environmentalists couldn't find anyone to listen to their emotional whining.

Anthropologists agree that our evolutionary history has bred our use of symbols into us. It's just the ability to separate symbols from realities that makes it possible for us to lie. How can you keep the signals that regulate ecological relationships from being lies? Rappaport said that's what ritual does. You can believe statements that ritual sanctifies. But if it doesn't work, if people lie anyway, the system isn't adaptive and won't work very well. People will notice, and they'll refuse to sanctify the rituals.

That part came to me later when I was riding with representatives of SEIU Local 1 in Chicago. Over the door of a sanctified hall of a Jesuit retreat near Chicago were inscribed words about justice and truth. The Jesuits were not about to provide either to their own workers without a fight. That's what the union guy was there to do. Deny the sanctity of their lies.

Before people can withdraw sanctity, they have to understand what is going on. Rappaport cautioned that some societies may be so mystified that it's difficult for people to understand the sources of their distress (233). It was pretty easy for the workers at the retreat and for folks in North Carolina and later in Iowa.

Rappaport said we continually change things to adapt to changing circumstances, but along with the adaptations come continual lies. Don't worry. People aren't fooled. A quote: "…the generation of the lie is continuously challenged by the living—by prophets, mystics, youth, revolutionaries, and reformers…" (p 233).

As Goldschmidt did. As Jules Henry did in his *Culture against Man*. Looking for inspiration for this talk, I opened the book at random. It was p. 271. He's discussing the narcotizing and anomic effects of teenage dance halls that promote consumerism. "A narcotizing machine for putting the powers of inquiry to sleep…" (263). He cites an advertisement from Standard Oil that lives revolve around cars for "shopping safaris, football games, dances and dozens of other 'musts'…." He comments, "I have spoken of pecuniary philosophy; let us call this *gasoline spirituality*. Is Standard Oil wrong? Can a billion dollars lie?" (emphasis original 273). Jules Henry spoke the words of a prophet. A billion dollar lie.

Well, that was 1963 so maybe it needs an update. Standard is now Exxon-Mobile. Last year its total sales were up 24 percent from the year before to $370 billion. Profits were up 44 percent to $59.4 billion. That's greater than the GNP of 125 of the 184 countries in the World Bank's statistics. It paid $23.3 billion in taxes for a net profit (up 27 percent) of $10.7 billion. So, no, it's not a billion dollar lie. It's somewhere between a $370 billion and $11 billion lie.

The theme I'm developing here is the anthropologist as prophet, the anthropologist as one who sees things as they are and sends the signals ricocheting through the system. Sometimes the signals are damped. But we keep on doing it. It's our job. It's anthropology that makes a difference.

Back in 1975, Miles Richardson (page 528-9) wrote that anthropologists stand on the fringes of our societies, at the edge of the light cast by the fire, and tell the stories of what we learn from moving with the people. With the passion of the radical, the practicality of the liberal, and the detachment of the scientist. (530).

Last week Suzan and I were in Vancouver for the annual meeting of the Society for Applied Anthropology. Over dinner with a colleague I mentioned my efforts to write this essay. He said that at meetings like that one and the AAA we hear lots about power, a little bit about class, and virtually nothing about struggle.

Like anything else, that can be over worked. Some of our union friends use that word "struggle" so much it gets comical, even to them. We started saying "Without struggle there is no struggle." People stop hearing the message. It's an important message. Anyone know the source? Abolitionist leader Fredrick Douglass.

If there is no struggle, there is no progress.

...Power concedes nothing without a demand. It never did and it never will. Find out just what a people will submit to, and you have found out the exact amount of injustice and wrong which will be imposed upon them; and these will continue till they are resisted with either words or blows, or with both. The limits of tyrants are prescribed by the endurance of those whom they oppress.

That was 1857. Sounds contemporary doesn't it? He also said that to want freedom without agitation is to want crops without plowing, rain without thunder, and the sea without the noise of the surf.

It seems to me that Douglass is saying pretty much the same thing Rappaport was saying about challenging the sanctity of systems that aren't working for the people in them. Later (1993) Rappaport said that real-world problems and research on American issues should be the center of anthropology because American problems reverberate around the world and affect many people.

Anthropology grew in the U.S. after World War II and exploded in the 1960s. By the 1970s anthropologists were working outside the academy (Parades and Higgins 2000:3). Nowadays fully half of us work somewhere outside the universities. In that we make a difference. We have to ask, make a difference for whom?

Some of us work for National Marine Fisheries Service. In 1976 Congress passed a law that set up the management of fisheries. A number of anthropologists were already working on those issues and helped set up fisheries management from the beginning. We're the ones who busted the economists' myth of the tragedy of the commons and showed how people are sufficiently reasonable to manage their own resources. The economists' myth couldn't stand the test of ethnography.

A number of us work for the Agency for International Development. One of my classmates left the academy in disgust at its petty politics and the power of undistinguished people who set themselves above more accomplished scholars. He took refuge with AID. He told me that we now have the tools to forecast famine and the means to prevent it. We can see civil strife coming a mile away. It's absurd not to use that knowledge in the furtherance of the wellbeing of our species.

We work with the Centers for Disease Control to figure out how people think about health and sickness. And what they do. We helped to create needle exchange programs to staunch the AIDS epidemic.

We work with businesses to figure out how people shop and what kinds of cars people like. We help the priests of gasoline spirituality figure out how to keep that religion alive. The only profitable airline, Southwest, has an anthropology department. So do Motorola, GM, Intel, and Xerox.

Like the species as a whole, Anthropology goes in contradictory directions, but it does make lots of differences. All of these folks share a concern with justice, equality, fairness. And most of them share a concern for scientific inquiry. Where anthropology makes a difference, we have to get it right.

Where does all this come from? Where did I get it? From what I learned from my first intro course through graduate school. From doing ethnography and reading ethnographies. From listening to you. From moving with the people of the planet and providing those signals to the powers that be. It comes from anthropology that makes a difference, anthropology that is part of the human ecology of the planet.

We learn it and then we teach it to those who follow. Southeast Asians who have learned any skill from ritual to carpentry pay respects to their teachers before they start a project. It behooves us all to pay respect to all of our teachers. Part of that respect is to pass on what we've learned with the same passion, wit, and dedication with which they gave it to us. Some of the lessons of a four field approach:

We are all one species. We are all related. We are truly brothers and sisters. When others speak of homelands we envision the whole species standing on each other's shoulders back at that original homeland of Olduvai.

We know about the role of cooperation in the evolution of our species. We know that societies are not based on the "application of scarce means to differentially graded ends to maximize the position of the actor vis-à-vis others" (Rappaport 1979:236). We know, in short, that economists are wrong, if powerful. Imagine patents on the atlatl, the Folsom Point, the Acheulean hand axe, wheat, rice, or the horse.

We know that our cultures define the worlds we live in. That idea has been enormously successful, even if not always in ways we imagined or favored. Did Boas imagine such rhetorics of corporate culture or multi-culturalism? But we have separated race from culture and shown that ways of thinking cannot be related to biology. That makes a difference.

And it is that half of anthropologists who work in the academy, who teach the intro courses, the capstone courses, the intermediate courses, the seminars and supervise honors, MA, and PhD theses who develop, test, and pass on these powerful ideas.

Anthropology gives us the empirical basis for a powerful ethical and political stance.

Every person deserves one share of the planet by virtue of being a person.

We document the social, political and economic arrangements people have devised and we understand departures from that measure. And why they failed. In our professional and personal lives we can move toward that ideal. In our academic and civic lives, we can enter the struggle for justice.

We can go through the curtains of the cultural dreamworks and see the systems behind them and how they operate to the benefit or detriment of our species.

All of this makes a difference in a society as dedicated as ours is to gasoline spirituality and the perpetuation of ignorance, fear, and conflict from which Marvin Harris said politics fashions our collective dreamwork. It is that dreamwork that prevents people from understanding what their social life is all about and keeps them mystified. That's why my students get increasingly uneasy as they read *Cows, Pigs, Wars and Witches* and have to confront their own dreamwork as dreamwork.

We can even show how corporations created the discipline of economics as an ideological bulwark to make their machinations seem natural, inevitable, and acceptable at the turn of the 20th century as

Dimitra Doukas did in her book, *Worked Over*. We can show that economics is a religion to sanctify corporate and government policies that have led our land and the rest of the world into unprecedented poverty and injustice.

We provide the empirical work that challenges these doctrines and brings to consciousness the sources of distress. Insofar as our work as anthropologists does that, it makes a difference.

So far I've been talking about ideas in books. Some people think of anthropology as a dialogue among books. I'm not one of them. I think of it as an active engagement with the realities of social, political and economic systems.

One of the challenges I face right now is how to approach the intro course. It's my turn again. I face a mass of students as consumers of education. These are the youngest kids or earliest grandchildren of the narcotized anomic teenagers Jules Henry studied. University administrators think they understand their market. They think students are there to consume a product. The administrators call on me to deliver the product.

I'm supposed to teach students how to serve their corporate masters. I'm supposed to persuade them they're consuming the product they're paying for. That it's OK to live in the dreamworld. They've grown up in the electronic age of not just television but the Internet where the attention span doesn't even need to stretch to the ten minutes between commercials but is more likely to be the thirty seconds of a commercial. I am supposed to be a component of their portfolio mass media entertainment along with their Gameboys, Ipods and instant messaging cell phones.

I'm not sure I'm up to the challenge. When it comes to other courses, I can structure discussions of books and carry on the dialogue. But in the intro course how do I get behind the dreamwork? How do I still the fear and conflict and dispel the ignorance?

I'll tell stories and show pictures and make graphs and explain things and hope some of it takes. I'll ask my teaching assistants to take the students into the real world to observe, record and understand what they see.

A challenge to all of us is to be able to articulate these ideas in a way that's as compelling in fifty years as Jules Henry and Walter Goldschmidt are today.

But we face a lot of the same challenges our ancestors did. We understand better than Boas could the realities of institutional racism, how a bunch of really nice people can perpetuate a system that discriminates against people because of the color of their skins. We understand how that system works, how schools belong to neighborhoods and depend on local taxes, how poor neighborhoods have poor schools and rich neighborhoods have good ones that get their kids to college to sit in my intro courses. That system doesn't depend on anyone's ideas. It doesn't depend on how nice the people are. If we want to change the realities of racism, we know it won't suffice to change anyone's ideas, we have to work to change the system itself.

We know better than Rappaport could have about the deterioration of the environment and the suppression of the signals in the regulatory system that could control it. We know about the suppression of science in favor of ignorance and conflict that benefits corporations and intensifies global warming. We know about the right wing think tanks that generate mind-fog and mystification as news and current events. We know about the mechanics of power that established them. Our challenge is to figure out how to change those.

Some of us try. Kendall Thu, Joe Heyman and others worked for years to establish a public policy institute within the American Anthropological Association. The idea is to make available what we know so that there is a point where it can enter the policy processes via grass roots organization, court cases, legislative decisions, agency rule-making, and executive understanding of phenomena. CSAS members supported these efforts with donations of money. It's taking shape. It's coming into being. One day it will be up and running and it will make a difference.

We know about globalization. We see it wherever we do fieldwork. We see the peasants we used to plant rice with working in factories. We see the migratory herders we used to ride with working in oilfields. We wear the clothes they make and burn the fuel they pump. We know how international finance has replaced substantive capital with money shamanics. We surf the multinational waves of labor with our informants.

We know about corporate power and the growing gulf between the working class and the ruling class that Goldschmidt described. It's incumbent on us to articulate those realities as they are and not disguise them behind polite phrasings to please the ruling class. We need to understand the war against working people as class war. We need to not blame the victims of these structures and processes for making bad choices. We need rather to change the structures.

It's difficult to think of class warfare in a country that doesn't admit to having classes. When people accuse others of inciting class warfare, they usually mean to silence someone who is speaking on behalf of the working class. They accuse the combatant of left-wing polemics for recognizing the reality of the war. That's like a B-29 pilot accusing a third-world peasant with a rifle in her hand of bad manners while the plane sprays the area with burning napalm, bullets, Agent Orange and high explosives. Fire, poison, bullets, and concussion are only one kind of terror.

Another terror is the haunting insecurity of hunger and sickness that stalk those who have only their labor to sell for whatever they may glean from a system designed to make rich people richer.

Most people here today have not experienced that life. But most in our country have. Most people who have lived that life couldn't afford the registration fee or the college education that lead one to want to be here. Or their high school education didn't prepare them for college. They don't usually go to college or read books.

But isn't that middle class itself an argument against class warfare? Most of us belong to it, after all. That's what the dreamwork says. Eighty percent of Americans control six percent of the wealth. What part of that eighty percent is the middle class? The top part? The top 1 percent of our population controls more than half of our wealth. The next 19 percent controls 44 percent. Maybe that's the middle class? The ones who work for the capitalist class to manage the rest of the working class? Those are the students sitting in our classes. Those are the ones we're supposed to teach to manage workers.

They're just as much working class as the rest of us. Just paid better for their labor. All of the debates about the significance of occupation, education, residence, leisure choices, food consumption, clothing and income avoid these basic facts of class. A few own resources; the rest of us work for them. Lots of us have written about the realities, the ethnography of working America. Others have written about the stark relationships of power that underlie the system from the origins of the first states to now.

What can we do about any of this? The chief weapon of the working class in this incessant war is the labor movement. From the collective action of their members Unions create power to stand against the power of ownership and wealth. A sign of capitalist success in the class war is the reduced numbers of workers that unions represent. What we can do is to try to move those numbers up rather than down when we get the chance. And we get that chance more often than we might think.

When your graduate assistants or colleagues try to organize a union, help them. I got a union organizer from AFT to do a session at the SfAA meeting on how to organize a union.

It's been several years since the colleagues of the executive board of the CSAS authorized me as president to request that the AAA meet only in hotels whose workers are represented by a union. That led to a motion that was adopted by a vast majority of other sections and finally became AAA policy. That policy was first tested in 2004 when the AAA was scheduled to meet at the San Francisco Hilton.

UNITE-HERE represents the workers at the San Francisco Hilton. The union was negotiating a new contract. The workers struck. Then the hotel locked them out, told them they could not return to their jobs. That's what was going on when AAA was supposed to meet there.

I had organized a session on unions. I polled the participants and we decided we'd do anything except go into that Hilton hotel to do an academic session on labor unions. We'd walk the picket line. We'd do our session on the sidewalk or in a park or a union hall, but we wouldn't go into that hotel. Many other colleagues felt the same way and let the AAA know it. Finally, the meeting was canceled and moved to Atlanta where the Society for Cultural Anthropology sponsored a session on the AAA and unions. That was the best attended session of the meeting.

AAA's canceling that contract with the San Francisco Hilton led a sea change among organizations as other academic organizations saw what we'd done and followed suit. It made a difference. It's still making a difference. The AAA established a Labor Relations Commission to keep the members and leaders informed about labor situations.

Nothing had changed by 2005 and the AAA had agreed to meet in the San Francisco Hilton again in 2006. It soon became clear that the Hilton chain had declared San Francisco a battle ground. They want to break the power of UNITE-HERE. Their strategy is to start unraveling the union by busting Local 1 in San Francisco. UNITE-HERE is strong in San Francisco. They're not going to be busted.

When the new Labor Relations Commission reported this situation, AAA leadership again canceled the contract with the San Francisco Hilton and moved the meeting to San Jose, California.

We, CSAS, led the way in this struggle. I'm proud of that. That is anthropology that makes a difference. And we did it. We are doing it.

Some may say what goes on with unions and hotels is none of our business. We're not union organizers, we're academics. We don't get involved in politics. That's fine. But then you can't be doing your job as an anthropologist either, not if it's anything like I've been talking about. Not if it involves being part of the feedback loop, not if it involves seeing things as they are and acting on that knowledge.

We can do other things as well. The Coca-Cola Corporation is busily busting unions in Columbia. One of the techniques they use is assassination. You can check various websites for the details. A number of universities have banned their products as a result of such draconian corporate policies. Penn State was already a Pepsi campus long before these facts came to light, so it's not been problematic there. They say the P of PSU stands for Pepsi. On that campus, it's a revolutionary act to drink a Coke. Such are the contradictions of human adaptation.

But the Labor Relations Commission has also recommended to the AAA leadership that we not allow contracting hotels or agencies to supply Coke products when we contract services with them. There are things we can do that can make a difference.

Suzan and I have been working with unions and telling their stories. Doing the ethnography. I've seen the class war in action at the negotiating table when management presented its proposals in terms of the corporate budget and workers presented theirs in terms of household needs. I've seen the economists try to convince the workers that they have to be "realistic," to confirm to a reality their religion defines, a religion the workers do not sanctify.

Our current project is telling the story of the longshoremen in Charleston, South Carolina. They joined the NAACP to demonstrate against flying the Confederate flag over the State House in Columbia late in 1999. At the same time, a Danish shipping company was trying to reduce its budget by contracting with a stevedore who promised to use non-union labor to unload the ships. The longshoremen picketed the non-union workers. The picketing continued until the Danish company felt threatened and asked for protection. Then the Ports Authority called the cops and 600 of them showed up in riot gear and black uniforms with dogs and helicopters.

The longshoremen responded and in the end there was an altercation. Rocks were thrown. Shields were lifted. Rocks were deflected. Tear gas was used. And so on. In the end the magistrate who heard the case found that there were misdemeanors, but nothing more. A second local magistrate agreed.

But the Republican Attorney General of the state had also been George Bush II's campaign manager. He was running a tight race against McCain. The next year, this Attorney General ran for the Republican nomination for governor. He wanted to use the case for publicity for his political campaigns. In this, perhaps the most anti-union state in the United States, this attorney general brought felony charges against five of the longshoremen. The president of the local union could not let his brothers lose their livelihoods, as they would if they were convicted. This move radicalized an otherwise easy-going if reform-minded union president. The militant ILWU in California immediately offered their support. The local president began looking for support in the labor movement and within his own union. The most responsive people were other dockers in other countries.

These dockers were organizing themselves at the time. In 1995 a group of longshoremen in Liverpool had been fired for refusing to cross a picket line. They never did get their jobs back. But, unemployed, they began to learn to use computers and the internet and began to organize other dockers in Sweden, Spain, Korea, Japan, Australia, and California. These dockers let it be known that if their brothers in Charleston went to trial, the world's ports would shut down and the global movement of containers that hold all of the consumer goods so dear to the hearts of consumer economies would halt in its tracks. The business community of Charleston pressured the Attorney General and he dropped his case against the five.

Those stories illustrate the structures of class and race, of business and unions so starkly and vividly that we want to tell them. They have a promising ending too, an ending where the good guys win.

Aren't my working class values getting in the way here? Nope. We're telling a story truthfully from all points of view. We've interviewed folks from the religious right that backed the attorney general's race for governor (he didn't win the primary to get nominated). We interviewed right-wing politicians. One in a quaint restaurant-bar. After he and his pal finished their lunch, he invited me to go fishing with them. I declined. As Suzan and I walked from the restaurant I explained to her that while I've done a lot for anthropology, there are some things I won't do. And going fishing with that individual was one of them. But we did interview him. He's on the record.

We interviewed clergy and in service of this project, we even went to church. With black folks and with white folks. But not at the same time. It is South Carolina. We've talked to legislators and business people. We've talked to folks from old families and interloping business people from the north. We're studying up. We went high up in a glass building that towers over the State House in Columbia to talk with the leaders of the Chamber of Commerce and learn about their jihad against labor. We went to Liverpool to a meeting of the international dockers to talk to the Spanish, Australian, and Californian dockers who were involved. So we don't see the story from just one point of view. If we did, it wouldn't be much of a story.

In our other work, we've used a lot of fancy statistics and methods to test any number of hypotheses about class and unions. We thought union members would be aware of their unions. They are not. Some anthropologists say that working people were more realistic in their thought processes than middle class managers. We wondered if they were right. They aren't. We thought class and union consciousness would go with activism. We were wrong. In short, in this project, every hypothesis I developed was proven incorrect. But that's how we know what we're talking about. That's what anthropology is all about. The one time our hypothesis was correct, we wished it wasn't.

The other day in a class on religion I asked students to think of a formulaic secular ritual they might have participated in. They immediately jumped to the pledge of allegiance. "Did you ever feel sort of funny when you said it?" I asked. Many nodded and some said they had at some point. I asked why. They said that it felt funny to pledge allegiance to a flag of a country that did the things our country was doing. There was some discussion of that.

Then I told them about using the word "republic" in a Scrabble game with my step-daughter and how we'd looked it up. She wanted to check the spelling because she doesn't accept my word for spellings. At least not in Scrabble games. I wanted her to think about the definition of the term. She was puzzling over it when I pointed out its role in the pledge of allegiance. Of course, she'd never actually *heard* the word.

But in my class I said that I don't mind pledging allegiance to a republic with liberty and justice for all. In fact I think that's a good idea. I think we ought to bend all of our efforts and all of our work to making that a reality.

Anthropologists know from our ethnographic work in this and other countries that the "realities" of the economists are corporate propaganda. We know that we don't in fact have a republic with liberty and justice for all any more than we have a government of the people, by the people and for the people. Our ethnography tells us that our self-image of one big prosperous if insecure middle class is inaccurate. We have many other ethnographic examples of inauthentic folk models. We know that people's cultures can and often do misrepresent realities.

We also know the process by which these misrepresentations are magnified and heightened and used against people in our own country. It's part of our jobs to continue to teach those realities to our students, to write them in our books. If the emperor has no clothes, why are we so bad at saying so?

Part of it is because of the language we use. A young colleague sent me a paper of his to read. He's working with a union and was talking about union matters. I read it and it was full of philosophical and ethnographic insights. But it was damned near unintelligible. I sent it back to him and told him to write it so one of his union sisters or brothers could read it and know what he meant. He admitted he was trying to be fashionably academic in his writing. I said it was more important to be clear and understood.

Later on I had occasion to give a talk near where he was working. He came to the talk with a friend of his, a union steward. After the talk, they came up to the podium to say hi. The young colleague introduced his union friend, a guy about my age.

The union guy said he'd read our book, *Class Acts*. He said, "That part about union politics?" That's where my breath caught in my throat for a minute. He continued, "You got that part about union politics just right. That was good to see. I'd often thought that myself but I never read it anywhere."

And, my friends, that's the best review Suzan and I could ever get for that book. My young colleague got the message of that review as well.

So I think we should keep on talking about power. But I think we should talk a good deal more about class. And I think we should engage in the struggle to make meaningful changes. That's what Suzan and I do in *Anthropology Unbound*. We hope lots of students will read it and learn from it. We hope it will help them see clearly as much as Marvin Harris's *Cows, Pigs, Wars and Witches* does. And we hope it will spur them to action—to enter the struggle.

As long as we do these things, I think we're doing anthropology that makes a difference. And we're fulfilling the promise of our ancestors and being worthy of the lessons they taught us.

We're far from the only ones. You're all involved in the effort as well and we thank you for the ideas, the exchanges, the critiques and the help we've gotten from each of you. It's at meetings like this that we huddle together at the edge of the camp fire and tell the stories of our species. It's here that we learn new stories to tell our students. It's here that we all make a difference. Thank you all.

Thank you.

References Cited

Doukas, Dimitra. 2003. Worked Over: The Corporate Sabotage of an American Community. Ithaca, Cornell University Press.

Durrenberger, E. Paul and Suzan Erem. 2005. Class Acts: An Anthropology of Service Workers and their Union. Boulder. Paradigm.

Goldschmidt, Walter. 1978. As You Sow: Three Studies in the Social Consequences of Agribusiness. Montclair, N.J., Allanheld, Osumn & Co.
2006. The Bridge to Humanity: How Affect Hunger Trumps the Selfish Gene. New York. Oxford University Press.

Hernry, Jules. 1963. Culture Against Man. New York, Random House.

Paredes, J. Anthony and Patricia J. Higgins. 2000. Introduction: Context and Vision for *Practicing Anthropology*. IN Classics of Practicing Anthropology: 1978-1998. Edited by Patricia

Higgins and J. Anthony Paredes. Oklahoma City, Society for Applied Anthropology. Pages 1-9.

Rappaport, Roy. 1979. Ecology, Meaning, & Religion. Berkeley, North Atlantic Books.

1993. The Anthropology of Trouble. American Anthropologist Vol 95. No 2:295-303.

Richardson, Miles. 1975. Anthropologist-The Myth Teller. American Ethnologist. Vol 2. No. 3:517-533.

Anthropology into the 21st Century:
Where we are and Where we're Going

2007 Keynote Address, Icelandic Anthropological Association[1]

Philip K. Dick was a science fiction writer of the late mid-20th Century who wrote on futuristic themes. Several of his stories have been made into films such as *Minority Report, Paycheck, Through a Scanner Darkly, Bladerunner (Do Androids Dream of Electric Sheep), Total Recall (*"We Can Remember it for you Wholesale"). Some of the social developments that he accurately foresaw were the warfare state, state spying, individual insecurity and socially induced paranoia and the related horrors that we see unfolding before our eyes in the first years of the 21st century in the U.S.

He had a sense that computers would somehow be important, but he failed to anticipate the most revolutionary changes in technology. The moviemakers have corrected for this by updating the technology, but in his books and stories, characters use typewriters, mainframe computers with punch cards that record data on spools of tape, telephones with wires and rotary dials, pay phones, cameras with film, and people smoke self-igniting cigarettes. Today the settings seem like curiously anachronistic worlds.

To emphasize the importance of technology in social evolution in the mid-19th century Karl Marx said that the windmill gives us feudalism but the steam mill gives us capitalism. In the 21st century, we have to ask what does the microchip give us beyond executives such as Bill Gates and Steve Jobs? Heaps of rubbish as cell phones and other devices that Philip K. Dick couldn't even imagine become instantly outdated? Everyone talking with someone else on cell phones? People doing everything on the internet?

Anthropologists understand lineages, clans, and moieties where they are the predominant social forms. One thing is certain about the 21st century: corporations have become dominant institutional form. Way beyond any kind of kinship organization; beyond even states. To understand anything else, we have to understand corporations.

[1] I gave a similar keynote address for the annual Pennsylvania State System of Higher Education Undergraduate Anthropology Conference at Mansfield University in 2008.

Canadian Jurist Joel Bakan argues that if they were persons, as U.S. law makes them to be, then we would have to diagnose them as being psychopathic because of the social damage they do in the pursuit of their own self-interest.

We know how corporations work and how they can create both upward and downward spirals of prosperity. Because anthropology is comparative, we know about economies that are not based on markets, even states whose systems of production were not based on markets. We know that states create markets via policy—and that a group of states recently created the global system via the Bretton Woods Agreements of 1944 that created WTO, World Bank, and IMF toward the end of the Second World War. We know how international finance works and how finance controls substantive economies in the global system. The Nobel laureate economist, Joseph Stiglitz, has written a couple of books about that.

We know how the global system works—we know the causal relationships and we know that they are complex and contradictory so that the whole system is chaotic, unpredictable if understandable.

Noble prize winning Turkish author Orhan Pamuk wrote of his homeland of Turkey:

> Their first step would be to establish a new state along the Bosporus and Dardanelles. But instead of bringing in new settlers as their predecessors had done a thousand years ago, they would turn old inhabitants into new people to serve their purposes. No need to read Ibn Khaldun; those charged with this task would quickly guess that the only way forward was to rip away our memories, our past, our history, leaving us with nothing to share but our misfortunes . . . . the new plan was to erode our collective memory with movie music.
> . . . women as beautiful as icons, the hymnlike repetition of images, and those arresting scenes sparkling with drinks, weapons, airplanes, designer clothes—put these all together and it was clear that the movie method proved far more radical and effective than anything missionaries had attempted in Africa and Latin America." (*The Black Book* 126-127)

He wants a coat worn by a new beautiful creature from a distant unknown land, so he can convince himself that he, too, can change, become someone new, just by putting on this coat…Turks no longer wanted to be Turks, they wanted to be something else altogether." (*The Black Book* 61)

It's the same in China where magazines and billboards portray glamorous working girls, *dagonme*, but where living conditions in factory dormitories are horrid as Pun Ngai describes in her ethnography of Chinese factory life, *Made in China*.

We anthropologists used to study peasants and tribesmen in faraway villages but now we study their daughters who are factory workers who make the electronic components for the world market for corporations or clothing in Sri Lanka, China, Thailand, Indonesia, Mexico.

Corporations spread to low wage areas where governments, in the control of elites who work with the corporate planners, insure a supply of stable and cheap labor, more people are more poor. Isn't it good for people to have a low paying job rather than no job at all? Anthropologists have studied communities where people grow everything they need to eat, communities where no one has anything like a job, where people get to keep what they produce. All of the gains in world income of the last decade went to the richest 20 percent while incomes at the bottom declined. So, no, it's not better to trade the poverty of self-sufficiency for the poverty of factory work, especially when it is accompanied by pollution and assaults on human rights.

The Gini coefficient measures inequality of income—the higher the coefficient, the greater the inequality of income. Northern Europe has the lowest Gini coefficients. Latin America and Africa have the highest inequality but the U.S. is not far behind with a rank of 92 between Costa Rica and Guinea-Bissau. And it's been getting higher and higher every day.

This system of global production that now includes us all gives us plentiful manufactured goods, corporate profits that a few at the top share, great poverty for most people on the planet, and massive pollution of waste products.

There has been a backlash in various populist movements in Latin America. The U.S. was so concerned by the success of Hugo Chavez in Venezuela that they sponsored a coup in 2002 similar to the 1973 CIA coup against Chile's Salvador Allende that replaced him with the military dictator Pinochet. In Niagara and Bolivia there have been widespread popular protests against attempts to privatize access to water.

Because of the backlash that shook the United States in 9/11/2001, the U.S. became obsessed with homeland security. The Patriot Act in the U.S. was part of a massive legal and propaganda program to quash dissent, legitimize a group of right wing radicals in the U.S. that stole two elections, and spread the American military-petroleum complex to the rest of the world by the terror of fire, bombs and bullets while keeping Americans compliant through fear of terrorists and of each other. Today's alert color is orange. Fear your neighbor.

That's why my wife, Suzan Erem and I wrote *Anthropology Unbound*, to move anthropology in the direction of addressing issues such as race, class, state propaganda, the religious right, the comparative study of states, corporations, the world system, and the production of poverty and ignorance—at the level of introductory courses. This is where we think anthropology should begin—we know the answers to the questions of the causes of poverty, war, and injustice. These are not mysteries. We need to teach them as the realities they are for the people of our planet.

One of the few balances to corporations is labor unions. Suzan and I started our study of them in 1995 in Chicago. When we found that their organization was highly centralized, we wanted to compare them with more democratic unions such as 1199P in Pennsylvania that organizes health care workers and Teamsters local 705 in Chicago that organizes truck drivers. So we discuss these results in the introductory book, again, to make it apparent that such topics have become the usual ones for anthropology—to move anthropology away from the image of the exotic savage to that of the person next door who used to have a job.

We continued the participant observation in union meeting rooms and picket lines and strikes even in our hometown of State College, PA where we kept up our blend of qualitative observation and participation with quantitative work. We're convinced that it is more than ever necessary to be able to state more than opinions and do more than tell stories.

The whole global system rests as much on container shipping as it does on computer chips. If information, orders, and capital can be sent with the speed of light anywhere on the planet, the same is not true of what comes out of the factories. Those products have to be put into containers that are stacked onto huge ships for shipment around the globe.

In Charleston, S.C. longshoremen are organized as part of the ILA. When a Danish company tried to use non-union labor, the longshoremen picketed and a massive police response in January 2000 escalated into what some call a riot. An ambitious state's attorney who was running for governor made this into a major case.

Listen to Orhan Pamuk again:

> You can even imagine your own face in those faces, can't you? How many we are, how much anguish we all carry, and how helpless most of us are in the face of the world! (*The Black Book* 269)

Meanwhile, dockers around the world were organizing and formed the International Dockers Council which threatened to shut down world ports if the prosecution continued. Dockers in Spain, Sweden, Korea, Japan, California, and other lands organized together to form a network of locals in spite of their own larger national and international organizations.

That's the story Suzan and I tell in our new book, *On the Global Waterfront*. It is a story about race, class, political ambition, the religious right, and corporate power and labor in the global system, a story with an optimistic end. The reason we decided to tell the story is because it's so difficult to find optimism in today's world.

Meanwhile, income inequality in the U.S. and around the world increases and people respond—starting with demonstrations at the WTO meeting in Seattle in 1999 when labor and environmentalists made an alliance against the WTO and continuing until the G8 meeting last year in Germany. And armies of police meet these people with tear gas and clubs.

So, as we move into the 21st century, we already know the dynamics of corporations, states, wealth and poverty. It's up to us to provide the ethnographic details, and we can and must do that. But in addition, many of us understand that it's not enough to provide information to policy makers, it's up to us to help organize as well—to use the technological revolution of the microchip to organize via the internet, via cell phones, and via face to face connections to continue and enlarge the resistance to these negative processes so that more of us can benefit from the positive things we find in the systems. The immediate objective must be to get the U.S. out of Iraq. That war is destroying our economy, the credibility of our government, and the people who serve in the military. It's killed more than 4,000 of our people and more than half a million Iraqis. It has made some corporations that produce nothing very rich through various forms of corruption that have looted the American treasury.

How do we bring them home? As one Marine officer who had just returned said, "With ships and planes." But not to quibble about when or how. That just reflects corporate power. And that's what anthropology needs to understand, communicate, and organize to resist.

By the end of the century we may all be buried in garbage, but there's always optimism in anthropology because one century's garbage is another's archaeology.

Last Wall to Fall:
The Anthropology of Collective Action and Unions in the Global System

2009 *Journal of Anthropological Research* 65(1).

Preface

I want to talk about how in the process of my quest to understand economic systems from the worm's eye view of fine-grained local ethnography I went from the exotic borderlands of Southeast Asia to the mundane heartland Chicago labor unions and learned the necessity of understanding local events in terms of global processes. I'll show the role of collective action theory, critique that theory, discuss barriers to collective action and show and how in my most recent work, it's been necessary to keep both the local details and the global processes in focus to understand the reasons that there is still one barrier to otherwise unbridled neoliberal free marketers. To show relationships among states, class structures, global process and locales requires attention to the details of local ethnography as well as the larger scale causal forces.

Southeast Asia

My first fieldwork was in highland Southeast Asia, in the Golden Triangle where the borders of Burma, Laos, and Thailand come together just south of China.

During the Second World War, British anthropologist Edmund Leach was in the highlands of Burma organizing Kachin guerillas against the invading Japanese. He later used that experience, his twice reconstructed notes, and archival materials to write *Political Systems of Highland Burma* (Leach 1954) which challenged the varieties of functionalism then current in the U.K.

He argued that highland ethnic groups and locales were so dynamically involved with lowland Buddhist kingdoms, lowland Shan principalities, and the Silk Road from China that they could only be understood as a region. He gave us the notion of Kachin villages oscillating between hierarchic *gumsa* and egalitarian *gumlao* forms and under certain conditions *gumsa* groups becoming lowland Shan.

Political Systems was published in 1954 and described a fairly orderly if dynamic region. Highland Burma had been conquered by the

British, then invaded by the Japanese who helped nationalists such as Ne Win and Aung San organize an army contra the British. The army changed sides to help the British against the Japanese, and became the backbone of the new independence government under U Nu before it split. Finally, the army took complete power in 1962. The army remains in power today. After the coup, virtually all of the ethnic states went into armed rebellion that continues to this day. Add to this the arrival of the American backed Nationalist Chinese Kuomintang (KMT) in 1949 after the victory of the Communists in China and we see a dynamic region that is incorporated into the ebbs and flows of global historical developments.

So, far from a stable system of any kind, from this vantage point, we see a series of local polities forming and reforming as they alternately resist or abet British and Japanese invaders, elements of the independence government, a military dictatorship, long-standing revolutionary actions against it, and a drug-dealing armed force with sometime American backing.

I read about these things in books and journal articles and heard about them from my professor, Kris (F.K.) Lehman at the University of Illinois and from my Burmese teacher, Maran LaRaw, himself a Kachin who had close up knowledge of the violence in Burma that cost him one hand.

These events and ideas were interesting background for area studies, but never entered my understanding of the anthropology of the place except insofar as fieldwork in Burma was impossible while Ne Win was in power. Current events were the stuff of political science or journalism, a parallel track that did not intersect with ethnography.

I see the problem

I first went to Thailand in 1967 under Kris's tutelage. I had heard about the various rebellions in Burma as soon as we arrived in Chiangmai. Kris even called on the Burmese consul to assure him that we would be not fomenting rebellion just across the border in Thailand. We took up residence in a Shan village not far from the border. At that time there were no bridges across the rivers or roads beyond the province capital of Maehongshon. My main disappointment was that nobody spoke Burmese. So I started learning Shan.

One morning, I saw elephant tracks in the muddy trail that led to a gasoline-powered rice mill. People answered my inquiries about the elephant with blank stares and denials. I pointed to the piles of dung among the tracks and met with shrugs. Another morning, I saw the elephant patiently chewing on the thatched roof of the miller's house while waiting to be loaded with bags of milled rice. I learned that in fact every other day the elephant came to the village to carry rice to the Shan States Army (SSA). As it turned out, a number of residents of the village were former SSA soldiers.

In 1968, I returned to Northern Thailand, this time to the highlands where I lived in a Lisu village where people grew opium that they sold to the KMT. One day, a KMT horse caravan from the lowlands delivered my mail from Chiangmai.

In the mail was a news magazine with an article about heroin in New York. Some Lisu asked what it was about. I said it told about what happened to opium when it reached my country. They asked what price it would fetch. The article quoted the street price in New York. I did some calculations to convert raw opium to number 1 heroin base and then to street heroin and then converted dollars to baht and then baht to silver in the form of India rupees and calculated the volume of the silver in them and finally announced that the local unit, a *joi*, about 2.2 kg., would fetch silver enough to fill the house to about knee level. There was a long silence before one old man asked, "How long does it take to walk to New York?"

This village in the back end of nowhere was even then part of a global system, whether its residents knew it or not. The price of a *joi* of opium varied with the intensity of U.S. Drug Enforcement Agency (DEA) enforcement efforts and the cooperation of Thai officials, often themselves involved in the trade. By then, the CIA was actively running drugs from Thailand into Vietnam to help fund Marshall Ky and arms were flowing from Laos and Vietnam in return for heroin and opium from Thailand and Burma. The revolutionary groups battled with the KMT for control of the trade and the right to tax it. To them, opium meant access to food and arms with which to continue their struggles against Ne Win's dictatorship.

Refugees flowed from Burma into Thailand to establish new villages or to join existing ones. Across the highlands there was a boom in population as refugees from an American secret war began to stream in from Laos. Scouting parties from the village where I lived would go in search of better lands and return with news that they had only met other scouting parties from other villages. There were no new forests to which to move.

I visited a number of Lisu villages and found that the longer a village had been in place, the more opium it grew and the less rice. Their swiddening had exhausted the possibilities for rice, but, since they could grow opium poppies repeatedly on the same fields, they turned to opium to get money with which to purchase rice from lowlanders (Durrenberger 1979a, 1979b). Leach was right; I couldn't comprehend the economy of any village without appreciating its position within the whole region (Durrenberger 1974).

I was aware of the connections between Lisu opium growers and an American War in Southeast Asia, but even when I read McCoy's work (1972, 2003) on the global narcotics trade, I had not incorporated a global perspective into my ethnographic work. None of this—Lisu opium production, KMT trafficking, CIA involvement, Mafia networks, "the French Connection"—was anything economists could discuss. It was the informal economy that you can only see from the streets, villages, and war zones.

By the time I returned to Shan in 1976 there were a paved airstrip, roads, bridges and regular transportation into the hinterlands of Maehongson Province. Shan had stopped double-cropping rice and started growing vegetables to sell in the capital. The KMT and SSA were still active however, and now and then the Thai would send some Border Patrol Police or some helicopters to check out the situation on the border. One generation gave way to the next, who grew up with the new realities that continual revolution established. Shan villagers who owned irrigated fields routinely recruited refugee Shan from Burma for contract or wage labor and many people in the Shan village where I lived had no proper identity papers because they'd come from Burma or China.

Perhaps because he was forced to be mobile, Edmund Leach had managed to transcend the village as a unit of analysis to discuss the region, but he could not foresee what was to come, even as he was writing his book, because he did not situate the Shan States of Burma in the context of events or structures in China, Britain, France, the U.S. or Thailand, or take into account state polices or responses to them.

That may be asking a bit much for an anthropologist cum intelligence officer organizing irregular forces behind enemy lines, but at about the same time half-way around the world in Libya, E. E. Evans-Pritchard was posted as a political officer to the British Military Administration of Cyrenaica, where he traveled among the Bedouin tribes.

Evans-Pritchard discusses (1949) the last days of the Ottoman Empire, the young Turks, the new Republic, British and Italian Colonial ambitions in the context of Europe, the rise of Fascism, evolving Ottoman and Italian policies, administrative systems and styles, and how the relationships between the Sanusi religious order and tribal Bedouin developed in response to these global processes-- resulting in the formation of the state of Libya.

His book, *The Sanusi of Cyrenaica* was published in 1949, but there was no way he could foresee the discovery of oil in the region or the impact of American oil interests and geopolitics in the area, the army's revolution of 1969 or their impact on Bedouin herder-agriculturalists (Benhke 1980). Philip Carl Salzman (2001:37) sums up the contribution of Evans-Pritchard's Cyrenaican work well when he writes that he, "...demonstrates that an understanding of culture and structure alone are not sufficient for explaining human destinies; as well, we must take into account the agency and acts of the multiple parties and the events these generate."

Anthropologists know things the same way other people do—by doing. Leach and Evans-Pritchard were learning by their engagement in intensely political processes, not just by interviewing. Questions of investigator-or objectivity may only come up when the results lend credence to subordinate rather than more powerful groups, but many argue that involvement can only increase validity and reliability (Singer 1995).

Whatever your own sense of involvement or agency or causality, if you act according to local ideas of gods, you may get treated like a god. But if you act like a god who doesn't know how to be a proper god you get killed. While Captain Cook may have died of it, it probably wasn't an issue for many of his sailors (Sahlins 2000).

This reminds me of the story about the execution of the priest, the drunk, and the engineer during the French Revolution. The executioner takes them to the guillotine and asks the priest, "Face up or face down?" "Face up," he says, "so I can look toward heaven." The executioner pulls the lever and the blade rushes down...but stops just short of the priest's neck. The executioner says, "It must be divine intervention," and frees the priest. The drunk figures he'll try the same thing, and it works for him. Then comes the engineer, who has been watching intently. He also opts to be face up. The executioner hoists the blade and it's almost ready to drop when the engineer says, "Wait! I see the problem."

If our problem as anthropologists has been insufficient concern for global processes, we have to be careful that we don't sound our own death knell and forget the value of ethnography. Local ethnography is often one end of a thread that leads us into a complex web of relationships of locales, governments, corporations, NGOs, and international agencies, none of which are very accessible to our favorite methods of participant observation, though those methods do reveal ways to understand agencies' documents and statistics (Haraldsdottir 2002)

Without the worm's eye view of local ethnography, we would not even be able to ask questions about gods because all we would have is measurements determined by someone else's sense of what to count. Do economists count gods? Without ethnography, we would be more or less like economists expecting reality to conform to their airy abstractions because in some sense, it just should, and we would be just as surprised or unfazed when reality fails to comply and the gods all die or the economists all get lynched.

To understand events such as these in Burma and Thailand requires more than more ethnography, even ethnography in many places. We need to change our perspective so we can see the causal forces and how they interact with local people and cultures.

I want now to turn to a theory of collective action.

Collective action theory

Anthropologists agree that culture is collective, though we may question what group of people shares it (Hannerz 1996). But there's quite a leap from collective thought to collective action. We often talk about collective action without theorizing it explicitly. Many discussions of states contain the nucleus of Morton Fried's (1967) definition of the institutional structures that guarantee to one class privileged access to resources. That definition suggests collective action on behalf of a ruling class. As railroad baron Jay Gould said more bluntly in 1896 during a strike, "I can hire one half of the working class to kill the other half." He was aware of class. But collective action theorists don't seem to raise their gaze beyond the horizon of face-to-face communities.

Malinowski (1922) called his external understandings of Trobrianders "sociological" to distinguish them from Trobrianders' internal views that he termed "ethnographic." Economic theorists generally assume that the world mirrors their own constructions and don't make such fine distinctions. But political economists such as Elinor Ostrom distinguish categories of goods according to two continuous criteria which they take to be intrinsic to the things themselves:

• Excludability—how easy it is to deprive others from using the resource and

• Subtractability—the extent to which one person's use of a resource precludes someone else using it (Ostrom et alia1994).

The intersection of these two criteria defines a four by four table of possibilities (Table 1):

Subtractability

	high	low
Excludability difficult	common pool	public
easy	private	toll

Table 1
Four Possible Categories of Goods

Those goods from which it is difficult to exclude others' use and are highly subtractable are common pool resources. The classic example is fisheries resources (Acheson 2003). If one person takes fish from the sea, there are fewer for the next person, and it is difficult to police the seas. Theoretically, there need be no institutional structure associated with common pool resources and economists usually assume that there is none.

Goods of low subtractablity and difficult excludability are public goods. Police protection and education are examples that Ostrom (1997) develops. If everyone enjoys the good and it is not possible to exclude anyone, there must be some way to fund its production—typically via taxation—which assumes functioning institutional structures to organize the production of public goods and to tax those who benefit. The other two categories of goods are private property (high subtractability, easy excludability) and toll goods (low subtractability, easy excludability).[2]

---

[2] I can't fully develop this idea here, but I want to mention that I missed the mark in my critique of Ostrom. The night after the lecture, I awoke in the middle of the night with the thought that I'd used the standard anthropological critique that in her definitions of terms Ostrom had not honored the cultural variability that we see ethnographically. There's nothing wrong with that critique; it is what brought some reality to the discussion of the tragedy of the commons and showed that it isn't necessary or universal. But I think that Ostrom's arguments are more deeply flawed than just taking insufficient account of ethnographic facts in the definitions of her categories. Economists Stiglitz and Galbraith are some who have suggested that if economics had a feedback loop between theory and fact in the manner of scientific inquiry, it would have ceased to exist. That it hasn't suggests that it is an ideology akin to religion rather than a science.

The main flaw is in the basic assumption of economics, methodological individualism, the idea that institutions are the totality of individual decisions and their outcomes. Other anthropologists have argued more eloquently than I can that this assumption is a cultural artifact of capitalism, not a fact or even a reasonable assumption. Sahlins (2000) devotes an essay to the cultural matrix and history of the underlying assumptions of the dismal science. Doukas (2003) shows that economics as a discipline is an important component of the corporate sponsored cultural revolution that I discussed in the lecture. It was promoted by the backers of the revolution to achieve scientific status for the doctrine of wealth that would serve their purposes so well. Rappaport (1979:236) points out that economics defines rationality as competitive activities that pit people against each other and is, by necessity, anti-social.

Thus economics defines a kind of humanity that is quite different from the social animals that anthropology knows—creatures that evolved over five million years. The evolutionary view of humanity has the strong helping the weak in the image of the kind of solidarity that I discussed. Goldschmidt argues that what made us human is the selective advantage that flexibility conferred on groups whose members could be more committed to serving group interests than replicating themselves—groups that were more committed to collective action than individual advancement.

Everything human, Goldschmidt argues, takes place in the "gap between the encoded genetic instruction and behavioral performance" (18) In that fissure is culture, collective thought Goldschmidt argues that we learn culture because of an inborn necessity to please those who are trying to teach—affect hunger. The individuals and groups that could not transcend the first competitive evolutionary imperative—the selfish gene--with cooperation—collective action-- have long since perished, unable to be sufficiently responsive to changing conditions of time and space.

In this sense collective action is part of our species evolutionary history. What needs to be explained is not collective action, but any departures from it. Thus, the question we should try to answer is, "Why are there economists?" and other *departures* from collective action.

As anthropologists, we understand that cultural usage defines subtractability and excludability and that different practices may define the same goods in different ways. Or, as Marx (1976) put it, property is a social relationship. For instance, in medieval Iceland, land was not a good that was easy to exclude others from using because there was no institutionalized state to make it so. The only means for enforcing claims to exclusivity was whatever force one could muster through coalitions of armed fighters, which was costly even though it did result in lots of good stories that come down to us as sagas.

Policy can change a good's position in the matrix. For instance, fish were a common pool resource in Iceland until 1990 when the government enacted a system of Individual Transferable Quotas (ITQs) that redefined them as private property.

Bonnie McCay (1998:193) observes that the limitations of the work of the "political economy" theorists is their "high and sometimes misleading levels of abstraction from empirical cases" which often omit what we learn via ethnography—significant details of how political and economic factors are embedded in social relations and cultural constructs.

This is perhaps an inevitable consequence of our anthropological penchant to relativize everything, or, conversely, to economists' proclivity for ethnocentrism, projecting capitalist ideological categories as absolutes. Anthropologists are likely to ask where slaves fit and who says so. And so with the labor that each person controls.

We can understand excludability and subtractability in material terms such as arable land and fish. But what happens when we move into the more rarified atmosphere of finance in which even the "objects" are abstractions of abstractions such as shares of corporate stock, or financialized bundles of mortgages? By definition, and only by definition, things like money and stocks are commodities that people buy and sell on markets. That they are so by definition makes them cultural constructs akin to gods. But upon them are built global financial markets.

The owners of capital are the ones with the power to define such objects. Out of such definitions they have created great wealth. At least lots of money. Whether money is the equivalent of wealth is a different matter, but it does pretty well here in the U.S. even in the early 21st century. This manipulation of cultural categories and objects is collective action on behalf of the capitalist class.

In the 1980s the finance economy built of these fictions became more important than the substantive economy of producing things. In 2004-6 financial services represented 21 percent of the U.S. GDP and manufacturing 13 percent (Phillips 2008). With their talk of realism and bottom lines, the money shamans took over corporations (Durrenberger and Erem 2007: 236).

When there's something like the sub-prime mortgage melt-down of the early 21st century, when the market shamans and priests start lying and cheating until they can't even believe themselves any longer, the whole system collapses. It's as if our gods have abandoned us.

How are we to imagine massive government transfers of money into the system in terms of common property? If the money is public funds, a public good in Ostrom's terms, and the public now has controlling interest in the financial sector, do we not in some sense own it? That must have Marx and Lenin dancing in their graves. For all the bad-mouthing of these founders of Communism, capital eventually consolidated itself and fell right into collective hands, though not in the way Marx and Lenin anticipated. So, as the headline of the conservative British newspaper, *The Daily Telegraph* of October 9, 2008, dryly proclaimed, "We're all Socialists now, Comrade." Just what kind of socialists remains a bit unclear.

The provision of public goods may engender debate about just how to achieve the goals, but most academic work does not acknowledge what we see ethnographically and historically— opposition to collective goals. No one, the collective action literature suggests, opposes the existence of community police forces, fire departments, or schools, though they may oppose taxation. Nor has there been meaningful opposition to the global financial bail-outs of recent days. On the other hand, Jay Gould was a harbinger of things to come: there is massive and sometimes violent opposition to unions.

The collective action theorists do not discuss collective action on behalf of classes, but what else is the National Association of Manufacturers or the Chambers of Commerce that represent corporate interests (Fones-Wolf 1994) other than collective action to transform our culture (Doukas 2003) and to use the collective means of government for their own corporate ends?

Nor does the academic literature discuss the consequences of the capture of public apparatus for the benefit of private interests—e.g. the so-called "out-sourcing" of functions such as police, prisons, education, and military or government bailouts of irresponsible lending agencies to preserve their grasp on wealth at public expense. The collective action theorists seem to see these matters as parts of natural processes rather than historically given cultural or political ones or as collective action on behalf of one class.

Labor and collective action

Slaves are private property by definition. In the U.S., abolitionists tried to change the ownership of the person and his or her labor from the master to the slave but in a market system, the individual's labor was still a private good. Labor unions originated to amplify the negligible power of individuals who have nothing but their labor to sell. By joining together, such individuals can bring the force of their collective action to represent their interests versus the owners of capital. As in the segmentary lineages Evans-Pritchard described, the byword for unions is solidarity, because their strength depends on the joint action of all in the support of any individual. The slogan, "an injury to one is an injury to all," characterizes the central role of solidarity. To be effective, action must be collective.

Eugene V. Debs articulated this in 1905 at the organizing meeting of the Industrial Workers of the World (IWW) in Chicago when he said "The Industrial Workers is organized not to conciliate but to fight the capitalist class…." (quoted in Kornbluth 1964:1) Bill Haywood was blunt in stating the IWW goal of overthrowing rather than negotiating with in the capitalist system to replace capitalist class with working class control of the political economy Kornbluh1964: 1).

But today, conciliation and negotiation are the unions' stock in trade. Fifty years ago, C. Wright Mills observed that union members were interested in unions as a means to the individual goal of increasing their remuneration rather than as a "collective means of collective ascent" (Mills 1951:309). There is little ethnographic evidence to suggest any difference today (Durrenberger and Erem 2005). From the point of view of workers, unions are like insurance companies to protect them individually. For their part, unions became professionalized bureaucracies whose leaders are hard to distinguish from their counterparts in the corporate world.

How did this transformation from a social movement on behalf of a class to a self-satisfied bureaucracy happen?

There were at least three related processes:

1. violent opposition

2. a corporate-sponsored cultural revolution to redefine economic consciousness to focus on individual rather than collective interests

3. a corporate legislative program to redefine labor's legal position.

The violent chapters of our history have largely been purged from our consciousness, but archaeologist Dean Saitta (2007) is reviving some of them by his work at the Ludlow massacre site in Colorado. Jay Gould wasn't just kidding about hiring half of the working class to kill the other half. But if he did that, he would kill the goose that laid his golden eggs because there would be nobody to work for him. The job was to kill and imprison enough to intimidate the rest and buy off the rest of them with privileges.

The IWW came out against the First World War on the principle that working people should not fight a capitalists' war. The socialist slogan was, "A bayonet is a weapon with a working man at both ends." In 1917 the Justice Department simultaneously raided forty-eight IWW halls and arrested 165 leaders for conspiring to hinder the draft and encourage desertion. A hundred of them were tried and convicted in 1918 and given prison terms of up to 20 years. Bill Haywood jumped bail and went to the Soviet Union. The rest were lynched or arrested during the Palmer raids of the 1920s (Boyer and Morais 1955)

Rather than killing half of the working class, the owners of capital could hire them to manage the other half of the working class, offer them sufficient privileges that they would not continue to identify with the working class, and define an appropriately comfortable and self-congratulatory individualistic ideology for them to live by within the capitalist system.

Since the turn of the 20th century, there has been what Dimitra Doukas (2003) calls a cultural revolution in the U.S. to replace the "gospel of work," —the idea that labor creates all value—with the "gospel of wealth," namely the notion that capital creates wealth. I'll come back to the gospel of work. Unstintingly sponsored by trusts and fledgling corporations, this cultural revolution has been largely successful (Durrenberger and Doukas 2008). The American working class concurred with the self-congratulatory ideology of individual merit that the cultural revolution and the managerial class promoted (Durrenberger 2001).

The Wagner Act of 1935 gave labor the right to organize, but the corporate-sponsored Taft-Hartley Amendments of 1947 redefined the role of unions as negotiating and enforcing contracts on behalf of their members to specify the terms and conditions of their work. This legislation made unions responsible for seeing that their members adhered to the contracts, especially that they did not strike during the term of the contract. Corporate America had bought labor peace and unions became bureaucracies for resolving grievances that arose between workers and management.

So together, the focused violence, the cultural revolution and the legislative campaign redefined unions from social movements to benefit the working class to allies of corporations to provide contracts for and to control their members. This alliance disguised and denied both the existence of classes and the necessity of class struggle and curtailed traditions of direct action. The Cold War enhanced this partnership between labor and capital, and union leaders even joined in the "red-baiting" and purges of progressives from the labor movement to inculcate a climate of fear that was consistent with the McCarthy period (Fletcher and Gapasin 2008)

From the point of view of union members, the contract is a public good analogous to community police services, and unions face some of the same problems that communities do, for instance, how to finance the institutional means for producing the public or collective good. As with many other goods, policy defines whether union representation is a collective good or not.

In the 1950s, corporate interests began to support so-called "right-to-work" laws that passed in a third of the states. In these states, unions can represent workers, but workers are not required to pay for union services. Thus, only that portion of workers who are union members pay for the services such as increased wages and benefits that benefit their non-dues-paying fellow-workers. Imagine opting out of paying your local property taxes and still having police and fire protection and sending your children to public schools.

Other states, without "right-to-work" laws, require that workers pay at least their "fair share" of the costs, usually a large portion of union dues. Still other states require that if workers at a site elect a union to represent them, all workers must be members and pay dues (i.e., "closed shops").

An argument for closed shops, based on the logic of provision of a public good, is that all should pay for the benefits they receive. An argument against them, based on individualistic ideology, is that to require such payment is an infringement of individual rights.

For unions, the financial issue includes the institutional wherewithal to pay people to negotiate and enforce contracts. The riddle for unions in "right-to-work" states is whether to expend resources to bargain on behalf of *all* workers in a worksite where only *some* of them pay for the benefits, or to not represent any of the workers. Many opt to represent all workers in the hope that in the long term, the majority will pay their way, and that the union may grow strong enough and have enough political influence to change the "right-to-work" law. Clearly this approach imposes costs on current members for longer term goals that benefit non-members. This is also collective action to influence government on behalf of one class.

One of the problems of the contemporary union movement is that the ability to negotiate and enforce contracts depends on the power of unions to control certain segments of the labor market. For instance, if all janitors in an area belong to a union, that union has the power to negotiate good contracts for all. But if only some janitors belong to the union, employers have the option of using non-union workers or contractors. This was the difference between the very favorable pay and benefits in the late 1990s that downtown Chicago janitors enjoyed, compared to the unhappy conditions of work of suburban ones. Thus one of the goals of Chicago's Service Employees International Union (SEIU) Local 1, which I studied in the late '90s (Durrenberger 2002) was to organize all suburban janitors in an effort to protect the higher wages and benefits of the downtown janitors. To protect themselves, the strongest—the downtown janitors—had to extend protection to the weakest, the suburban janitors.

But such organizing requires resources that might otherwise be used to provide services to current members. This poses a collective action dilemma because it imposes costs on current members for the long term future benefit of the collective. With their dues, current members underwrite the organization of future members.

The confluence of the violence, the cultural revolution and corporate sponsored policy was not sufficient to obliterate the union movement. Another policy change undid even the pretense of the power of labor. Since President Reagan busted the air traffic controllers union in 1981 with the use of replacement workers, there has been an organized attack on unions in the U.S. Having become as complacent as Mills suggested they would, unions failed to respond effectively to the assault and corporate interests organized even more virulent means for attacking unions (Brodkin and Strathmann 2004). A multi-million dollar industry of anti-union consulting has grown in the U.S. since the 1990s. Two out of three organizing efforts face the opposition of such firms (Logan 2002, 2006) and unions have yet to organize a successful response beyond collusion with management in so called top-down organizing. The labor movement's loss of class focus has translated into a loss of political power.

The last wall

The Berlin Wall and then the Soviet Union fell. In succeeding years, the walls of currency restrictions and tariffs fell. There was little to restrain the neoliberal free markets. Some saw the withering away of the state, but a withering that Marx never could have imagined as the World Bank and the IMF assumed financial power over previously independent states (Durrenberger and Erem 2007).

As the microchip revolution made speed of light communication possible corporations began to relocate manufacturing to low-wage and low-regulation areas. When currencies were freed to float against each other on the world market, finance took on new importance, and soon finance gained ascendency over management in corporations and the substantive economy of production was uncoupled from the dynamics of money (Durrenberger and Erem 2007).

Even if money could be abstracted from substance to flow at the speed of light, material goods still had to be moved around the planet. The spread of systems of container freight facilitated the consolidation of shipping into fewer hands as corporations began to move their wares and raw materials around the planet in giant ships piled high with large boxes that could be identified by barcodes, loaded and unloaded by massive cranes, and delivered almost anywhere by attaching them to trucks or railcars.

In 1995 dockers in Liverpool were fired for not crossing a picket line. A new Thatcher administration policy made it legal to fire them for upholding such a basic tenet of union solidarity. Finding no support in their own national union (the Transportation and General Workers' Union of Great Britain and Ireland, TGWU) or the international federation to which it belonged (International Transport Workers' Federation, ITF), they continued to search until they found other dockers in Europe who were also in search of alternatives to their ineffective national and international unions, as they faced the prospect of the privatization of dock facilities in the European Union (EU).

During the next six years, representatives of the Liverpool and other European longshoremen met to organize an alliance of longshoremen's locals that went "under" the national and international organizations to create solidarity among locals without higher level intermediaries. This is the International Dockworkers Council (IDC). They were not the only ones to try to deal with ineffective union organizations.

In early January of 2000, four members of Charleston, South Carolina's mostly Black International Longshoremen's Association Local 1422 and one member of its sister union Local 1771 were arrested and charged with felony crimes for their protests against the Nordana Shipping Company (a Danish concern) using non-union workers. Their dock-side action was a response to what many saw as a provocation in the massing of a police force of more than 600 to confront their picketers. Knowing that he could not weather the coming fight alone, the local's newly elected president, Ken Riley, began to search for solidarity. It was no more forthcoming from the civil rights movement than from his own International Longshoremen's Association (ILA) or the overarching American Federation of labor-Congress of Industrial Organizations (AFL-CIO).

Because Ken Riley was active in a movement to reform the notoriously organized crime-affiliated East Coast ILA, he was anathema to the incumbent power structure. When he asked for their support, they were slow to respond. The AFL-CIO pled that they were bound by protocol and procedural rules and could not respond without the sponsorship of the national level union to which the local belonged.

The January 2000 events on the Charleston docks captured brief national media attention in the U.S. The morning after the arrests longshoremen in a California International Longshore and Warehouse Union (ILWU) local, heirs of the IWW, offered their support and, in the tradition of independent and direct action defied their international union association.

Meanwhile, by 1999, the European dockers were ready to incorporate the International Dockworkers Council. One of the ILWU activists suggested that IWW-style direct action would win ILWU's support of the IDC.

Meanwhile, an expatriate American in England had worked with the Liverpool dockers to develop a web-based clearinghouse for international labor news. He found that a Nordana ship that had loaded in Charleston was to call at Barcelona and Valencia, two key IDC ports.

Four months after the confrontation on the Charleston docks, when the Nordana ship arrived, Barcelona dockers refused to unload it. Because the ship had not been professionally loaded, they explained, they could not safely unload it. This action put the company on notice that Spanish union members would refuse to work ships that had been loaded by non-union workers on the legally acceptable grounds that it would be unsafe. Furthermore, the company's ships would meet the same response in other European ports if it did not resume using ILA workers to load their ships in Charleston.

Unaware of the IDC, Riley was surprised when the shipping company quickly agreed to resolve its differences with the union. The IDC had shown that dockworkers' locals responding to each other with direct action was more effective than the moribund national and international federations and associations of the Cold War era. So, in June of 2000, when the IDC held its founding convention in the Canary Islands, Ken Riley and the ILA 1422 Vice President attended and met their fellow workers from 85 ports in 13 countries. The west coast ILWU came on board as well.

The independence of West Coast ILWU locals allowed them to respond quickly, and its open and democratic nature allowed the international association to follow suit after its initial objection. On the contrary, the personalistic and hierarchical organization of East Coast ILA not only paralyzed it, but also moved it to act counter to the interests of its members and made it impervious to their influence.

The lesson is the same one we learn from the ethnography of fisheries and water management, namely that while democratic and independent organizations can extend flexible and timely responses, hierarchic and personalistic ones cannot.

Global solidarity has been born of waterfront unions because of the inadequacy of the response of their national and international organizations that become bastions of conservative and reactionary thought and action, rather than instruments of the working class whereby to assert their interests against those of the capitalist class. If such efforts at solidarity maintain power and use it as an organizing base, collective action can expand. But to do so requires solidarity of other transportation unions and other kinds of unions. Given current failures of the labor movement, both in the U.S. and internationally, this is uncertain.

However, there is room for hope in developments such as the IDC, the outcome of the protracted struggle around the Charleston 5, and the chances for reform both within unions such as the ILA and international organizations as current leadership is replaced by younger, brasher, more combative leadership from the ranks of workers who understand their common interests and act upon them following the example of the ILWU (Erem and Durrenberger 2008).

The organizing task is so immense as to be almost unimaginable. It requires linking low-wage factory workers in Sri Lanka, China, Latin America, Indonesia and other slave labor emporia with highly-paid labor, such as the unionized longshoremen of the First World into a group who understand and act upon their common interests as a class in the global economy.

In short, it requires a rebirth of the vision of organizations such as the IWW and the ILWU and replacement of those leaders that are corrupt and unimaginative with people that share such a vision. This kind of rebirth will not result from self-congratulatory conferences, nostalgia for days of yore or from incorporating better studies of industries. It will only result from a rebirth of the spirit that the IWW displayed in 1905.

The heirs of the IWW have built the last wall brick by brick. And they are maintaining it with due vigilance, waiting for the day when their fellow workers join them in a world-wide social movement. *This wall has not yet fallen.*

Process and prognosis

More than a hundred years after the organizing meeting of the IWW in Chicago, in the summer of 2005, the venerable AFL-CIO split into the successor AFL-CIO and the Change to Win (CTW) movement. So much for solidarity on behalf of the working class. In 2008, the organizing of nurses became a battleground between the two labor federations (AFL-CIO and CTW) as some within the SEIU began to question the wisdom of "top-down" organizing, in which unions enlist the cooperation of management in return for concessions from the union. The slogans of class struggle have been replaced by a reality that some call "class snuggle" (Durrenberger and Erem 2005).

And now, CTW is facing an internal crisis as one of its main constituent unions (SEIU) is busily pulling its own house down around its ears in an internal political battle. Though we can see echoes of social movements in small places within the labor movement (Durrenberger and Erem 2005) there is little reason to suppose that it will become a significant social movement. Generations have grown up with its co-opted leaders and the structures of power have shifted too significantly toward capital. Self-interested leaders have lost any ability to sway their members to anything but their own self-interest.

Individually focused union practices have not inculcated in members the view that their own collective action creates the power to stand against the power of ownership and wealth. But the cultural revolution has not expunged the experience of class. The "gospel of work" is based on that experience. As a working class interloper, I still feel it every time my office key jams in the lock and the thought flashes through my head that they've finally found out that I don't really belong in this privileged post in the academy and they've changed the locks.

The "gospel of work" is formed from that experience of class and those injuries of class (Sennett and Cobb 1993). And comparing the experience of class to the denial of class that we encounter in academic and popular writing and media creates a disjunction from which the old spirit of the IWW is continually remade, even though people may not know what to call it or even what it is. That's why Joe Hill will never die[3]. That spirit is alive and well in the labor movement. I saw it when I rode with union people of all stripes. That's where the hope of

---

[3] Joel Emmanuel Hägglund, aka Joseph Hillström (died November 19, 1915). A Swedish-American labor activist, songwriter, and IWW member-organizer. He was executed for murder after what many consider false charges in Utah. The reference is to the song, " I Dreamed I Saw Joe Hill Last Night" by Alfred Hayes (c 1930) set to music by Earl Robinson in 1936. The lyrics are:

the labor movement lies—with those leaders in the movement who foster and develop that spirit in their organizations. There are some; the cynical and self-interested aren't the only ones.

Labor activists Bill Fletcher, Jr. and Fernando Gapasin warn (2008:141) that until and unless labor can reorient itself and represent the interests of the working class as opposed to simply representing employees in contract negotiations there is little likelihood that U.S. unions could be capable of internal much less national or global solidarity.

Codicil: anthropologists and collective action

Solidarity, whether in unions or segmentary lineages, is people exercising their analytic abilities and their agency to join with similarly situated people to defend the weakest among them because they know that an injury to one is an injury to all. California longshoremen supported their threatened fellow-workers in South Carolina; dockers in Europe joined them. This is at the same time both self-interested and radical. The loss of the longshoremen's local in Charleston would be a loss to all longshoremen. By supporting those who are most threatened, those at the bottom, the interests of all workers are served. Ourselves included, whether we be janitors, anthropologists or longshoremen. This outlook of taking care of others to take care of ourselves challenges people to understand and join in radical struggle to support transformative movements.

For one brief moment in 2004, we anthropologists showed sufficient courage and leadership to join the struggle when we refused

---

I dreamed I saw Joe Hill last night,
Alive as you and me
Says I "But Joe, you're ten years dead"
"I never died" says he.

"In Salt Lake, Joe, by God" says I,
Him standing by my bed
"They framed you on a murder charge"
Says Joe "But I ain't dead."

"The copper bosses killed you Joe,
They shot you Joe" says I
"Takes more than guns to kill a man"
Says Joe "I didn't die."

And standing there as big as life,
And smiling with his eyes
Joe says "What they forgot to kill
Went on to organize."

"Joe Hill ain't dead" he says to me,
"Joe Hill ain't never died
Where workingmen are out on strike
|Joe Hill is at their side."

From San Diego up to Maine,
In every mine and mill,
Where workers strike and organize,
Says he "You'll find Joe Hill."

Hence, the slogan, "Don't mourn. Organize."

to honor our contract to hold the annual meeting of the American Anthropological Association (AAA) in the San Francisco Hilton Hotel as long as their management refused to negotiate with the UNITE-HERE local union that represents its workers. That proved to be a pivotal point in the negotiations, as other associations followed us and forced the Hilton to the table.

But immediately thereafter, we stepped back with a vote that approved a change in our policies from a *requirement* that our meetings be in union organized facilities to a *strong preference* as though solidarity means only when it's easy or cost free. Our association created a Labor Relations Commission and then proceeded to marginalize it and isolate it from any decision making or planning role.

Most academics come from the managerial middle class and share and perpetuate its self-congratulatory cultural dream work, as Marvin Harris (1974) called such delusions, for instance, about class. Academics with tenure have learned to politely defer to power. Those without tenure are fearful and incapable of inciting meaningful change. Perhaps the experience of contract and adjunct academics with no tenure to hope for will clarify their class positions to them.

Decades of experience with the AAA tells me that while we can tolerate identity politics, the way to get along is polite accommodation. Noisy trouble-makers outside the familiar register of identity politics can't make it past the nominations committee to get on a ballot. So much for open, transparent and free elections. That means that there's probably no hope that anthropologists' collective action in solidarity with other workers.

Persuade those in decision making positions in the AAA? It's like Iowans say about teaching pigs to sing. It's a waste of your time and it annoys the pig.

Even so, Leach and Evans-Pritchard worked behind the lines in the last great war on fascism. I think we should be worthy heirs to that tradition and continue the struggle, even if it does annoy the pig. After all, we are all in this together.

References Cited

Benhke, Roy. 1980. Herders of Cyrenaica: Ecology, Economy and Kinship among the Bedouin of Eastern Libya. Urbana. University of Illinois Press.

Boyer, Richard O. and Herbert M. Morais. 1955. Labor's Untold Story. New York. United Electrical, Radio & Machine Workers of America.

Brodkin, Karen and Cynthia Strathmann. 2004. The Struggle for Hearts and Minds: Organization, Ideology, and Emotion. Labor Studies Journal 29(3): 1-24.

Doukas, Dimitra. 2003. Worked Over: The Corporate Sabotage of an American Community. Ithaca: Cornell University Press.

Durrenberger, E. Paul.1974. The Regional Context of the Economy of a Lisu Village in Northern Thailand. Southeast Asia 3:569-575.
1979a. An Analysis of Shan Household Production Decisions. Journal of Anthropological Research 35:447-458.
1979b. Rice Production in a Lisu Village. Journal of Southeast Asian Studies 10:139-145.
1987. Reflections on the Absolute. Anthropology and Humanism Quarterly 12: 38-41.
2001. Explorations of Class and Consciousness in the U.S. Journal of Anthropological Research Vol 57(1): 41-60.
2003. Global Processes, Local Systems. Urban Anthropology Vol 32(3-4):253-279.

Durrenberger, E. Paul and Suzan Erem. 2005. Class Acts: An Anthropology of Urban Service Workers and Their Union. Boulder: Paradigm Publishers.
2007. Anthropology Unbound: A Flied Guide to the 21st Century. Boulder. Paradigm Publishers.

Durrenberger, E. Paul and Dimitra Doukas. 2008. Gospel of Wealth, Gospel of Work: Hegemony in the U.S. Working Class. American Anthropologist 110(2):1548-1433.

Erem, Suzan and E. Paul Durrenberger. 2008. On the Global Waterfront: The Fight to Free the Charleston 5. New York. Monthly Review Press.

Evans-Pritchard, E.E. 1949. The Sanusi of Cyrenaica. Oxford. The Clarendon Press.

Fletcher, Bill and Fernando Gapasin. 2008. Solidarity Divided: The Crisis in Organized Labor and a New Path toward Social Justice. Berkeley, University of California Press.

Fones-Wolf, Elizabeth A. 1994. Selling Free Enterprise: The Business Assault on Labor and Liberalism 1945-60. Urbana. University of Illinois Press

Fried., Morton. 1967. The Evolution of Political Society: An Essay in Political Anthropology. New York. McGraw-Hill.

Galbraith, John Kenneth. 1992. The Culture of Contentment. New York. Houghton Mifflin.

Goldschmidt, Walter. 2006. The Bridge to Humanity: How Affect Hunger Trumps the Selfish Gene. New York. Oxford University Press.

Hannerz, Ulf. 1996. Transnational Connections: Culture, People, Places. New York. Routledge.

Haraldsdottir, Gudrun. 2002. Cooperation and Conflicting Interests: An Ethnography of Fishing and Fish Trading on the Shores of Lake Malawi (Malawi). PhD Dissertation in Anthropology. Iowa City. University of Iowa.

Harris, Marvin. 1974. Cows, Pigs, Wars and witches: The Riddles of Culture. New York: Random House.

Kornbluh, Joyce L. 1964. Rebel Voices: An I.W.W. Anthology. Ann Arbor. University of Michigan Press.

Leach, Edmund R. 1954. Political Systems of Highland Burma: A Study of Kachin Social Structure. Boston. Beacon Press.

Malinowski, Bronislaw. 1922. Argonauts of the Western Pacific: An Account of Native Enterprise and Adventure in the Archipelagoes of Melanesian New Guinea. Long Grove, IL: Waveland Press (reprinted).

Marx, Karl. 1976. Collected Works: Karl Marx and Fredrick Engles. Vol 5:1845-47. New York. International Publishers.

McCay, Bonnie. 1998. Oyster Wars and the Public Trust: Property, Law, and Ecology in New Jersey History. Tucson, University of Arizona Press.

McCoy, Alfred. 1972. The Politics of Heroin in Southeast Asia. New York. Harper and Row.

2003. The Politics of Heroin: CIA Complicity in the Global Drug Trade. Chicago. Lawrence Hill Books.

Mills, C. Wright. 1951. White Collar: The American Middle Classes. New York. Oxford University Press.

Nordstrom, Carolyn. 2004. Shadows of War: Violence, Power, and International Profiteering in the Twenty-First Century. Los Angeles. University of California Press.
2007. Global Outlaws: Crime, Money, and Power in the Contemporary World. Los Angeles. University of California Press.

Ostrom, Elinor. 1997. The Comparative Study of Public Economies. Memphis, Tennessee. Rhodes College. Acceptance paper for the Frank E. Seidman Distinguished Award in Political Economy.

Ostrom, Elinor, Roy Gardner, and James Walke. 1994. Rules, Games, and Common-Pool Resources. Ann Arbor. The University of Michigan Press.

Phillips, Kevin. 2008. Bad Money: Reckless Finance, Failed Politics, and the Global Crisis of American Capitalism. New York. Viking.

Rappaport, Roy. 1979. Ecology, Meaning, & Religion. Berkeley. North Atlantic Books.

Sahlins, Marshall. 2000. Culture in Practice: Selected Essays. New York. Zone Books.

Saitta, Dean. 2007. The Archaeology of Collective Action. Gainesville. University Press of Florida,

Salzman, Philip Carl. 2001. Understanding Culture: An Introduction to Anthropological Theory. Prospect Heights. Waveland Press.

Sennett, Richard and Jonathan Cobb. 1993. The Hidden Injuries of Class. New York. W. W. Norton & Company.

Singer M. 1995. Beyond the Ivory Tower: Critical Praxis in Medical Anthropology. *Medical Anthropology Quarterly* 9(1):80-106.

Stiglitz, Joseph. 2003. Globalization and its Discontents. New York. Norton.

Existentialism

Icelandic Saga Heroes:
The Anthropology of Natural Existentialists

1984 *Anthropology and Humanism Quarterly* 9:3-8.

Philosophers live in the subjunctive realm of "what if"; anthropologists, in the experienced realities of other people. If philosophers outline various possibilities for the human experience, anthropologists should be able to find them as they are lived rather than as they are reflected upon. Iceland was formally converted to Christianity in 1000, but because the institutional structure to support it was lacking, the everyday outlook remained pagan. This outlook has much in common with modern existentialism. Neither allows the leap of faith that Christianity demands. The sagas depict life without the leap of faith. Such a life is heroic.

Norse settlers came to Iceland from Norway, Ireland, and Scotland beginning in 870. The establishment of the general assembly or *Althing* in 930 marks the end of the period of settlement and the beginning of the free state or commonwealth period. Icelanders adopted Christianity in 1000. From 1220 to 1262 the Church struggled against the chieftains, the chieftains struggled against each other, and the Norwegian king strove to establish his power in Iceland. This was the Sturlung period, named after its dominant family. In 1262, civil strife began to abate when the *Althing* recognized the Norwegian king. The sagas were written in the 13th century about events and people of the tenth century. Among the most famous of saga heroes is Gunnar Hamundarson of Hlidarend (Magnusson and Palsson 1960). The following is a brief summary.

Both abroad and in Iceland, Gunnar has won fame and honor for his exploits. With the help of his friend Njal, he has won many lawsuits and negotiated many settlements. He has killed those who have trifled with him, although he is reluctant to take their lives. At each success the numbers of his enemies grow. He defends himself when they first ambush him. He wins his law case against them. He defends himself the second time they ambush him but is outlawed as a consequence and must leave Iceland. He refuses to leave, even though his life is forfeit. He knows his enemies will attack. He refuses offers of help twice and sends his own supporters away when the time for the attack draws near. He elects to die. To quote from the saga:

> He kept on fighting until exhaustion brought him down. His enemies then dealt him many terrible wounds, but even then he got away from them and held them at bay for a long time.
>
> But in the end they killed him (Magnusson and Palsson1960, 171).

Gizur the White, the leader of the attackers, says, "We have felled a great champion, and we have not found it easy. His last defense will be remembered for as long as this land is lived in" (17 1). After he is buried in a mound, Gunnar is heard to chant of himself, "He would rather die than yield, much rather die than yield" (17).

One of the perpetrators of Gunnar's death, a chieftain, is jealous of the influence of Gunnar's friend Njal in the district and plots Neal's death to restore the chieftain's own position. Neal's sons become involved in other killings and plots that lead to an attack on Njal and his family. Njal and one of his sons debate tactics.

Njal decides not to offer a resistance in the open, but to withdraw to the house, knowing he will be burned. When the attackers give him and his wife a chance to leave the burning house Njal replies: "I have no wish to go outside, for l am an old man now and ill equipped to avenge my sons; and l do not want to live in shame" (267). Njal's son-in-law, Kari Solmundarson, escapes the fire and avenges the killing of his own son and Njal's family.

This account touches only some of the high points of a subtle and complex saga. Not all saga characters are heroic. Some are drawn in stark contrast to the heroic figures. Whether the characters contrast with, or exemplify the heroic image, the saga writers seem intent on representing it.

The sagas emphasize the hero's willingness to accept death rather than compromise, to yield nothing (Gordon 1957: xxx). When he hears of an impending ambush, Gunnar says, "Death will catch up with me wherever I am when it is so fated" (156). Even his enemies admire Gunnar. Saga characters say they will rely on their own strength and cunning, that they will act in terms of what they can know and risk the outcomes.

During the commonwealth period of Iceland there was stratification and there were classes, but there was no state. There was indeed an anti-state ideology, as many settlers had come to Iceland to escape the stare formation process underway in Norway in the time of Harald Finehair. If the settlers were anti-state, they were nor egalitarian. There was no question of establishing an egalitarian society, but rather of preserving the autonomy of petty chieftains who thought they had something to lose by subordinating themselves to a central authority. They immediately reestablished themselves as chiefs, *godar,* when they set foot on Iceland by claiming land for themselves and then apportioning it to their followers. They even maintained the ritual justification for claims to chieftaincy by preserving the priestly components of their roles and building temples in Iceland.

Although many Icelanders had been Christians before they settled in Iceland, the contradictions between the stateless chieftaincies and Christianity were strong enough to obliterate Christian traces in favor of paganism. Many who write about Icelandic history and literature make much of the conversion to Christianity in the year 1000, only 70 years after the founding of the *Althing.*

This episode was not the exchange of one system of belief for another. Belief was not at issue. As with the political system, the pagan religion of Iceland had much in common with other "primitive" religions, religions of people who do not participate in state systems. Turville-Petre (1953) offers a convincing view. The hierarchy of gods changed from time to time. In Iceland, Odin was largely neglected in favor of Thor and Frey. Odin was associated with kings. There was no doctrine. The gods could grant favors and were propitiated but not worshipped. Gods could avenge insults to themselves. There was no moral code implicit in the religious system, nor were morals the concern of the gods. "The fundamental distinction between paganism and Christianity was in the conception of the deities. The one religion was dominated by a single god, who was all-powerful and all good; but the other knew no supreme god. None of its gods were all-powerful, for like men they were the playthings of an impersonal fate" (Turville-Petre 1953:-49-50). Fate was impersonal and indifferent to the affairs of people. People neither could nor influence it by sacrifice or invocation. The religion was like other primitive religions, simply an aspect of the social order, nothing to be propagated or defended.

The priestly functions of the *godar* had nearly been forgotten by the time of the conversion, and it is not difficult to see why their authority survived the transition of Christianity. As Christians, the *godar* were hardly less powerful than they had been as pagans. This shows that, however great the spiritual importance of the conversions, it was not, as in some lands, a social and cultural revolution. This may help to explain why the traditions of pre-Christian Scandinavia survived the conversion in Iceland, as they could not survive in Norway or in any other Northern land (Turville-Petre 1953:69).

"Northern paganism had, thus, more in common with atheism than with Judaism and Christianity" (Turville-Petre 1953:50). I think this is one key to understanding the sagas that has not been much emphasized. The sagas were written in Christian times. Some, Palsson (1971), for instance, consider some sagas to be Christian stories in local form. I think there is sufficient evidence to suggest that the sagas were not heavily influenced by Christianity.

There is really no mystery about Iceland's becoming Christian by arbitration in the year 1000. First, paganism did not demand orthodoxy or conformism. Second, although Christianity was a state doctrine and could not therefore be tolerant, it was introduced into a stateless society without the institutional structure that Christianity was designed to support. Thirdly, the Icelanders were not self-sufficient. They needed grain from Norway as well as timber and other goods (Foote 1963:98). The choice facing the Icelanders was not only the oft repeated one of whether to have one law for the whole land or two, one for Christians and one for pagans, but also whether to maintain contact with Norway. It was really no choice at all. It was precisely the same sort of choice King Olaf presented potential converts when he burned coals on their chests and invited them to convert.

Just as there were instances of individuals who had no truck with pagan gods (Adalsteinsson 1978:26), there were many in the twelfth century "who were untouched by the Christianity of the twelfth century. In this century there existed a way of thinking that was native and but little affected by Christian influence" (Venison 1953: 110-111).

Njal and his sons were burned to death, the saga related, by their enemies taking justified vengeance on them. "Like the traditional Icelandic chief Njal was noble and upright, and uncompromisingly loyal to his friends and relatives. But he also had many Christian virtues. He was generous to those in distress, and faced death submissively like a martyr. Since he could see into the future, he must be a fatalist" (Turville-Petre 1953: 251). Martyrs were burned, but not everyone who has died that way has been a Christian martyr. To be generous was a characteristic of pagan chieftains, as it is of all similar chieftains in similar political and economic systems whether they be in pagan Iceland, high land Southeast Asia, or Melanesia. This is not an especially Christian virtue. By Njal's reckoning, his sons had caused enough havoc and were justly killed. This makes him responsible, as an honorable person, for his deeds and his sons' deeds. This does not make him a paragon of Christian virtue.

I think the changes in outlook with conversion were minimal (Palsson and Edwards 1968: 12). My general argument is that religious ideologies are not independent of their social, economic, and political contexts, but rather serve particular functions. Christianity, for instance, is an ideology of states. Wherever we find pre-state forms of organization, we find similar modes of political, social, and economic organization that co-vary systematically as Fried (1967) argues. Wherever there are similar forms of organization, there are similar religious forms. It follows that religion does not change *unless* there are fundamental changes in these other realms. Religion is not an independent variable, but a dependent one. Where there are similar social arrangements, there are similar kinds of repetitious events and actions. To explain the similarities we do not have to appeal to archetypes or literary convention or borrowings.

Of all the possible social and political arrangements, the stratified system without a state is the most unstable. A stratified society is one in which access to resources (land, for instance) is limited to certain people. Those who claim rights to access to resources must be able to enforce that claim if need be. The people who claim differential access to resources must sooner or later either relinquish that claim and allow universal access or band together to enforce their claim. The Icelandic commonwealth was unstable, and, as it could not be self-sufficient, it was literally fated to fall into foreign hands sooner or later. The instability of the system is exhibited in the upheavals of the Sturlung period:

By this time the power of individual chieftains has multiplied one man may rule entire districts or quarters or even the whole country. Some of the chieftains are possessed of greater wealth than their grandfathers dreamed of, others must provide for their initial establishment by forcible means. A considerable number of the common people are destitute (Sveinsson 1953:2).

Sveinsson (1953:5) continues:

> Quarrels, incursions, manslaughter, battles, burnings. The districts change rulers constantly. One year a chieftain has most of the country in his power, the next he has gone abroad to the royal court, and his greatest enemy is in complete control. The time-honored bonds that link *thingman* and *godi* [follower and chief] creak under the strain. All the pristine virtues totter. The extravagant ambition of the chieftains overthrows the nation's independence.

The structural transformation that makes Christianity possible, incorporation into Norway, happens more than 200 years *after* the conversion of Iceland. Before that time, the notion of a Christian Iceland is a contradiction in terms. The values and outlook of the saga writers were essentially the same as those of their characters. Textual arguments cannot well decide this point, but the kind of comparative and structural argument I have developed here makes the assumption overwhelmingly plausible.

The people who wrote the sagas were writing about people just like themselves living in the same social situations, although the political balance was different. The audience for the sagas was similar to what it would have been 200 years before. I think Halldorsson (1976:74) presents a most convincing conclusion. He rejects both the idea that Hrafnkel's saga is a Christian story and that it is remade heroic mythology.

According to this interpretation, the saga assumes the worldly morality of power-seeking, not the moral code of mediaeval Catholic Christianity. Both the description of characters and the conclusion show that the cold-blooded men of reason (Hrafnkel, Bjori, Thorgeir) prosper at the expense of those who allow their action to be governed by their emotions. Thus the author's view of life appears to be based, not on the ancient belief in fate or on hero-worship, but on the experience contemporary events have taught him. By this treatment the ancient Frey-Worshipper is transformed into a 13th century chieftain who realizes what really matters in the last resort is the aid of other men.

People who disagree about everything else concerning the sagas agree on their style. The essence of the saga style is the tension between the demands of an accurate historical rendering of events and the demand for an entertaining story. When the demands of entertainment outweigh the discipline of history, the sagas lose their power. By the beginning of the 14th century the balance is destroyed.

"The saga is plane narrative with no vertical dimensions . . . . The subject is supreme; the author never intrudes and the reader is never apostrophized directly or indirectly" (Andersson 1967: 32). The sagas are not idealistic, didactic, satirical, or sentimental. "In short, the saga comes very close to pure narrative without ulterior aims of any kind . . . ." (Andersson 1967:32). There are only brief descriptions of characters when they are introduced into the sagas. Their characters and personalities are not described, but shown through action. "They describe the heroic mentality incapable of deception and unwilling to take refuge in secrecy" (Andersson 1967:45). Although the sagas are full of omens and dreams, witchcraft and sorcery, the saga characters indicate a consistent skepticism toward all of it and repeatedly emphasize their reliance on their own wit and strength. They operate in a strong system of honor, are vulnerable to others' opinions and judgments, which the saga writers recorded side by side with the actions so judged. There was a system of law, not merely custom, but formal law that had been self-consciously designed and formulated. Even when the consequences of action are ambiguous or unclear, the characters indicate their willingness to accept the risk, to chance the outcome. They do not shirk responsibility for their actions.

This objectivity and the other elements of saga style were consequences of the general outlook of the period. This was still essentially a pagan outlook, an outlook that in our terms had more in common with atheism than Christianity, as Turville-Petre put it. Existentialism is a modern philosophy that seems to embody many of the features of this pagan outlook.

Sartre (1957:5) argues that "Existentialism is nothing else than the attempt to draw all the consequences of a coherent atheistic position." If there is no god, then there are no a priori values of legitimate conduct nor any fixed given human nature (23). People are free and responsible for their actions. People are responsible for their passions, choose their passions. So actions cannot be explained by reference to passion (23). No future state provides goals for actions for, "I've got to limit myself to what I see" (31). "Actually, things will be as man will have decided they are to be . . . . I should involve myself; then act on the old saw, 'nothing ventured, nothing gained'" (31). Action is the only human reality, and humanity is nothing else than the ensemble of acts. Sartre scoffs at circumstances as a justification for anything (32). Historical situations are objective because they are universal constraints. They are "subjective because they are *lived* and are nothing if a man does not live them, that is, freely determine his existence with reference to them" (38-39). For individuals there is no determinism, no excuse, no recourse (44-45).

Compare Sartre's characterization of existentialism with Foote's description of the sagas (1963: 104-105). The saga writer's outlook entailed a "humanism which is at once deep and expansive and narrow and stern." The characters come from every conceivable social stratum: they are individual characters, not stereotypes. "And they apply one standard to all: they approve when a man, slave or freeman or noble behaves like a man; they have no sympathy when he fails to do this, however much such failure might be attributed to externals or involuntary causes" (Foote 196.1: 104). "Everywhere we find the same essential respect for the boundless freedom and power of the individual human will" (105). Saga writers never describe internal states, or except for brief introductions, the characters of individuals, but describe only speech and action, what an observer could hear and see, nothing else. There are no monologues; Icelanders did not talk to themselves. These Icelanders had created their own social system, political system, and law by negotiating with each other. Although they built their society from the materials of "custom," they consciously shaped its form and content, and things were as they had decided they would be (Foote 1963:95-97).

Camus (1955) derives the consequences of "the absurd," which he sees as the inescapable contradiction between reality and human representations of reality, none of which is capable of encompassing it. The absurd is a relation, the relation between humanity and reality, the world as it is. "The Absurd is not in man. . . nor in the world, but in their presence together" (23). This is an indivisible trinity—humanity, the world, and the presence of humanity in the world. "To destroy one of its terms is to destroy the whole. There can be no absurd outside the

human mind . . . . There can be no absurd outside this world either."
For Camus, "the sole datum is the absurd" (23). If humanity cannot
capture reality in its representations, and if humanity exists in the
reality of the world, the absurd is the fundamental principle from
which all else follows. To define away one aspect of this trinity is to
negate reality, to demand "a leap" (25). Camus resists the "sacrifice of
the intellect" required to accept God and the sacrifice of life in suicide.
Either course destroys part of the equation of the absurd = reality.
Camus says, "I want to know whether I can live with what I know and
with that alone" (36). "Gods change with men. There are many ways
of leaping, the essential being to leap" (17).

Refusing to "leap," Camus can understand only in human terms.
"What I touch, what resists me—that is what I understand" (38). He
does not want to do anything he does not understand, to leap. The
person who understands the absurd, who lives only with what he
knows, must accommodate "himself to what is, and to bring in nothing
that is not certain" (39). He wants to live without appeal. "Living an
experience, a particular fate, is accepting it fully" (40).

Doctrines that demand a leap and explain everything debilitate,
relieve one of the responsibility for one's life (41).

"Once and for all, value judgments are discarded here in favor of
factual judgments. I have merely to draw the conclusions from what I
can see and risk nothing that is hypothetical" (45).

People may be responsible, but not guilty. One is simply
responsible for the consequences of actions and "is ready to pay up"
(50). The consequences of actions are equivalent; one is simply
responsible for them. "The absurd mind cannot so much expect ethical
rules at the end of its reasoning as, rather, illustrations of the breath of
human lives." Past experience is a guide to future actions. Ethics
cannot be formally derived, nor values, but truth "unfolds in men"
(50).

The saga writers clearly accepted this view. They do not preach,
they illustrate in concrete instances. One scribe wrote:

If people want to listen to old stories they should first of all bear
in mind that most sagas are made out of certain specific materials.
Some are about God and His holy men, and a great deal of wisdom can
be gained from these, although not many people get much
entertainment from the Lives of the Saints. Then there are sagas about
mighty kings, and from these we can learn courteous and courtly

behaviour, and how a man ought to serve outstanding chieftains. The third type of saga tells about those kings who find themselves in great danger, and the various ways they get themselves out of it. Kings like these are for brave men to model themselves on (Palsson and Edwards 1971:37-38).

The sagas are stories of people. They illustrate all varieties of behavior and the consequences of it. They present the past actions of people as guides for the future. There is no a priori ethical system here, only example.

Sartre's philosophy is not individualistic but social. One is responsible for one's actions and their consequences. One takes responsibility in terms of consequences for others and in one's actions, represents all humans, acts as an example for others. Others are "the condition of his own existence. He realizes that he cannot be anything . . . unless others recognize it as such. . . . The other is indispensable to my own existence, as well as to my knowledge about myself" (Sartre 1957: 37-38). This outlook is clear in the sagas in the importance of public opinion, and in terms of reporting the consequences of actions for others, how one character's action determines another's response, and the responsibility of the first.

Sartre is concerned to draw the consequences of not supposing there is the higher authority of a god. Camus is concerned to draw the consequences of the absurd, one of which is a rejection of higher authority and its consequences. Neither is concerned to prove the existence or non-existence of god. These concerns are elevated to philosophy and intellectual manipulation because they are not obvious. They are not obvious because the assumptions were not widely shared when and where the existentialist philosophers were working. They were reactions to other formulations that started from other assumptions. Sartre and Camus refuse to take any leap of belief and they derive the logical consequences of such a refusal. The refusal is only significant because they were different from others who were content to leap in to one belief or another. Existentialism is the struggle to recreate a pre-state, pagan outlook from within a state system.

Sartre and Camus are relevant to anthropology because they draw the consequences of non-belief. To Needham (1972), the fact "that men can be said to believe, without qualification and irrespective of their cultural formation, is an implicit premise of anthropological writings of the most varied kinds." He concludes that belief "is not a discriminable experience, it does not constitute a natural resemblance among men, and it does not belong to the common behaviour of mankind" (188).

Anthropologists often assume a straightforward relationship between social system and religion. A denial of religious beliefs must be evidence for a denial of the society, an incomprehensible dilemma. If religion provides an analysis of the world that makes it comprehensible and livable (Geertz 1966; Spiro 1967) or codifies social relations, then it follows that people must believe its postulates or enter the morass of insanity or social chaos. The notion of belief follows from the very concepts of the functions of religion. The attribution of belief often contradicts ethnographic evidence. Analyses of religion need not rely on the notion of belief but can treat religion as a logical system that takes as its premises the theorems of the axioms of social, political, and economic action, logical consequences of other logics (Durrenberger 1980). I think a detailed analysis would show that the notion of belief, attributed to all humanity, is an ethnocentric idea based on the necessity for belief in some of the world religions such as Christianity and Islam. Religions that have evolved as state religions require the leap of belief. They are aspects of the ideological negation of real social and economic conditions that state organizations required for their existence (see Harris 1971:406). Pre-state or non-state organizations do not require such negations. They do not therefore require belief. Not requiring the "leap" of belief, these ideological systems ought to have common elements with existentialist philosophy, which draws the logical implications of not believing. One such society was Iceland during the commonwealth period before the introduction of Christianity in the year 1000 and before its incorporation into Norwegian hegemony in 1262.

The saga characters were, as Palsson points out, farmers, sheep-herders who lived in poor houses and had to struggle for their subsistence from one year to the next in the inhospitable setting of Iceland with its unpredictable weather and poor prospects. Sometimes they traded and raided. Palsson wonders where there is room for heroes in such a pedestrian setting. There are none of the ingredients for romance.

"In the sagas," writes Palsson (1975: 15), "the heroic image was superimposed on an essentially unheroic situation. The literary convention accepted by some of their authors demanded the transformation of farmers and peasants into idealised warriors and adventurers, worthy descendants of the great heroes of the legendary past." Palsson, like Andersson (1967:65-91), follows Ker's notion that the sagas are prose versions of the old heroic poems with historical personalities from Iceland's past in the positions of the original characters, the retellings of a more ancient set of stories with tenth and eleventh century characters set in Iceland. Palsson (1975: 16) provides a character sketch of the typical legendary hero.

He is a man of exceptional qualities, brave and strong. He abides by a code of honor and is loyal to friends. "His greatness is realised through valorous deeds, fighting hopeless battles against overwhelming odds" (16). "The descriptions of Icelandic saga heroes often generate a similar kind of emotional response in the reader, and it is this aesthetic sensation that has created the illusion that people in tenth-century Iceland lived and died like legendary personages" (16).

Perhaps the saga people were not romantic heroes, but they were heroic. By virtue of the nature of their ecological, economic, and political situation they were pagans, they could not take any kind of leap from the immediate and real as they perceived it. There was no place to leap to, intellectually or ethically. They designed their own laws rather than receiving them from a god or a king. Because of their unromantic and impoverished lives they were forced to live lives of no recourse. Having no refuge, no place to leap, they were forced to be heroic. Their heroism is not as improbable as Palsson suggests; it was a consequence of their situation. Their heroism is not in their deeds, but in their approach to life, an approach they did not choose, for there were no alternatives. They were heroes in the same sense that other people of stateless societies are, people who struggle to create meaning rather than to accept it as created; people who confront each other in human terms rather than through bureaucratic structures; people who must live with the consequences of their actions.

Today one may choose existentialism, because there are alternatives. For the saga people there were no choices. They were "natural existentialists" as people of other pre-state societies are. Perhaps they were not romantic. Direct confrontations with reality allowed little room for flirtations with fantasy. They demanded maintenance of the balance Camus speaks of, not destroying any of the aspects of the trinity of human existence in reality and the consequent absurdity. Saga people were heroes, existentialist heroes in an absurd world. As such they were not loath to engage in hopeless struggles against overwhelming odds, and if need be, to die.

References Cited

Adalsteinsson, Jon H. 1978. *Under the Cloak: The Acceptance of Christianity in Iceland with Particular Reference to the Religious Attitudes Prevailing at the Time.* Uppsala: Acta Universitatis Uppsaliensis, Studie Erhnologica Upsaliensia, 4.

Andersson, Theodore M. 1967. *The Icelandic Family Saga: An Analytic Reading.* Cambridge: Harvard University Press.

Camus, Albert. 1955. *The Myth of Sisyphus and Other Essays.* Translated by Justin O'Brien. New York: Vintage.

Durrenberger, E. Paul. 1980. Belief and the logic of Lisu spirits. *Bijdragen Tot de taal- , Land-en Volkenkunde* 136: 21-40.

Foote, Peter. 1963. An essay on the saga of Gisli and its Icelandic background. In *The Saga of Gisli,* translated by George Johnston. London: Dent.

Fried, Morton. 1967. *The Evolution of Political Society.* New York: Random House.

Geertz, Clifford. 1966. Religion as a cultural system. In *Anthropological Approaches to the Study of Religion,* edited by M. Banton. ASA Monographs No. 3. London: Tavistock.

Gordon, E. V. 1957. *Introduction to Old Norse.* 2d ed. Revised by A. R. Taylor. London: Oxford University Press.

Halldorsson, Oskar. 1976. *Upprnniog Thema Hrafnkels Sogu.* Reykjavik.

Harris, Marvin. 1971. *Culture, Man, and Nature.* New York: Crowell.

Leach, Edmund R. 1954. *Political Systems of Highland Burma.* Boston: Beacon.

Magnusson, Magnus, and Hermann Palsson, translators. 1960. *Njal's Saga.* New York: Penguin.

Needham, Rodney. 1972. *Belief, Language, and Experience.* Chicago: University of Chicago Press.

Njardvik, Njordur P. 1973. *Birth of a Nation: The Story of the Icelandic Commonwealth.* Translated by John Porter. Reykjavik: Iceland Review.

Palsson, Hermann. 1971. *Art and Ethics in Hrafnkel's Saga.*
     Copenhagen: Munksgaard.
Palsson, Hermann. 197 5. *The Confederates and Hen-Thorir.*
     Edinburgh: Southside.
Palsson, Hermann, and Paul Edwards, translators. 1968. *Gautrek's
     Saga and Other Medieval Tales.* New York: New York
     University Press.
Palsson, Hermann, and Paul Edwards, translators. 1971. *Legendary
     Fiction in Medieval Iceland.* Studia Islandica 30.
Sartre, Jean-Paul. 1957. *Existentialism and Human Emotions.* New
     York: Citadel Press.
Spiro, Melford. 1967. *Burmese Supernaturalism.* Englewood Cliffs,
     N.J.: Prentice-Hall.
Sveinsson, Einar Ol. 1953. *The Age of the Sturlungs: Icelandic
     Civilization in the Thirteenth Century.* Translated by Johann S.
     Hannesson. Ithaca: Cornell University Press.
Turville-Petre, G. 1953. *Origins of Icelandic Literature.* Oxford:
     Oxford University Press.

AT THE FOOT OF THE MOUNTAIN
Existentialism, Anthropology and Life

I leave Sisyphus at the foot of the mountain....The struggle itself toward the heights is enough to fill a man's heart. One must imagine Sisyphus happy.

Albert Camus, *the Myth of Sisyphus*

Prologue

In the deep of the night, images form in my sleeping mind, a moving cubist painting of multiple shifting impressions.

I walk to the podium in front of a lecture hall full of newspaper-rustling, chatting and bored-looking kids, plug in a thumb drive, connect the microphone, clamp it to my shirt and put up the first slide of the hour.

"Good morning. Today I'll...."

Some kids nod off; my eyes dwell on the few who are wide awake, eagerly writing in their notebooks. My energy level rises as I make connections and a thousand others explode in my mind.

"This is the beauty of anthropology," I conclude, "All things are connected."

I'm walking up a hill in the rain, my feet slipping in the red mud. My legs are cramped from a day of walking. The night is dark. I cannot see the surrounding hills, only the ever present endless mud underfoot. I welcome the sounds of a dog's bark and a rooster's crow that tells me that the village of grass thatched bamboo huts where I live is close.

I'm sitting in front of a typewriter stand in a small stuffy office crammed with books and computer print outs, pounding on an old fashioned typewriter as the pages of manuscript pile up on the desk beside me. I am lost in an abstract world of words trying to make all of the connections make sense.

I am running up the long incline of a sidewalk in the gathering dusk as storm clouds come together and lightning begins to flash with the crash of nearby thunder. Large cold drops spatter on my arms, legs and face. I am flying through the night, a spirit accepting the offerings of the aromas of cooking meals in the houses I pass.

I'm in the middle of a table in front of a small room where a scattering of people sit in folding chairs as a colleague at the podium changes the image on the screen and reads an academic paper in a monotonous drone. I look at the pile of transparencies in front of me and review the connections I want to draw from the figures.

I'm lost in an infinite kiss with a beautiful dark-haired woman stretched out naked on the bed beside me as I caress her breast.

I stand on the shoulder of the two-lane asphalt road, my right hand extended toward the sparse traffic to ask for a ride. Loneliness envelops me. The pang of hunger doesn't bother me. A melancholy song begins in my mind, "I've hungered for your touch a long lonely time. Time goes by so slowly, and time can do so much…." Time is like water. I think of the old Taoist philosophers talking about how yielding the water is as it carves magnificent canyons. It does nothing, but nothing is left undone.

I am walking on the docks in front of a shrimp processing plant looking for human figures among the shrimp boats and their apparatus spread along the wharf. I've become a father confessor to these anonymous men trying to make their livings in the Gulf of Mexico as they tell me their life stories.

I am standing in a large room drenched with blue-white neon light as a cop rolls my thumb on an inkpad and then on a card. I am proud to be among those imprisoned for opposing an unjust war.

I squat on a one-legged stool strapped to my hips to dip a rag in a bucket, clean the teats of a cow and attach the sucking cylinders of the milking machine as I hear the news on the radio in Icelandic.

We lash the dead leopard's feet to a pole and carry it back to the village where we skin it and eat it.

Times, moments, places cascade over one another as the images form in my mind.

One dream, one long restless night, one long restless life. I stare into the darkness, turn over, and hope that sleep may return. It does not. My mind free wheels.

How many times have I asked myself, "What am I doing in this world of academics?" From time to time I walk like some storied vizier among the people of the planet and then return to this abstracted realm of the irreal. My feet belong on the ground. I am the son of a working man.

I grasp a handful of tall rice stems in my left hand, pull them toward me, cut them with a sickle in my right hand and toss them behind me. On either side of me across the whole field people methodically do the same thing. The field of gently swaying rice seems endless.

The professor checks his watch, picks up the pace of his lecture filling in date after date, place after place until I fall behind and cannot keep up. I wonder what I am doing here in the first place as waves of frustration well up and cascade through my body to snap the pencil in my hands. I see a look of puzzlement on the face of the departing professor and slump in my chair.

I hear myself saying that something is useless and recall the Taoist's answer. "You use only the area of the path that your foot occupies. Is the rest then useless?"

I climb metal stairs to a catwalk high above the giant pots of molten chocolate and the black people dipping ice-cream cones into them to the offices of the white supervisors with elves embroidered on their golf shirts. "I might as well be in apartheid South Africa," I think as I talk to one of the elves.

On a manual typewriter I pound out answers to questions my elders and betters have handed me for that day. The anger comes through my fingers, through the machine and flows onto the pages as they fall one upon another.

At the end of one of my classes, a student snaps a pencil in frustration. On my way out I invite her to come to my office to talk.

I walk with a group of villagers to find the carcass of a horse that a leopard has left the night before. We surround it with shotguns and rifles rigged to fire at any tension on a web of strings surrounding the dead horse. "That's so tight," my companion, Fish Man the shaman says, "A fly landing on it would set it off." He taps the string with a finger and the gun discharges. Everyone else jumps up to see who has been shot. Then we re-do the work.

I am in the Icelandic National Library copying out numbers, deep in the basement of the University of Illinois library reading old French journals, in the stacks of the University of Texas library, head buried in a microfilm reader in the Mobile, Alabama Public Library.

Two teamsters walking with me to an office building in Chicago explain that you don't need a necktie if you have a good union. They teach me how to swagger like a teamster. If the outsized wooden doors, paneled walls and posh offices of the lawyers negotiating on behalf of British Petroleum were meant to intimidate, they failed with these truck drivers.

A dean explains to me why all of the colleagues in my department cannot be equal.

A group of villagers approaches the thatched teak house where I am drinking tea to ask me whether my people actually believe that all people are created equal.

An archetype of a union boss wearing a necktie, shiny Italian suit and fancy shoes explains to me why the centralism is the important part of democratic centralism and why the democratic part of it won't work.

I recoil at the cannon-ball pain of my wife's revelation of her infidelity. "It's been almost forty years," my internal voice says.

"Some wounds are too deep to be forgiven."

"Forgiveness is the only release."

"Forgive us our trespasses as we forgive those who trespass against us."

"What doth the Lord require of thee but to do justice, love mercy and walk humbly with thy God?"

Humbly. Walk. Justice. Mercy.

Words of an ancient mad prophet railing against the injustices of a system he did not create.

Echoes of scripture from my childhood.

"The most important teaching of the Buddha?" an orange-robed village monk repeats my question. "Do good; avoid evil." The Buddhist scriptures say past actions determine your current level of enlightenment, your progress along the long road to enlightenment and release from the continual cycle of rebirth and suffering. The monk says do good, avoid evil. He's pitching it to my level of enlightenment.

Unready to roll out of bed and resume the tasks of this life, I turn over to ease the pain in my back and stare at the insides of my eyelids. I feel the warmth of my wife beside me and understand why Orpheus would brave the land of the dead to retrieve his. I want to prolong that moment, project it into an infinite future. My mind tells me I cannot.

A self-indulgent tear forms behind my eyelid and I smile in the knowledge that as a thoroughgoing materialist I will cheat the endless cycles of rebirth and yet achieve nirvana, enlightened or not.

My eyes flutter open as the pale light of the rising sun crosses my face. Words form in my mind. This is the last chapter. Here, on this bluff above this river, with this woman, finally, with my feet on the ground. The first chapter was so long ago....

About the Author

Paul Durrenberger is a retired anthropologist who has lived and done research among the peoples of Southeast Asia, Iceland, and the U.S. He was a professor of anthropology at the University of Iowa for 25 years and Penn State for 15. He now lives on a farm in rural Iowa.

For his personal story, see *At the Foot of the Mountain: Existentialism, Anthropology and Life* (2014) also from Draco Hill Press.